American Evangelicals

Critical Issues in History
Series Editor: Donald T. Critchlow

American Evangelicals

A Contemporary History of a
Mainstream Religious Movement

Barry Hankins

ROWMAN & LITTLEFIELD PUBLISHERS, INC.
Lanham • Boulder • New York • Toronto • Plymouth, UK

ROWMAN & LITTLEFIELD PUBLISHERS, INC.

Published in the United States of America
by Rowman & Littlefield Publishers, Inc.
A wholly owned subsidary of The Rowman & Littlefield Publishing Group, Inc.
4501 Forbes Boulevard, Suite 200, Lanham, Maryland 20706
www.rowmanlittlefield.com

Estover Road
Plymouth PL6 7PY
United Kingdom

British Library Cataloguing in Publication Information Available

Library of Congress Cataloging-in-Publication Data
Hankins, Barry, 1956–
   American evangelicals : a contemporary history of a mainstream religious movement /
Barry Hankins.
     p.   cm.
   Includes bibliographical references and index.
   1. Evangelicalism—United States. 2. United States—Church history. I. Title.
BR1642.U5H36 2008
277.3'082—dc22   2007044222

ISBN-13: 978-0-7425-4989-0 (cloth : alk. paper)
ISBN-10: 0-7425-4989-5 (cloth : alk. paper)
ISBN-13: 978-0-7425-7025-2 (paper : alk. paper)
ISBN-10: 0-7425-7025-8 (paper : alk. paper)
ISBN-13: 978-0-7425-7026-9 (electronic)
ISBN-10: 0-7425-7026-6 (electronic)

∞™ The paper used in this publication meets the minimum requirements of American
National Standard for Information Sciences—Permanence of Paper for Printed Library
Materials, ANSI/NISO Z39.48-1992.

For Dixon, Johanna, Coleman, Hunter, Michael B., and blended (or collided) families everywhere.

Contents

~

Preface

When postmodern theorist Stanley Fish was asked in 2007 what would replace race, class, and gender as the centerpiece of scholarship, he answered like a shot, "religion. That's where the action is." This book intends to join that lively conversation within the American academy, particularly with reference to American evangelicals. Evangelicals are everywhere in the news these days, and what one reads in newspapers or sees on television is often unflattering to say the least. As portrayed there, evangelicals often seem angry about something—the teaching of evolution, the removal of Ten Commandments monuments, gay marriage, abortion, and any number of other issues. While it is true that the many activist evangelicals are angry about such practices and determined to do something politically to stop them, these highly visible activists represent only a small fraction of one of America's two largest religious subcultures, the other being Roman Catholics with whom evangelicals have much in common.

The structural approach of this book is to take a number of highly contested issues and show where evangelical views and positions on such issues started historically, how they developed over time, and what this means today. In the process of these overviews, it will become apparent that there is much more complexity and diversity among evangelicals than one might expect. This is because evangelicals in America are quite at home in the culture, even as some of them insist that the culture is hostile to them.

This at-homeness is the result of the fact that American culture itself was shaped substantially by evangelical Protestants, especially in the nineteenth century. While the evangelical dominance of that era is long past, American culture still bears the marks of evangelical Protestantism, often in secular guise. A key example would be the American emphasis on freedom of choice. Most evangelicals believe, or at least act as if they believe, that the most fundamental aspect of human life, one's relationship with God, is a matter of choice. One chooses to be born again. Beyond this life-changing decision, evangelicals tend to take their religion into their own hands, shaping it accordingly. They are innovative rather than traditional, populist rather than elitist, intuitive rather than scholarly, activist rather than conformist, and individualistic rather than hierarchical. In short, they are quintessentially American in their quest to shape their own destinies, religious or otherwise. All this has led sociologist of religion Alan Wolfe to write recently, "We're all evangelicals now," a remarkable statement from a nonpracticing Jew.[1]

Wolfe's point is that evangelicals are not fundamentally different from other Americans, at least when it comes to a highly individualistic view of life. Many evangelicals do not like to hear this because they believe the Bible teaches them to be different from the rest of the world. And that's the rub. This quest to be different and outside the mainstream is so American that when people succeed in being unique, they have conformed to a key component of the American way. As one scholar of religion argued in the 1980s, virtually all the significant religious groups in America, including evangelicals, have at one time or another cast themselves as outsiders, and the reason is that being an outsider is the way to be American.[2]

This book, therefore, attempts to take what seems clearly distinctive about evangelicals—their theology, scientific views, political action, gender relations, scholarship, etc.—and show historically the ways that evangelicals are sometimes mainstream and sometimes rather distinct from cultural norms. The book is not a systematic rendition of the sweep of evangelical history; there are a number of other books that do that well. Rather, the chapters are topical and organized around issues that animate evangelicals today and result in their being in the media frequently. Nevertheless, the book does seek to explain historically who evangelicals are and where they have come from while organizing that effort around the issues that make evangelicals so interesting. This book is for any reader who has ever seen a news item on evangelicals and wondered, "Who are these people?" or even, "Am I an evangelical?" The resulting picture reveals that evangelicals, when viewed historically, have been and continue to be part of the wide mainstream of American culture.

Preface Notes

1. Alan Wolfe, *The Transformation of American Religion: How We Actually Live Our Faith* (New York: Free Press, 2003), 36.

2. R. Laurence Moore, *Religious Outsiders and the Making of Americans* (New York: Oxford University Press, 1986).

~

Acknowledgments

I would like to thank Baylor University and the University Research Committee for a one-semester research leave during which I wrote the first draft of this book. Baylor's Institute for Studies of Religion, under the leadership of Bryon Johnson, provided a 2007 summer grant to support the book's completion. I would like to acknowledge my colleagues in the Baylor history department, especially Chair Jeff Hamilton and Tommy Kidd. Tommy listened to and critiqued many of my interpretative ideas and provided helpful insights on a variety of matters. Michael Hamilton of Seattle Pacific University read the entire manuscript, made helpful suggestions, and saved me from some embarrassing errors. I am solely responsible for any errors that remain.

I also would like to thank Critical Issues series editor Donald Critchlow and acquisitions editor Laura Gottlieb for their encouragement when the book was just an idea and editor Michael McGandy, who offered helpful ideas for final revisions when the manuscript neared completion. Finally, as always, I would like to express my gratitude to my wife Becky, who never seems to weary of hearing about American evangelicals and how they might be understood and explained. I dedicate this book to my son and daughter and Becky's three sons.

CHAPTER ONE

~

Awakenings and the Beginning
of American Evangelicalism

According to the best sociological data available, just under one-third of Americans are evangelicals or "conservative Protestants," as they are also called.[1] Evangelicals and fundamentalists are highly visible during political campaigns, especially presidential races every four years. A key question for every would-be Republican presidential candidate is how well he or she will appeal to evangelical voters, especially those associated with the Christian Right political movement. Because evangelicals have become the most reliable and influential voting bloc in the Republican Party, many in society fear their power and are convinced that evangelicals are intolerant and a threat to democratic values. Recently, author Chris Hedges referred to evangelicals and fundamentalists in the Christian Right as "American fascists." This was just three years after Alan Wolfe made his "We're all evangelicals now" quip (see Preface). The irony is that the same book publisher published these two widely divergent views.[2] So which is it? Hedges's threat to democracy or Wolfe's quintessentially American? Better yet, who are the evangelicals, and what do they want?

Among historians and other scholars there has developed a fairly strong consensus as to what defines evangelical Protestantism, at least in terms of theological beliefs. British scholar David Bebbington has nicely summarized the four essentials of evangelicalism as (1) Biblicism, (2) crucicentrism, (3) conversionism, and (4) activism.[3] Biblicism simply means the reliance on the Bible for religious authority above all other authorities. Put simply, evangelicals hold all beliefs up to the test of scripture. If a belief is deemed to be

1

unbiblical, it should be rejected. If a belief is considered biblical, it must be believed. The Bible is the highest authority in matters of faith.

Crucicentrism, while an unusual word, refers simply to the emphasis on Christ's crucifixion on the cross. Traditional or orthodox Christians of all sorts have always emphasized the importance of Christ's death and resurrection, but some modern forms of liberal Christianity have stressed Christ's moral witness more than his crucifixion. Liberal Christians sometimes interpret Christ's death on the cross as a symbol of Christ's selfless love that humans should emulate. Although not alone, evangelicals are among those Christians who continue to believe that the cross is more than a symbol. Jesus's crucifixion was a sacrifice for the sins of humankind followed by Christ's literal and bodily resurrection without which there is no hope for the salvation of humans.

The third component of Bebbington's four-fold definition of evangelicalism is conversionism. This term refers to the life-transforming and supernatural experience that evangelicals believe is central to the Christian faith. For most evangelicals, conversion is a singular and immediate event, although a minority of evangelicals believes that individuals can grow into conversion over a span of time. Some liberal Christians, who are discussed in chapter two, see little need for conversion since all people are children of God all the time. Most evangelicals, by contrast, believe that the conversion experience itself is a life-transforming event. This feature of evangelicalism is a product of revivalism that is discussed below. Of course, evangelicals also believe that once a person converts he or she should grow in relationship to God through Christ, but the conversion experience itself is most often considered a one-time event that marks the beginning of one's Christian walk.

Activism, Bebbington's fourth marker for evangelicalism, refers to the belief that Christians should be involved in the world. The primary form of activism is evangelism, which is the spreading of the Christian faith through preaching, witnessing, and missionary work. While not synonymous, the terms *evangelical* and *evangelism* are related. Both come from the root word *evangel*, which is usually translated as "good news." Evangelism is the spreading of the good news that Christ's death took away the sins of the world so that individuals who accept Christ can experience salvation. Activism can also take other forms of cultural engagement including moral and political reform. As discussed below, nineteenth-century evangelicals started a strong reform tradition that continues in many evangelical quarters today.

An evangelical, therefore, is a Christian who believes two things and experiences two things. He or she believes that the Bible is the supreme and authoritative foundation for truth and that Christ's death on the cross was a sacrifice for the sins of the world. As a result of these two beliefs, an evangelical experiences conversion through Christ and is then empowered to engage in an active and holy life of evangelism and service to humankind. Beyond these beliefs and experiences there is a dizzying array of diversity among American evangelicals. The best way to illustrate Bebbington's four components in action is to look at some history.

The First Great Awakening

Evangelical Christianity in a sense got its start in the Protestant Reformation of the sixteenth century. On October 31, 1517, Martin Luther posted his 95 Theses to the door of the Castle Church in Wittenberg, a small German town in the region of Saxony within the Holy Roman Empire. The 95 Theses constituted Luther's protest against the medieval Roman Catholic Church's insistence that people needed not only to confess their sins but also do penance to show they were genuinely contrite in order to experience salvation. Penance was one of the seven sacraments, and the Catholic Church taught that salvation comes to individuals by faith and participation in the sacraments. In opposition to this view, Luther and all Protestants after him came to believe that salvation was by faith alone. The first rallying cry of the Protestant Reformation, therefore, was *sola fides*, meaning "salvation by faith alone." In other words, a person could do nothing to contribute to his or her own salvation. Rather, an individual could only accept by faith that Christ had already done all that was necessary by dying on the cross—crucicentrism. While participating in the sacraments might be a means of worshipping God, Luther and the Protestants believed that salvation came to human beings only by faith in the grace of God; nothing else is required.

The second great rallying cry of Luther and the Protestants was *sola scriptura*, and one could argue that chronologically this belief came before *sola fides*. Through years of study, both of the Bible and the history of the church, Luther concluded that scripture was the highest authority in religious matters—Biblicism. As with *sola fides*, this contradicted the medieval Catholic Church, which taught that both the Bible and the church were authoritative. Luther and the other Protestants rejected the idea that the traditions and teachings of the church were authoritative in the same way the Bible had authority. While Protestants divided into several different groups or denominations based on secondary beliefs, virtually all Protestants from the sixteenth century to the early twentieth century held to *sola fides* and *sola scriptura*, which were essentially crucicentrism and Biblicism. During much of this period, the term *evangelical* was used as a synonym for Protestant.

Modern evangelicalism, as the term is used today, may have gotten its start during the Protestant Reformation, but evangelicalism received its distinctive shape in the English-speaking world during the awakenings of the eighteenth century. The First Great Awakening was a series of revivals that swept across the American colonies, up and down the eastern seaboard, from the 1730s into the 1760s and beyond. These American revivals occurred simultaneously with the Wesleyan revivals in England and what were called the Pietistic revivals on the continent of Europe. The two key figures associated with America's First Great Awakening were Jonathan Edwards and George Whitefield.

Edwards is often considered one of America's truly original thinkers. Born in East Windsor, Connecticut, he was the grandson of the Congregational preacher Solomon Stoddard, whom Edwards would succeed as pastor in Northampton, Massachusetts. The Congregationalists of the early eighteenth century were the immediate descendents of the New England Puritans. Puritans came to New England in the early seventeenth century seeking to construct a godly commonwealth that would become a model Christian society. They received their name from their efforts to purify the Church of England. Massachusetts was the largest of the Puritan colonies and for two generations the church and state, while separate entities, sought to work together to fashion a godly society based on biblical principles. This effort was modeled after John Calvin's work in sixteenth-century Geneva, Switzerland, and the Puritans were Calvinist in their theology and politics. By the time Edwards was born in 1703, the dream of a commonwealth where only the godly were politically enfranchised was just about finished, having been killed off by increasing diversity and the need for tolerance of nonbelievers and a variety of Christians who were not Puritans. If New England were to ever be a godly place, it would have to be through voluntary, not legal, means.

Edwards was a precocious and brilliant child who grew up in an era when science, or natural philosophy as it was called then, was becoming a prominent intellectual activity. This was the era when the great Isaac Newton was still alive and president of the Royal Society in England, a prestigious community of scientists and philosophers. Edwards himself wrote a scientific treatise on spiders when he was a seventeen-year-old senior at Yale. He even performed an experiment shaking spiders off sticks to see how they could fly through the air from tree to tree. He concluded that the web material the spiders emitted was lighter than air and thereby allowed the creatures to stay aloft. Edwards graduated from Yale at the age of seventeen and received his master's degree at nineteen. He continued educating himself for the rest of his life and became conversant with the most important intellectual works of his time, including those written by John Locke, Newton, Rene Descartes, and others of the early Enlightenment period. His brilliance was manifested in his ability to rearticulate Calvinist theology in light of modern modes of thinking without compromising biblical orthodoxy, but for our purposes here, we are most interested in his role as a revivalist.[4]

Edwards became an assistant to his grandfather Solomon Stoddard at the Northampton Congregational Church in the late 1720s and succeeded him when Stoddard died in 1729. When he became pastor he encountered a myriad of social sins, including drunkenness and sexual promiscuity in Northampton and the surrounding New England towns. As he said in one sermon, "Licentious and immoral practices seem to get great head amongst young people. And how little appearance is there of a spirit of seriousness and religion to be seen among them? How little concern about their salvation and escaping eternal misery?"[5] Edwards set out to correct this through careful preaching and attention to the spiritual welfare of his parishioners. In 1734, the first revivals began. These spontaneous outpourings of the Holy Spirit touched the lives of hundreds, then thousands, of New Englanders. Within three months, Edwards estimated that 300 people had been converted, bringing the total membership of the Northampton congregation to over 600, nearly every adult in the town.[6] As word spread of the stirrings at Northampton, so did the revival, and soon many other towns throughout New England experienced awakenings. Over the course of the next few years, it is safe to estimate that thousands were touched by these revivals that would later be viewed as the beginning of the First Great Awakening.

It is important to point out that Edwards was not a ranting evangelist that one might see on late night television today. He was not the least given to dramatic displays of preaching. Rather, he read his sermons either from a manuscript or from very detailed notes. When he looked up, some said he appeared to stare at the rope hanging from the church bell in the back of the sanctuary. Still, his sermons had a powerful effect on his listeners, who were often struck with a profound sense of conviction for their sins and their need for conversion. During one sermon in 1741, Edwards's listeners were so taken by the power of his words that they shrieked, groaned, and shouted out their fears, believing they were going to hell. So intense was the commotion that Edwards had to stop preaching so that he and other ministers present could go among the people and soothe their distress.[7] That sermon became known famously as "Sinners in the Hands of an Angry God," which is now a standard entry in many American literature and history readers. Recalling his treatise and scientific experiments as a teenager, Edwards used the imagery of spiders in this sermon. He told his hearers that their wickedness pushed them downward toward hell and that their good works could stop the fall no more than a spider's web could stop a falling rock. Referring again to spiders, he said, "The God that holds you over the pit of hell, much as one holds a spider, or some loathsome insect, over the fire, abhors you, and is dreadfully provoked." Continuing, he said, "His wrath towards you burns like fire; . . . you are ten thousand times more abominable in his eyes, than the most hateful venomous serpent is in ours. You have offended him infinitely more than ever a stubborn rebel did his prince."[8] This portion of the sermon was later criticized and even parodied by scholars who were products of the Enlightenment idea that human beings were naturally good but corrupted by unnatural institutions.

At some points in the sermon, Edwards seemed to present God as an oppressive, menacing, and frightful being. It is important to point out, however, that Edwards was not trying to convince his listeners of the reality of hell. They already believed that. He was attempting to show them that they deserved hell because their sin and rebellion against God made them truly guilty. Still, the very God whom they had offended so deeply was the one keeping them out of hell and the one willing to deliver them from the pit. This portion of the sermon exemplified the Christian belief articulated perhaps most powerfully by John Calvin that human beings are depraved sinners incapable of pleasing God. The evangelical message was that only the grace of God through Christ's sacrificial death on the cross can bring sinners into salvation. For this reason, Edwards presented not only the reality of sin and hell but also the other half of the revival message as well: "And now you have an extraordinary opportunity, a day wherein Christ has flung the door of mercy wide open, and stands in the door calling and crying with a loud voice to poor sinners; . . . many that were very lately in the same miserable condition that you are in, are now in a happy state, with their hearts filled with love to him that has loved them, and washed them from their sins in his own blood, and rejoicing in hope of the glory of God. How awful is it to be left behind at such a day."[9] This was the evangelical revivalist message: You are a sinner, but Christ calls you to salvation that comes through his death on the cross. By the time Edwards preached "Sinners in the Hands of an Angry God," the revivals were in their second wave and spreading across the American colonies.

While Edwards's preaching in Northampton may have served as the precipitating event of the First Great Awakening, no one was more influential than George Whitefield (pronounced Whitfield). This was largely because Whitefield was an itinerant evangelist—that is, one who traveled incessantly, preaching to multitudes across England and the American colonies. He was born in 1714 in Gloucester, England, the youngest of seven children. His parents owned an inn, but his father died when Whitefield was only two years old. His mother remarried when Whitefield was ten, but his stepfather abandoned the family after he was unsuccessful in taking control of the family business. Whitefield's mother was convinced that her youngest son was destined for greatness, and with the exception of a brief period in Whitefield's teens she would not let him work at the inn with his brothers, who eventually owned it. Whitefield's grandfather and great-grandfather had been Anglican ministers, a position of social standing, and the family hoped that the young Whitefield might go into the ministry and thereby recapture some of the family's prestige. Little did they know that Whitefield would become the greatest preacher of his era and one of the greatest in the history of English-speaking Christianity. As his principal biographer has written, while Whitefield would have equal success in Great Britain and America, in the latter he would become the "prototypical culture hero as well."[10] In other words, Whitefield was America's first media superstar.

As a boy, Whitefield was fascinated with the English stage, as he studied plays and acting. This experience would be formative for the dramatic preaching style he would develop later. In the early 1730s, he moved for a time to Bristol to live with one of his brothers. While there, he attended church regularly and came to view religion as less a matter of social status and more a matter of personal experience, primarily the experience of the sacraments and worship liturgy of the Anglican Church. After returning to Gloucester, he had a religious epiphany and concluded that God had a special calling for his life. Soon thereafter, his mother learned of a program whereby young men without means could attend Oxford University as the servants of wealthy gentlemen. She pursued this for George, and he was admitted to Pembroke College at Oxford. His university admission in 1732 made the ministerial career his mother had dreamed of a possibility for Whitefield, and his religious experience intensified as he embarked on higher education. He became a devout Anglican Christian, frequently experiencing not only the sacraments but also meditation, prayer, fasting, and even mystical dreams.

At Oxford, Whitefield met the Wesley brothers, John and Charles, who played the major role in the founding of Methodism. Charles invited Whitefield to join with John and some other students who, like Whitefield, were serious and passionate about their faith. In derision, other students called the group the "Holy Club," "Bible Moths," or simply "Methodists," the latter because of their methodical approach to religion. Students in the Holy Club were generally disgusted with the laxity of morals among the general student body and sought to lead more holy lives. They met daily for prayer, fasting, Bible reading, and the sacraments. Whitefield fit well with this group.

Midway through his university years, Whitefield took a brief hiatus from his studies to recover from illness. He returned to Gloucester and did volunteer work in the prison and among the poor. In the midst of this work, he had another profound religious experience that he interpreted as his conversion or "new birth," after which he ceased to doubt his salvation. He subsequently began preaching to the prisoners and townsfolk of Gloucester. A few years later, John Wesley would have a similar experience of "salvation by faith." Although an ordained Anglican minister, Wesley for years struggled with doubts about his salvation until feeling his heart "strangely warmed" at a Bible study and prayer meeting at Aldersgate Street in London in 1738. This "new birth" experience of salvation by faith would become a staple of the revivalist evangelicalism that Whitefield and the Wesleys would help establish in Great Britain and the American colonies. It was nothing other than the conversionism plank of Bebbington's four-fold definition of evangelicalism. It should be noted that from the Reformation forward Martin Luther and others had similar experiences, but the evangelical form of conversion took a distinct shape in the eighteenth century. The experience was more immediate than Puritans and many other English-speaking Protestants had known. Moreover, the conversion experience was noninstitutional—that is, it usually came outside of the sacramental institutions of the established churches and often even outside of church buildings.

Whitefield graduated from Oxford in the spring of 1736 and was ordained as a deacon in the Anglican Church in June (he would be ordained a priest in 1739). At the urging of Charles Wesley, who along with his brother John had recently done mission work, Whitefield decided that God was calling him to be a missionary in the American colonies. Georgia was founded in 1732, primarily as an outpost for convicts and assorted petty criminals and debtors and as a military buffer between Spanish Florida and the Carolinas. Populated by soldiers, ex-convicts, and other roughnecks, there was great need for religion there. It took roughly a year for Whitefield to get his affairs in order so that he could leave for America. During that year, he became a star preacher in London.

London was the largest city in Europe, home to one in seven who lived in England and the center of a thriving commercial revolution. Whitefield made religion part of that commercial revolution. Just as other elements of fashion, merchandise, and culture high and low started in the big city of London then were promptly exported elsewhere, so did the revivalist brand of evangelicalism that Whitefield was marketing. As his acclaim grew in the city, he published his first sermon, which bore the marks of evangelical conversionism. Titled "The Nature and Necessity of Our Regeneration or New Birth in Christ," it appeared in print in 1737. In the sermon he asked listeners to imagine what would happen if a person experienced a "thorough, real, inward change of heart?"[11] While there might not be much of a change in one's head knowledge of religion—that is, an individual may already believe all the necessary things of biblical religion—real conversion would result in a profound change in feelings and passions that would reorient one's entire life. This was the type of conversion Whitefield preached, usually to people already orthodox in their knowledge of theology and already of the belief that the Bible was the supreme authority in religious matters. In terms of revivalist evangelicalism, however, they were unconverted until they had an inward and supernatural experience of forgiveness of sins that was possible because of Christ's death on the cross.

Whitefield became well-known in and around London in the year leading up to his departure for the American colonies. Thousands attended services regularly to hear him preach. When he went to Georgia in 1738, his stay lasted barely longer than the voyage over, about three months, and his most significant act was to lay the groundwork for an orphanage that would be the object of his care and fund-raising for the rest of his life. The Bethesda orphanage, as it was named, is still in operation today near Savannah. Back in London by the end of the year, he resumed his revival preaching, which more and more was done outdoors in fields in order to accommodate the crowds that grew to well over 10,000 and sometimes possibly twice that. Calculating from Whitefield's estimates, often confirmed by newspaper reports, it is likely that in the summer of 1739 he preached to somewhere between 800,000 and 1 million people.[12] The scope of his preaching was unprecedented in the history of English-speaking Christianity, and he was also busy writing sermons and other tracts for publication, making him and his evangelical cause all the more famous.

All this drew Whitefield back to the American colonies, as he seems to have intentionally created a transatlantic, international revivalist evangelicalism. Landing in Delaware on October 30, 1739, for his second visit, he chose Philadelphia as his first preaching stop. He preached at Christ Church on November 6, then two days later, at the urging of supporters, moved outdoors and preached from the courthouse steps to an audience of 6,000. In the crowd that day was Benjamin Franklin, who although himself was not religious in any orthodox sense, would become a Whitefield supporter and friend. Having heard that Whitefield had preached in England to crowds approaching

30,000, the scientifically inclined Franklin performed an informal inductive experiment to test the theory that many people could hear Whitefield's voice. While Whitefield preached, Franklin walked away from the courthouse as far as he could while still hearing the sermon. Franklin then estimated how many people could fit between himself and Whitefield and concluded that indeed 30,000 or so would have been able to hear the sermon clearly.[13] Impressed by Whitefield's powers of persuasion, Franklin told of another time when he decided to attend a Whitefield revival but give no money at the end of the service. As he listened, Franklin said he softened and decided to give his copper coins. As Whitefield preached, Franklin was moved to give his silver, and by the time Whitefield completed the sermon, Franklin had decided to give all the money he had with him. Franklin also told of a friend who deliberately left his money at home to ensure he would give nothing. By the end of the sermon the friend was hitting up others in the crowd to borrow money to give.

By the end of November, Whitefield had preached from Philadelphia to New York and back, then he headed South, preaching his way down the coast to Georgia where he would survey the work of his orphanage. As he moved across the colonies, Whitefield became the first intercolonial megastar in America history. Newspapers gave his revivals major coverage, tens of thousands showed up to hear him, and the revivals themselves became the first major transcolonial event in American history. This was at a time when Americans were becoming more, not less, British, largely because the government in England had begun to tighten its administrative reigns over the empire through Navigation Acts and other laws geared toward integrating the colonies into the empire. At the same time, however, the revivals would help Americans begin to develop a sense of their own solidarity as distinct from the mother country. This being the case, the revivals were instrumental in the coming of the American Revolution, an event that could not have happened until the colonists had developed a sense of self-consciousness distinct from England. Some historians argue that without the revivals of the First Great Awakening, there could have been no American Revolution.

Whitefield did not create the First Great Awakening. Rather, he joined a revivalist movement that was already underway and gave that movement its greatest impetus. In addition to the revivals that occurred under Edwards's preaching in New England, the middle colonies experienced revivals precipitated by the preaching of the Tennents. William Tennent was a Presbyterian preacher who founded a "Log College" in New Jersey where he trained his sons and others to be revival preachers. His son Gilbert became a highly significant preacher, and revivalists replicated the Log College phenomenon elsewhere. Some of these rudimentary preacher-training schools would develop into fine colleges and universities. Also from the middle colonies was Theodore Frelinghuysen, a Dutch Reformed preacher whose preaching as far back as the 1720s had laid the groundwork for the revivals that the Tennents would lead. Such preparation in the 1720s was much like the revivals Solomon Stoddard recorded as "refreshing showers" that preceded the revivals in the 1730s under his grandson Edwards.

The revivals that created modern evangelicalism were controversial. Many revivalist features were unconventional, such as the preaching out of doors, preaching done by clergy who were uneducated, and public exhortation by women, much of which was essentially preaching.

There were signs, wonders, and emotions that conservatives viewed as extremist. Added to this were preachers who claimed that many of the ministers of the established churches were themselves in need of conversion. The classic example of the latter was Gilbert Tennent's "The Danger of an Unconverted Ministry," a sermon in which he urged people to judge for themselves whether their ministers were truly converted and to leave churches where ministers had not experienced the new birth. Over time, revivals became so prominent and so much a staple within American Christianity that much of the controversy was between moderate revivalists and more radical elements, as the voices of those opposed to revivals got lost in the shuffle.[14]

If it is difficult to pinpoint exactly when the First Great Awakening began, it is even more difficult to say when it ended. While the most intense period of revivals took place from Edwards's preaching in 1734 through Whitefield's visits to the colonies in the 1740s, revivals continued into the 1750s and 1760s, perhaps trailing off somewhat during the American Revolution (1775–1783), resuming sporadically thereafter, then exploding again in the Second Great Awakening of the early nineteenth century.

The Second Great Awakening

The period from 1775 to 1800 used to be known as a time of religious decline in America. The standard interpretation was that because of the war and the influence of Enlightenment deism, revivalist evangelical Protestantism faded. Enlightenment deism is a religion of reason that posits a God who created the world, instituted the laws of nature, then stepped back to let things happen according to those laws. The deists' God is, therefore, not very involved in the world. The Enlightenment had significant influence during the Revolutionary period, and some of the leading Founding Fathers of the nation seem to have been substantially deistic in their religious beliefs, notably

Thomas Jefferson. The deistic notion of religion would hold fast to traditional notions of morality that were considered part of the natural law, but there is little room for an activist God who sends His spirit in revivals. In this story of decline, revivals subsided only to explode onto the scene again during the Second Great Awakening of the early nineteenth century. More recent scholars are now challenging the declension motif. While acknowledging that the intensity of revivals may have been higher during the era of the First Great Awakening than after 1760 or so, it is now difficult to identify a period after 1740 when revivals were not a normal part of the American religious scene. It may well be that the period of the Revolution only looks less religious because it came in between the First Great Awakening of the 1730s and 1740s and the Second Great Awakening that began in the early nineteenth century.

At the dawn of the nineteenth century, the West was the least religious area of the country. Before the Revolution the British government had used the Appalachian Mountains as the Line of Demarcation beyond which American colonists were forbidden to settle. When America gained its independence as a result of the war, settlers began to pour into the region beyond the Appalachians, often moving westward faster than their churches and preachers could keep pace. When the first U.S. Census was taken in 1790, some 94 percent of the U.S. population lived in the original thirteen states along the eastern seaboard. By 1820, about one-quarter of the population lived outside the original thirteen states, and it is estimated that 800,000 people migrated West from New England during the intervening period. By 1850, more than half the U.S. population lived outside the original thirteen states. Andrew Fulton, a missionary, said it well when he wrote, "[In Nashville] and indeed almost all the newly formed towns in this western colony, there are few religious people."[15]

The revivals of the 1790s have traditionally been viewed as forerunners to the Second Great Awakening, which began in earnest on the Kentucky frontier in 1800 and 1801. The earliest revivals on the frontier took place under the preaching of James McGready or his associates. McGready had gone to Kentucky from North Carolina where his revivalist preaching had run afoul of conservative elements in his Presbyterian congregations. In Kentucky he pastored three congregations simultaneously, one of which was Gasper River. Kentucky was experiencing an influx of immigrants. The population of the state swelled from 73,000 in 1790 to more than 220,000 by 1800. Most of the settlers were young adults, and several revivalist preachers came with them, some of whom had been trained by McGready.[16] After some preliminary stirrings at two of McGready's churches, he sent out advance notice of a meeting to take place in July 1800 at Gasper River. The meeting turned into a three-day revival on the frontier, and the Gasper River revival is usually viewed as America's first camp meeting. People traveled as far as 100 miles to attend. An estimated forty-five people converted. By the end of the summer of 1800, revivals were percolating across Kentucky and Tennessee, and these would set the stage for the Great Revival at Cane Ridge the following year.

The key figure in the organization of the Cane Ridge revival in the summer of 1801 was Barton Stone, who was a McGready protégé. Stone pastored Cane Ridge and another church in Bourbon County and had gone over to McGready's revivals in Logan County to observe. He wanted nothing more than to see the revival spirit enter his own frontier area, so he scheduled a camp meeting revival for Cane Ridge that was to begin on August 6, 1801. He sent word out and expected people to come, but neither Stone nor anyone else could have predicted the numbers. Eyewitness estimates ran from 10,000 to 25,000 in attendance. Although organized by a Presbyterian, Baptists and Methodists attended the Great Revival at Cane Ridge as well. For several days multiple speakers preached from platforms set up at various locations across the encampment, and hundreds converted. As was usually the case at revivals, emotions ran high, and there were a variety of manifestations of religious experience, including crying, shouting, jerking, falling, and, according to some witnesses, even barking. While conservative critics derided these as excessive, those present believed the emotional outbursts were true manifestations of the Holy Spirit's work.

While usually dating the beginning of the Second Great Awakening with the Great Revival at Cane Ridge in 1801, it is increasingly difficult to say when the Second Great Awakening came to a close. The businessmen's revivals of 1858 are sometimes used as the late date for the end of the Second Great Awakening, but such a historical judgment seems driven more by the coming of the Civil War in 1861 than anything else. Whatever periodization one wants to use for the Second Great Awakening, the primary point is that revivalist evangelicalism that had begun during the First Great Awakening had become the dominant form of religion in America by the mid-nineteenth century.

If there was a peak during the era of the Second Great Awakening, it probably came during the urban revivals of the 1820s and 1830s, especially those led by Charles Grandison Finney. Finney trained as a lawyer before converting in the early 1820s. Following his conversion he allegedly told a client, "I have a retainer from the Lord Jesus Christ to plead his cause, and I cannot plead yours."[17] He began preaching revivals in 1824, and over the next decade led crusades in the major urban centers of America. More than anyone else, Finney helped move revivals from the frontier to the cities and thereby made revivalist evangelicalism a staple of American culture. Just as White-field had in some ways set the stage for Finney, Finney continued the re-vivalist tradition that would include Dwight L. Moody in the late nineteenth century, Billy Sunday and Aimee Semple McPherson in the early twentieth century, then Billy Graham in the second half of the twentieth century and into the twenty-first. Such individual preachers, however, were merely the most public of the evangelical figures. Through the rest of the nineteenth century, until the advent of theological modernism (to be discussed later), all the Protestant denominations were broadly evangelical as defined by Beb-bington's four components. The Methodists grew to be the largest Protestant denomination, Baptists made great gains throughout the century, and Pres-byterians held a significant share of members as well along with many smaller denominations.

There has been a historical school of interpretation, sometimes called loosely "the social control school," that has interpreted revivals as conserva-tive events. Essentially, the argument is that business leaders in urban areas promoted revivals as a means of controlling the behavior of their workers. They wanted to keep them sober, honest, and hardworking, in other words, to control them.[18] This interpretation was most influential in the 1970s and into the 1980s, but more recent scholars have argued that revivals were so-cially unsettling events that often empowered working-class people and women. In other words, revivals led to progressive reform. In particular, some studies show a correlation between urban revivals and worker activism that led to the formation of unions. As historian William Sutton has written in challenging the social control school, "[Evangelical artisans] provided an op-positional language and legacy to challenge the rising hegemony of laissez-faire economics and industrial capitalism."[19] Indeed, as Sutton argues, re-vivals empowered workers by giving them a language of justice and morality that they could use to resist unjust demands made by business owners.

Revivals also carried a sense of social equality that was a result of the evangelical notion that all people are sinners in need of salvation. Using the crucicentrism plank of Bebbington's four evangelical components, this is sometimes stated, "All are equal at the foot of the cross." For example, the Finney revivals seem to have accelerated women preaching in both the re-vivals and antislavery meetings. The Grimké sisters, Sarah and Angelina, are the most famous examples. Certainly, there were conservative elements within evangelicalism that resisted women preachers. In fact, both those such as Finney who supported female preaching and those who were scan-dalized by the practice were often evangelicals, and very few women were actually ordained as ministers. Still, to the extent that women were empowered spiritually, the revivals were usually responsible.[20]

Thus, we see that while all four of Bebbington's evangelical components were at work in the Second Great Awakening, the activism plank was especially prominent. When Finney and other revivalists preached, they assumed that a life of reform activism would follow conversion. Many of the antislavery reformers were Finney converts, and evangelicals also led in the area of women's rights, education and prison reform, and temperance. Blurring the social distinctions between men and women, the revivals had a similar effect on the class distinctions between urban workers and the owners of the industries where they worked.

If there is an event that marked the end of the Second Great Awakening period, it was probably the series of revivals of 1858. Like Finney's meetings, these were mostly urban revivals, and like the earlier eras of revival intensity, they were preceded by spiritual stirrings before the revival fervor broke with great intensity. It should also be said that as was often the case with revivals, the 1858 outpouring occurred simultaneously in a variety of places. Sometimes historians can trace influences from one area to another, but at other times the outbreak of revivals in unrelated locations at roughly the same time defies historical explanation. In the autumn of 1857, Jeremiah Calvin Lanphier began noon businessmen's bible and prayer times in New York City. By the following spring, these meetings, which had started with five or six men, were being attended by as many as 50,000 people across the city. A March 20, 1858, *New York Times* article reported: "We have seen in a business quarter of the city, in the busiest hours, assemblies of merchants, clerks and working men, to the number of 5,000, gathered day after day for simple and solemn worship. Similar assemblies we find in other portions of the City; a theatre is turned into a chapel; churches of all sects are opened and crowded by day and night."[21] These businessmen's revivals spread to Philadelphia then across the nation with even liturgical denominations such as the Episcopalians and Lutherans affected significantly. These revivals were reported quite positively in newspapers across the country, many articles noting the drop in violence and crime in the areas most affected. Revivals were mainstream American events by midcentury, and as was the case during the First Great Awakening, the revivals of 1858 were a transatlantic phenomenon with British cities also experiencing revivals. Evangelical Protestantism was entering a period when it would be the dominant form of religion in America and Great Britain. That period would last until the turn of the century and would see another of America's great revivalist evangelical preachers rise to prominence, Dwight L. Moody (who is discussed in the next chapter).[22]

Conclusion

Today there is a fairly strong consensus that evangelical revivals gave American Christianity a distinctly populist and democratic cast. In revivals, the audience was sovereign, historian Nathan Hatch has argued. By this, Hatch means that in a revival setting the common people decide which preachers have authority and legitimacy. The audience bestows the mantle of authority on the preachers who best stir the people's hearts and minds. This mantle of authority was not given to preachers because they had education or social status but rather because they could communicate effectively with the masses. They won the right to be heard. Many of the preachers of the Second Great Awakening period were not highly educated elites. Rather, they were from common stock and were able to preach salvation in a way that grabbed the attention of common listeners.

This "democratization of American Christianity" has continued even to the present, as often preachers who have little formal theological education and are not credentialed by major religious denominations lead the largest megachurches and television ministries. This distinctly democratic feature has helped religion remain influential among the majority of Americans. Common people in America often identify with religion over the dominant institutions of society such as the state, the media, the universities, and corporations. Religious institutions are their refuge against power. They feel empowered by religion against other forces that sometimes seek to dominate their lives. By contrast, in Europe, where churches are often supported by the state, common people view religion as aligned with the institutions that seek to dominate them. They, therefore, turn to secular and sometimes antireligious organizations for empowerment, labor unions and political parties in particular.[23] So it is that evangelicalism, as the most popular and influential form of religion in American history, has usually been a religion of the people and for the people. A new form of liberal or modernist Protestantism would challenge nineteenth-century American evangelicalism, however.

Notes

1. Christian Smith, *Christian America?: What Evangelicals Really Want* (Berkeley: University of California Press, 2000), 16–17. Smith puts the percentage of evangelicals at 29 percent. This is a judicious, perhaps even conservative, estimate based on polling data.

2. Chris Hedges, *American Fascists: The Christian Right and the War on America* (New York: Free Press, 2006); Alan Wolfe, *The Transformation of American Religion: How We Actually Live Our Faith* (New York: Free Press, 2003), 36.

3. David Bebbington, *The Dominance of Evangelicalism: The Age of Spurgeon and Moody* (Downers Grove, Illinois: InterVarsity Press, 2005), 22–23. I have listed these in a slightly different order than Bebbington does. Although the four appear here in this 2005 book, Bebbington first discussed these components in the 1980s. Other scholars of evangelicalism, such as George Marsden and Grant Wacker, have used similar three- or four-component lists. Virtually all scholars of evangelicalism stress the authority of the Bible, the conversion experience, and the impulse for evangelism as components of evangelicalism.

4. The standard biography of Edwards is George Marsden, *Jonathan Edwards: A Life* (New Haven, Connecticut: Yale University Press, 2003), 64–65.

5. Quoted in Marsden, *Jonathan Edwards*, 126.

6. Marsden, *Jonathan Edwards*, 160.

7. Marsden, *Jonathan Edwards*, 220.

8. Quoted in Marsden, *Jonathan Edwards*, 223.

9. Quoted in Marsden, *Jonathan Edwards*, 224.

10. Harry Stout, *The Divine Dramatist: George Whitefield and the Rise of Modern Evangelicalism* (Grand Rapids, Michigan: Eerdmans, 1991), xiv and 1–3; quote on xiv. Unless otherwise noted, the following material on Whitefield comes from Stout's biography. Stout makes Whitefield's dramatic interests central, as Stout's title reveals.

11. Quoted in Stout, *The Divine Dramatist*, 39.

12. This is Stout's estimate.

13. Benjamin Franklin, *The Autobiography of Benjamin Franklin* (New York: Simon and Shuster, 2004).

14. Thomas Kidd, *The Great Awakening: The Roots of Evangelical Christianity in Colonial America* (New Haven, Connecticut: Yale University Press, 2007).

15. Quoted in John Boles, *The Great Revival: Beginnings of the Bible Belt* (Lexington: University Press of Kentucky, 1972), 17.

16. See Boles 45–47 and Bernard Weisberger, *They Gathered at the River: The Story of the Great Revivalists and Their Impact upon Religion in America* (Boston, Massachusett: Little, Brown, 1958), 24–26.

17. Quoted in Keith J. Hardman, *Charles Grandison Finney, 1792–1875: Revivalist and Reformer* (Syracuse, New York: Syracuse University Press, 1987), 43.

18. A classic example of the social control school is Paul Johnson, *A Shopkeeper's Millennium: Society and Revivals in Rochester, New York, 1815–1837* (New York: Hill and Wang, 1978), 15–18.

19. William R. Sutton, *Journeymen for Jesus: Evangelical Artisans Confront Capitalism in Jacksonian Baltimore* (University Park: Pennsylvania State University Press, 1998).

20. See Catherine Brekus, *Strangers and Pilgrims: Female Preaching in America, 1740–1845* (Chapel Hill: University of North Carolina Press, 1998).

21. Quoted in Roy Fish, *When Heaven Touched Earth: The Awakening of 1858 and Its Effects on Baptists* (Azle, Texas: Need of the Times Publishers, 1996), 44. See also Kathryn Long, *The Revival of 1857–58: Interpreting an American Religious Awakening* (New York: Oxford University Press, 1998).

22. Bebbington, *The Dominance of Evangelicalism.*

23. Nathan Hatch, *The Democratization of American Christianity* (New Haven, Connecticut: Yale University Press, 1989).

CHAPTER TWO

~

The Struggle with Modernism

Origins of the Culture Wars

Beginning in the second half of the nineteenth century, a new approach to
theology developed within American Protestantism that seriously challenged the American evangelical consensus. Originally from Europe, modernist or liberal theology was articulated by scholars such as Horace Bushnell
and popularized by preachers such as Phillips Brooks and Henry Ward
Beecher. The evangelical response to this liberal challenge would result in
the fundamentalist-modernist controversy that would divide Protestantism
and shape twentieth-century fundamentalism.

The Rise of Theological Modernism

Theological modernism is best defined as (1) the adjusting of religious ideas
to modern ways of thinking; (2) the idea that God is immanent (meaning
close to humans) and is revealed in cultural development; and (3) the belief
that civilization was progressing toward the kingdom of God.[1] In short,
therefore, modernism meant adjustment, immanence, and progress. The discussion of modernism below will focus mostly on adjustment. The three most
important modern modes of thought to which modernism adjusted were Romanticism, evolutionary science, and literary criticism. In adapting to these
three intellectual movements, modernism developed its ideas of immanence
and progress. By the 1930s, theological modernism was known as theological
liberalism, and the terms are often used interchangeably.

Romanticism emphasized feelings and intuition as sources of divine truth. In America, during the era of the Second Great Awakening, transcendentalists such as Ralph Waldo Emerson and Henry David Thoreau reacted against evangelicalism and Enlightenment deism by arguing that truth was not something found in scripture, as evangelicals argued, nor something demonstrated through rational argument, as Enlightenment rationalists said, but rather was something that was experienced in the depths of one's soul largely through feeling and intuition. As is well known, Thoreau built a small cabin next to Walden Pond in Massachusetts and lived in solitude for nearly three years so that he could experience nature and the divine. This Romantic element, as presented in German theology and American transcendentalism, became part of the modernist Protestant adjustment to the evangelical idea of biblical authority. In other words, modernists moved away from the idea that theology was a fixed set of truths found in scripture and toward the notion that theology had to do with one's experience of God through feeling and intuition.

The Romantic component of modernism caught on first in America with some well-known and popular preachers in the second half of the nineteenth century. Episcopal minister Phillips Brooks is an example of the Romantic aspect of theological modernism in action. Brooks was born into an affluent, but not rich, Boston family in 1835. His mother was evangelical, his father Unitarian, and for a time while Brooks was growing up the family attended a Unitarian Church. Unitarians were the New England liberals of the day. They rejected many traditional evangelical beliefs, most notably the trinity, hence the name Unitarian. Largely because of his mother's dissatisfaction with the liberal Unitarian Church, the Brooks family joined St. Paul's Episcopal Church. Low-church evangelicalism dominated the Episcopal Church in New England at the time. This meant that there was less emphasis on the forms of liturgical worship and more on biblical themes and a heartfelt relationship with Christ—i.e., Biblicism, preaching, worship, and conversion experiences were all carried out with modesty and decorum fitting the rising middle class in New England. Episcopalian evangelicals were heartfelt believers, but they wanted nothing to do with anything that smacked of a frontier camp meeting.[2]

Brooks attended Harvard College then Virginia Theological Seminary, an Episcopal school in Alexandria. By the time he reached seminary he had been reading Romantic poets for many years—Coleridge, Wordsworth, Tennyson, and Barrett Browning among them. From these he absorbed the Romantic celebration of the self that was also a major part of American transcendentalism. Traditional evangelicalism, especially in its New England

Calvinist form, taught that human beings are inherently depraved by sin and in need of Christ's atoning work on the cross. Celebrating oneself, in the Romantic or transcendentalist way, was nearly the opposite. In ways he could not have known at the time, Brooks's reading of the Romantics paved the way for his modernistic preaching that would come later.

While at seminary, Brooks began reading Horace Bushnell. Bushnell was a theologian and pastor in Hartford, Connecticut, from 1833 to 1859, and he continued to write theology until his death in 1876. In one of his early books, Bushnell argued against the idea of revivalist conversion, saying that children could be raised in the faith from infancy and never need a dramatic experience. His central project early in the 1840s was to explore the nature of theological language. Bushnell and other modernists influenced by Romanticism would come to believe that all theological language, including the Bible, was figurative and symbolic instead of literal and historic. Real truth lay beneath words and concepts and had to be experienced. By the 1860s, Bushnell had rejected the crucicentric evangelical idea that Christ died on the cross as a substitute for guilty sinners. Rather, Christ's death was a symbol of God's love. As Bushnell put it, Christ's death was "not a sacrifice in any literal sense."[3]

Brooks's mother warned him against Bushnell, but in his surviving library, no books show more sign of use than Bushnell's.[4] The primary effect that Bushnell had was to make Brooks impatient with theological dogma. Brooks first soft-pedaled and then rejected the aforementioned Calvinist idea of the depravity of humans, and eventually he also rejected the Calvinist idea that God elects some people to be saved but not others. Brooks became fond of a quote from Henry Ward Beecher, another famous early liberal preacher: "The Elect are whosoever will, the Non-elect, whosoever won't."[5] In other words, Brooks and Beecher believed anyone could choose to experience God.

During his seminary training and first years in the ministry, Brooks came to believe that Christianity was essentially about feeling close to God and following the moral example of Christ's love. Brooks went on to become one of the nineteenth century's "princes of the pulpit" at Holy Trinity Church in Philadelphia, then Trinity Church in Boston, the most fashionable and influential church in the city. In their preaching, Brooks, Beecher, and the other Romantic liberals emphasized that individuals could have a direct experience with God that did not necessarily rely on the kinds of doctrinal formulations evangelical Protestants had derived from scripture. Of course, evangelicalism had always emphasized in its revivals that individuals could have a direct religious experience with God, and by the late nineteenth century, there were Romantic influences even within evangelicalism.[6] Romantic experience of an evangelical kind, however, was defined and limited by the doctrines of the Christian church. In evangelical revivals, individuals became aware of their sinful nature and the vast chasm that separated them from a holy God. They believed that Christ had died on the cross and rose from the grave so that human beings could be saved, and they confessed their sins to the risen Christ in order to experience forgiveness and the new birth. This was a supernatural experience. By contrast, Brooks and other liberal preachers spoke of a religious experience without doctrinal notions such as original sin and the bodily resurrection of Christ. Moreover, they did not believe there was a vast chasm between God and humankind because humans were basically good and God was immanent, or near to, each person. While the experience of God was spiritual, it was more natural than evangelical revivalists had believed. Experiencing God in this way was based on feeling and intuition, much like Thoreau's experience of nature. God was near, human beings were very much like God, and so the experience of God was a natural part of discovering and celebrating the religious sentiment present in the self from birth.

This sort of theological modernism presented a direct challenge to the evangelical idea of crucicentrism and to the traditional understanding of the incarnation. The incarnation is the historic Christian belief that Christ was God in the flesh. Evangelicals believe this, but they believe it was a supernatural event, and they tend to emphasize Christ's crucifixion and resurrection as the atonement for sin more than the incarnation. The only way for sinful human beings to be made right with God was for the incarnate Christ to die as a sacrifice for the sins of the world. Modernists, by contrast, emphasized Christ's life, not his death and resurrection, as a model of what humans could become through experience. Even the incarnation, in this way of thinking, was more natural than supernatural. The idea that Christ was God in the flesh was reinterpreted to mean that he was the best model of what a human being should be and that individuals should emulate Christ's life of love and service. Such emulation of Christ was possible because all human beings were children of God. As one modernist theologian wrote, "[M]an as man is the child of God. He does not need to become a child of God, he needs only to recognize that he already is such."[7] There was certainly a good deal of overlap between evangelical and liberal Protestantism, and it is hard to say whether someone like Horace Bushnell was evangelical, liberal, or both. Evangelicals believe that Christians should try to emulate Christ's life, but they also believe that the real crux of salvation is not in such emulation but in the supernatural work of salvation through Christ's death and resurrection. Only through a supernatural conversion, evangelicals believe, can an individual become a child of God.

For modernists, it was a short step from de-emphasizing Christ's death and resurrection to the de-emphasis of other fundamentals of the faith that evangelicals held dear. For example, evangelicals, like Roman Catholic and Eastern Orthodox Christians, believe that the incarnation necessitated a virgin birth of Christ. The baby Jesus was not the result of a natural sexual union of male and female humans but was literally the son of God born of the Virgin Mary. By the early twentieth century, many modernist theologians rejected the virgin birth, noting that the Greek term for *virgin* in the New Testament could mean simply "young woman." In addition to there being little theological need to retain the virgin birth in a naturalized form of Protestantism, modernist theologians also came to view such an idea as too fantastic to believe in a modern scientific age. As they adjusted Protestant theology in light of modern science, some modernists rejected not only the virgin birth but also most other miracles found in scripture as well, including Christ's literal resurrection. For some modernists the resurrection was a purely spiritual event that did not include the resuscitation of Jesus's body, while for more radical modernists, the resurrection was nothing more than the memory of Christ in the minds of his disciples and their desire to keep his teachings alive in the future. The resurrection in this way of thinking was figurative, not literal. In the end, modernists largely redefined Christianity as a religion where God is immanent, human beings are generally good, and the best way of worshipping is to focus on the incarnation and to do good works. The essence of religion is feeling, not theology, and good works, not supernatural new birth.

In addition to the Romantic element of early theological modernism, evolution was the second modern idea to which theological modernists responded. While the specific controversies about evolutionary science are addressed in the next chapter, it is important here to understand the effect Darwin's ideas had on all intellectual life in the late nineteenth century, including Protestant theology. Charles Darwin published *Origin of Species* in 1859 and *The Descent of Man* in 1870. While he was not the first to theorize on the evolution of species, his works nevertheless popularized evolution, postulated a particular theory as to how evolution took place, and presented a challenge to supernatural readings of scripture. Almost all areas of intellectual life soon applied Darwin's evolutionary model, including theology. Applied to theology, the evolutionary model essentially meant that Christianity, like everything else, evolved over time. This meant that the form of faith found in scripture was a rudimentary and basic form of Christianity that evolved over nineteen centuries into a more fully developed religion. This way of thinking was a direct challenge to evangelical Biblicism, which held that the Bible was authoritative in all matters pertaining to faith. Instead of the authority of scripture, modernist theologians believed that modern religious experience could transcend even the Bible. Modernist preacher Henry Ward Beecher put it best when he said that the oaks of civilization had evolved over time. He asked, therefore, why we should "go back and talk about acorns?"[8] The implication of such a statement was that the Bible represented the acorn, or seed, from which grew the fully evolved oak tree of Christianity in the late nineteenth century.

Religious adaptation to evolutionary development accounted largely for the idea of progress that virtually all western European and American intellectuals adopted in the nineteenth century. Modernist theologians were by no means unusual among academics in their belief that civilization was progressing toward virtual utopia. Modernists simply believed that such progress was part of God revealing himself through culture. Whereas evangelicals believed God revealed himself in scripture and in the person of Christ, modernists believed God revealed himself also in cultural development. Several theologians and preachers influenced by modernism became part of the Social Gospel movement. Washington Gladden and Walter Rauschenbusch, the two most prominent Social Gospel figures, spoke not just of the salvation of individuals but also the salvation of society. They believed that society's economic and political systems could experience social salvation that would result in justice and fairness for all people. Most modern thinkers in America also believed that God was being revealed in the march of democracy and civilization, and for this reason they usually supported American imperialism. When the United States colonized the Philippines after the Spanish-American War of 1898, for example, many modernists as well as evangelicals believed this would allow America to spread democracy to the Filipinos and thus advance the Kingdom of God.

As theological modernists adjusted Protestant theology in light of Romanticism and science, they also began to use modern literary criticism in their understanding of the Bible. Use of modern literary criticism was modernism's third adjustment. Modernist biblical scholars approached the text of scripture in its original languages (Hebrew for the Old Testament and Greek for the New) just as they approached all other ancient texts. All questions were fair game—the dating and authorship of various books of the Bible, the dating of biblical events, and even the question as to whether certain biblical events actually occurred. This approach to the Bible became known as "higher criticism." Like the evolutionary approach to the faith, higher criticism of scripture also came largely from German theological schools.

The "documentary hypothesis" that higher critics accepted was particularly alarming for some evangelicals. The documentary hypothesis concerned the Pentateuch, the first five books of the Old Testament. The traditional view was that Moses had authored these books. Through the use of higher textual criticism, nineteenth-century German scholars concluded that these books had actually been written over a long period of time by many different authors. Redactors then edited the various texts, creating the Pentateuch. Because the hypothesis cast doubt on the authorship of the Pentateuch, it seemed likewise to cast doubt on biblical authority. Rather than being authored by a well-known prophet of God, the books were authored by who knows whom and then edited by a second group of unknown individuals. This made the Bible much like other historical texts, rather than the specially inspired revelation of God.

Some evangelicals were able to use the methods of higher criticism without adopting naturalistic conclusions about the Bible. Other evangelicals, however, believed that the documentary hypothesis and other forms of higher criticism cast doubt on the Bible's historical reliability. Modernist biblical scholars interpreted many Old Testament events as mythology with little basis in historical fact. Some passages in the book of Daniel that had traditionally been interpreted as prophecy of future events were redated so that the so-called prophecy came after the event. Most higher critics became convinced that at least two different authors wrote the book of Isaiah, and so on. For some evangelical scholars the conclusions of higher criticism were less problematic than the modernist presuppositions employed by the critics. As one evangelical scholar put it: "If the critics were content with attempting a partition of Genesis . . . on purely literary grounds . . . this would be a matter of curious interest but nothing more. The serious aspect of the affair is that there are presuppositions involved in the arguments employed and there are deductions made which are prejudicial to or subversive of the credibility and inspired authority of the sacred record."[9] In other words, some evangelicals were not threatened by the idea that there were two authors of the book of Isaiah or multiple authors of the Pentateuch. Rather, they reacted primarily against the underlying naturalistic presupposition that the Bible was pretty much like other ancient texts and should therefore be interpreted naturally, not supernaturally. Still, for many evangelicals, especially at the popular level, the findings of higher criticism challenged the view that the Bible was a straightforward, historically factual rendition of ancient events that was reliable and without error in all of its details. Most evangelicals viewed higher criticism to be a direct chal-lenge to evangelical Biblicism.

By the late nineteenth century, higher criticism of scripture was be-coming more and more prominent in the theological seminaries of the northern and northeastern United States. Indeed, while in 1870 most Americans, including intellectuals in universities, agreed on what it meant for the Bible to be "the word of God," by 1900 there were a variety of interpretations within seminaries, divinity schools, and universities as to what this meant.[10] A typical modernist view expressed by William Newton Clarke was that the Bible was not itself authoritative. Rather, as Clarke wrote, "[T]he authority of the Scriptures is the authority of the truth that they convey."[11] Clarke argued that rather than a person's theol-ogy being dictated by the Bible, it "should be inspired in him by the Bible—or, more truly inspired in him through the Bible by the Spirit."[12] In other words, the truth was within humanity and was distinct from the Bible. The Bible gained its authority only because it gave testimony to the truth within. Evangelicals could not accept such distinctions between truth and scripture.

By the early twentieth century, modernists had stripped away a good bit of what had been considered essential to the Christian faith just a few decades before. In 1906, a book by University of Chicago Divinity School theologian George Burman Foster was described in the *Chicago Tribune* headline "Assails Canon of Bible . . . Declares Miracles Incredible and Says Proof of Resurrection Is Lacking." Foster had merely stated more rad-ically what many modernist theologians had believed for two decades, and the new thinking was making inroads into leading denominations and their seminaries.[13] Foster's home, the University of Chicago Divinity School, had been founded as a Baptist institution and endowed by entre-preneur John D. Rockefeller. The school had become a leading center for the development of modernist thought almost overnight. Other seminar-ies such as Union in New York City and Andover in Massachusetts were also well known for their modernist professors. Meanwhile, some leading big-city churches became well-known platforms for modernist preaching. The leading historian of theological modernism suggests that modernism substantially affected the major Protestant denominations of the North by 1920, especially among the theologians in the denominational seminaries, universities, and bureaucracies.[14] The inroads of modernism challenged the dominance of evangelicalism that had held sway in Great Britain and America during the nineteenth century. This challenge elicited a strong evangelical response.

The Evangelical Response to Modernism

Theological modernists believed that if not adjusted in light of modern science and literary criticism, Protestant theology would suffer an ignominious defeat and become the virtual laughingstock of the modern world. In short, they believed they were saving Protestantism. Evangelicals believed just the opposite. They viewed modernism as an attack on the Christian faith more serious than anything else in history. Some evangelicals believed they had a duty to defend traditional views in the face of the modernist challenge.

The leading evangelical preacher of the late nineteenth century was another of America's great revivalists, Dwight L. Moody. Moody was born in 1837 in rural Massachusetts and moved to Boston when he was seventeen. He was converted there and a short time later moved to Chicago where he became a successful shoe sales clerk. He was active in the Businessmen's Revival of 1857 and became a leader in the Young Men's Christian Association (YMCA), eventually becoming president. In Chicago in the 1860s he started a Sunday school for children that eventually became the Illinois Street Church with Moody as its pastor. The Chicago fire of 1871 destroyed the church, Moody's home, and the YMCA building. With little left in Chicago to tie him down, Moody accepted an invitation to preach a series of revival meetings in the British Isles. He hooked up with popular song leader Ira D. Sankey and had great success in Britain. Thousands converted under his preaching, and when he returned to the United States in 1875, he was a preaching star, much like Whitefield in the eighteenth century. By the time of his death in 1899 an estimated 1 million people had converted under Moody's preaching.[15]

Moody was in the revivalist tradition of Whitefield, Wesley, and Finney. He possessed a winsome personality and preached the love of God for sinners. His association with Sankey was reminiscent of John Wesley and his hymn-writing, song-leader brother Charles, as well as Billy Graham and his song leader George Beverly Shea nearly a century after Moody. Although orthodox and evangelical, Moody was relatively unconcerned about doctrine and had several modernist friends. Moody described his ministry as a lifeboat. "I look on this world as a wrecked vessel," he preached famously. "God has given me a lifeboat and said to me, 'Moody, save all you can.'" [16] Henry Ward Beecher used Moody's famous quote to describe the differences between himself and Moody, saying, "Mr. Moody thinks this is a lost world, and is trying to save as many as possible from the wreck; I think Jesus Christ has come to save the world, and I am trying to help him save it." The two statements point up the growing divergence between evangelical and modernist Protestants. Evangelicals were becoming increasingly premillennial. Premillennialism is the belief that the world will get worse and worse until Christ's Second Coming. In the meantime, the point of preaching is to get as many people saved as possible before Christ comes back. Liberals such as Beecher, holding to the idea of evolutionary progress, believed the world would get better and better. Evangelicals such as Moody retained the idea that salvation was for individuals, while civilization would degenerate. Liberals such as Beecher believed that civilization itself was in the process of being saved.

Moody was not a theological defender of the faith. Theological fights were not for him. In fact, he believed that such contentiousness stood in the way of spreading the love of God for sinners and convincing people of their need for conversion. Moody, however, founded two institutions that would become instrumental in the evangelical defense of the faith against modernism. The first was the Northfield Bible Conference, which Moody started in 1880 in his boyhood hometown. The conference attracted evangelicals from around the country, like a camp meeting geared toward Christian maturity and growth for those already converted. At the annual Northfield Conference, preachers and lay people alike heard evangelical preachers teach the Bible and prepare people for Christian service, many of them as missionaries. The conferences promoted the premillennial idea that Christ was returning soon, and so it was imperative that as many be converted as possible before that time.[17] Over time, the Northfield Conference and other Bible conferences built on the Northfield model became events geared toward defending evangelical views against the challenges of modernism by presenting what were believed to be the fundamentals of the Christian faith. These fundamentals often included the authority and inerrancy of the Bible, the virgin birth of Christ, Christ's bodily resurrection, and his literal second coming. Bible conference preachers stressed the literal and historical nature of the scriptures and the veracity of miracles and other supernatural elements in scripture. In stressing these traditional beliefs, Bible conference preachers refuted modernism and roundly criticized the schools that promoted the new theology.

Like the Northfield Conferences, Moody was also instrumental in the founding of the Bible institute that would later bear his name. Moody Bible Institute in Chicago was part of the Bible institute movement that flourished in the twentieth century. Bible institutes formalized and lengthened the Bible-training aspects of Bible conferences, and, like the summer conferences, eventually became centers where the evangelical defense of the faith against modernism would flourish.[18]

In the late nineteenth century, therefore, the stage was being set for a theological clash between evangelical and modernist Protestantism. Evangelicals in the Bible conferences and Bible institutes, as well as those at Princeton Seminary and other seminaries, were preparing their defense of the faith,
while the modernists were moving forward with their Romantic views of religion, their adjustment of Protestantism in light of modern science, and
their higher critical views of the Bible. There were skirmishes and even
heresy trials within some of the major Protestant denominations as evangelicals accused modernists of changing the essentials of the faith. As a result of
these early isolated battles of the first few years of the twentieth century,
Presbyterians wrote five essentials of Christian belief that would later become known as the "five points of fundamentalism."[19]

Presbyterians in America had always adhered to the Westminster Confession of Faith of 1644, which outlined the basic tenets of the Calvinist form
of evangelical Presbyterianism. Modernists, however, reinterpreted the Westminster confession in much the same way they reinterpreted scripture—i.e.,
in light of modern modes of thought. In response to modernism, the evangelical party of the northern Presbyterian denomination, therefore, per-
suaded the Presbyterian General Assembly of 1910 to adopt a concise and
unequivocal statement of the fundamentals of the Christian faith. The five
points were (1) the inerrancy and full authority of the Bible; (2) the virgin
birth of Christ; (3) Christ's substitutionary atonement; (4) the bodily resurrection of Jesus; and (5) the authenticity of miracles. While never intended
to be a complete or fully sufficient statement of Christian essentials, a variant of these five soon became known as the "five fundamentals" of the faith
that evangelicals were ready to defend. The variation, which developed in
the 1920s, was simply that Christ's literal Second Coming replaced the authenticity of miracles.[20]

The effort to reduce the Christian faith to its essentials was quite natural.
Even modernists attempted to do this. For them, religious experience inspired by the example of Jesus and expressed naturally through the development of civilization was the essence of the faith. This was wholly inadequate
for evangelicals because it left out nearly all the historic doctrines. Evangelicals believed that the threat of modernism could be resisted and battles
averted if everyone could just agree on a baseline of belief beyond which no
orthodox Protestant would be allowed to go. The question was simply, What
are the fundamentals of the faith? The term "fundamental" was not widely
used in 1910, and the five points would not become formalized as "fundamentals" until the 1920s. Another development would be more immediately
significant for the development of the term "fundamental." From 1910 to

1915 there appeared in print twelve paperback pamphlet volumes known collectively as *The Fundamentals of the Faith*. Sponsored by two California millionaire executives, they were sent free of charge to every pastor, missionary, theological professor, YMCA and YWCA secretary, college professor, Sunday school superintendent, and religious editor in the English-speaking world. In all, roughly 3 million individual copies of the various volumes were mailed.[21] *The Fundamentals* consisted of articles written by evangelical preachers, Bible teachers, and scholars, and they addressed every theological issue imaginable: evolution and higher criticism of scripture, the relationship of evangelical Christianity to science more broadly, daily Christian living, evangelism, missions, and so forth. Most of the essays in *The Fundamentals* were moderate and reasonable, and some of the authors would not identify with fully developed fundamentalism after 1920.

It should be noted that until the last few paragraphs the terms fundamental and fundamentalist have not been used in this book. This is because these terms were virtually unheard of and almost never used until 1920. Until that time, those who defended the faith against the perceived challenges of modernism were simply the conservatives or the traditionalists. It should also be noted that the two sides in this developing controversy over theology were not firmly set until after 1920. Many theologians and preachers accepted some of the modernist adjustments, but not all. As said above, some could accept the findings of higher criticism of scripture while still believing that the Bible was the specially inspired word of God and not merely like other ancient texts. These evangelical liberals or liberal evangelicals retained their belief in the supernatural aspects of the Christian faith, including the need for the new birth in Christ. While there was this middle ground among theologians and preachers, it is important to note also that most people in the pews of Protestant churches knew little of the particulars of theological controversy. Common people continued in the standard evangelical beliefs that had dominated the nineteenth century. If they knew of the fundamentalist-modernist controversy at all, as the battles in the seminaries and denominational bureaucracies came to be known, they thought of them as a preachers' fight that had little to do with their daily lives. World War I would change this.

The Fundamentalist-Modernist Controversy

All that was said in the previous section was part of the early fundamentalist-modernist controversy. World War I, however, served as the event that catalyzed the controversy. In short, the war turned what had been a preachers' fight into a culture war. During World War I and for a long time thereafter, common Americans and even many intellectuals believed that Germany was totally at fault for the war. In oversimplified fashion, Americans reasoned that the German government was militaristic and autocratic and had engaged in hostile and aggressive acts that left Britain and France no alternative but military defense. Although initially opposed to the war, the most conservative and fundamentalistic evangelicals began to reason that Germany's aggressive, militaristic, and might-makes-right philosophy resulted from German philosophy, particularly that of late nineteenth-century philosopher Friedrich Nietzsche. Even though Darwin was British, fundamentalistic evangelicals associated evolutionary thought with German intellectual life, largely because German scholars had been quick to appropriate evolution in the area of religion. One can see where this sort of thinking headed in popular circles. The reasoning went something like this: If German philosophy led to German militarism, which led to the Great War and ultimately Germany's defeat, and if that same philosophy led to theological modernism and the higher criticism of scripture, then, if the German theology is not defeated in American seminaries and in the Protestant denominations, America will end up just like Germany.[22] In other words, the fundamentalist-modernist controversy was not just about saving evangelical Protestantism, it was a full-scale war to save American culture.

In 1920, in a Baptist periodical known as *The Watchman Examiner*, New York evangelical editor Curtis Lee Laws coined the term *fundamentalist*. He defined a fundamentalist as one who was ready to "do battle royal for the fundamentals."[23] He seemed to have something like the five fundamentals in mind when he wrote these words. As scholars define the movement after 1920, a key component of fundamentalism became its "militant" defense of the faith. Leading scholar of fundamentalism George Marsden, therefore, defines historic fundamentalism as "militantly anti-modernist Protestant evangelicalism," and he says, "Fundamentalists were evangelical Christians . . . who in the twentieth century militantly opposed both modernism in theology and the cultural changes that modernism endorsed."[24] The fundamentalists were by no means the only militant ones in this fight. Many modernists were just as aggressive in their tactics. The fundamentalist-modernist controversy became a nasty fight on both sides.

From 1920 to 1925, it was not altogether clear who would win the fundamentalist-modernist controversy. The battle in the Presbyterian Church, for example, looked as if it could go either way, and the moderate fundamentalist J. Gresham Machen at Princeton Seminary seemed to many observers to have the best argument. In 1923, he published *Christianity and*

Liberalism, in which he argued that theological modernism was less a variant of Christianity than a whole new religion. He pointed out that historic Christianity had taught that the doctrines of the Christian faith made experience possible. Modernists, by contrast, reversed this, saying that experience gave rise to doctrine. The implication was that Christian doctrine could be relinquished as long as the experience was retained.[25] Moreover, historic Christianity had posited that human beings were fallen creatures in need of a supernatural experience of salvation wrought by the death and resurrection of Christ. Modernists, by contrast, taught a completely different form of redemption, requiring only that basically good human beings move naturally toward God. Machen and other thoughtful fundamentalists were particularly irritated that modernists had continued to use traditional theological language—resurrection, salvation, incarnation, sin, etc.—while covertly redefining these terms to mean something other than what was commonly understood by lay people. Machen said modernists were of course free to think as they pleased, but they should at least have the decency to start their own new denominations rather than trying to take over evangelical churches that had historically taught the fundamentals of the faith. Reviewing the book, the widely read secular journalist Walter Lippmann said that Machen's argument was "the best popular argument produced by either side" in the fundamentalist-modernist controversy.[26] The editor of the widely read magazine *The Nation* wrote, "Fundamentalism is undoubtedly in the main stream of the Christian tradition while modernism represents a religious revolution as far-reaching as the Protestant Reformation."[27] Lippmann and the *The Nation* editorial writer, while by no means fundamentalists themselves, agreed with Machen that liberalism, as modernism was then being called, was less a form of Christianity than a wholly different religion. It appeared briefly that the fundamentalists had the better argument and just might win the controversy.

In 1925, at precisely the time it appeared that fundamentalists may have been getting the upper hand in the controversy, fundamentalism experienced a spectacular defeat in the infamous Scopes trial. That event is discussed in detail in the next chapter, so suffice it to say here that the trial made previously respectable fundamentalists look like "rubes" and "yahoos" in full anti-intellectual rebellion against the modern world. By the 1930s, largely as a result of the way the Scopes trial was portrayed in the media and a popular textbook, fundamentalists who still believed the evangelical faith that had dominated late nineteenth-century American culture were viewed by many as cultural outsiders from a bygone era. Fundamentalists who stayed in the mainline denominations but continued to believe the fundamentals largely accepted that while their local congregation might be evangelical, their denomination as a whole was theologically liberal. Many other fundamentalists, however, began to accept and promote their outsider status, arguing that true believers should separate from the liberal denominations and the culture those denominations endorsed. Like the militant defense of the faith popularized in the twenties, in the 1930s separatism became another badge of true fundamentalism. Many of the fundamentalists who left mainline denominations did so in order to form separatist churches, schools, Bible colleges, and periodicals.

Although himself not a typical fundamentalist, Machen's experiences serve as a good example of separatism and where it could lead. As his book *Christianity and Liberalism* showed, Machen was an erudite scholar. Another of his books, his Greek grammar, was still being used as late as the 1970s by students studying New Testament Greek. Defying the stereotype of a rural anti-intellectual fundamentalist, Machen was reared in a prestigious home in Baltimore, the son of a Harvard-educated lawyer. He was neither a teetotaler nor a six-day creationist, as many fundamentalists were. He was, however, an orthodox evangelical Presbyterian. Machen attended Johns Hopkins University, where he majored in classics and graduated valedictorian of his class in 1901. He then attended simultaneously Princeton Seminary and Princeton University, taking philosophy and theology master's degrees in 1904 and 1905 respectively. Following his student years at Princeton, he studied for a year in Germany and was introduced to theological modernism, experiencing a crisis of faith that he resolved by adhering to Presbyterian conservatism and by taking a teaching position as instructor of the New Testament at Princeton Seminary in 1906.

Christianity and Liberalism made Machen a significant intellectual figure in the fundamentalist-modernist controversy. He was the best scholar on the fundamentalist side. In the 1920s, in the face of resistance from Machen and his conservative colleagues, Princeton moved increasingly toward a pluralist position that tolerated both the conservative and modernist positions. This was intolerable for Machen because he believed lax theological standards would result in the seminary becoming overwhelmingly liberal. In 1929 he left Princeton to form Westminster Seminary in Philadelphia, and in 1936 he was instrumental in the formation of the Orthodox Presbyterian Church, a new fundamentalist denomination.[28]

Machen exhibited clearly fundamentalism's militant defense of the faith and theological separatism, both in highly intellectualized form. There were others, however, more militant and separatist and less intellectual than he. In 1937 a group of Westminster professors and students left Machen's seminary to form Faith Seminary in Wilmington, Delaware, and the Bible Presbyterian Church, another new fundamentalist Presbyterian denomination.

The issues that divided the two groups were end-times prophecy (premillennialism) and Christian lifestyle. In the latter case, those who left Westminster were insistent on total abstinence from alcohol, whereas Machen and Westminster's position was moderation. One of the leaders of the group that left Westminster was Carl McIntire, who went on to become one of the twentieth century's most militantly separatistic and idiosyncratic fundamentalists.

Machen's departure from Princeton Seminary, then the split within his own ranks, revealed a growing penchant among fundamentalists in the 1930s to separate from liberals, then separate from each other. There developed in some quarters of fundamentalism a doctrine called "secondary separation." Those who believed in secondary separation taught that it was not only necessary to separate from liberals but it was also necessary to separate from fundamentalists who would not separate from liberals. In short, fundamentalism became highly schismatic. While Machen's foremost concerns were theological, other fundamentalists were far less noble in their militancy. One of these was J. Frank Norris from Fort Worth, Texas. Sometimes called the Texas Cyclone, Norris represented fundamentalism at its worst. He became pastor of the First Baptist Church of Fort Worth in 1909, and by the 1920s he had maneuvered himself into a leading position within popular fundamentalism. From 1919 on, he engaged in vitriolic attacks against the Baptist General Convention of Texas (BGCT) and the Southern Baptist Convention (SBC). The BGCT expelled his church from association in 1924, while SBC leaders worked together to ensure that Norris would have no power within the denomination. Undeterred, Norris eventually organized a rival denomination that held its meetings across the street or next door to the yearly SBC convention meetings.

In addition to lambasting liberals in a Southern Baptist Convention where hardly any existed, Norris also had several scrapes with the law. He was indicted for perjury and arson in conjunction with the 1912 burning of his own church but was acquitted on both charges. In 1926, he delivered a series of sermons against the Catholic mayor of Fort Worth, at one time accusing him of misappropriation of city funds to aid a Catholic school. On a summer Saturday a Fort Worth lumberman named D. E. Chipps telephoned Norris at the church and warned the pastor to leave the mayor alone. Shortly thereafter, Chipps arrived at Norris's study where the two exchanged heated words before Norris pulled a pistol out of his desk and shot Chipps three times, killing him. After a change of venue to Austin and yearlong delay that resulted from pretrial maneuvers, Norris was tried for murder. Arguing self-defense, Norris told a jury that he feared Chipps was going to attack him.

The defense was able to establish that Chipps had in fact threatened to kill Norris within earshot of individuals who testified at the trial. The jury responded with an acquittal.[29]

The murder trial and other controversies notwithstanding, Norris's church continued to grow. Norris seemed capable of capitalizing on even the most negative publicity, and his popularity increased to the extent that in 1935 Temple Baptist Church in Detroit invited him to be pastor, and Norris accepted. He refused to relinquish control of his Fort Worth church, however, and for the next fifteen years pastored both congregations. In the 1940s the two churches had a combined membership of roughly 25,000, allowing Norris to boast, as he often did, that he had more parishioners under his pastoral care than any preacher in America. He also had a seminary in Fort Worth and a quasi denomination with churches across Texas and the Southwest.

If Machen represented fundamentalism at its intellectual best, Norris represented the movement's schismatic dark side. It often seemed in the 1930s that fundamentalism was living down to the reputation the movement had taken on after the Scopes trial—kind of a self-fulfilling prophecy. The militancy and separatism that led to such a negative public image became problematic for those who were evangelical in belief but neither militant nor culturally separatistic. Many of these types of evangelicals were still in the mainline denominations while many others had left to form independent churches, denominations, Bible colleges, and parachurch ministries. The nonmilitant evangelicals were usually lumped together with fundamentalists, however, even if they desired a more peaceful, cooperative, and intellectually respectable approach to Christianity. Dissatisfaction with the worst aspects of fundamentalism led to the development of a renewal of evangelicalism known as neoevangelicalism. Neoevangelicals were those who wanted to retain an emphasis on the fundamentals of the faith while presenting an intellectually compelling case for a nonseparatist, culturally engaged gospel.

The Rise of Neoevangelicalism

Among a handful of events that were instrumental in the development of neoevangelicalism was the formation of the National Association of Evangelicals (NAE) in 1942. The NAE was modeled after the New England Fellowship (NEF), a regional organization of evangelicals led by J. Elwin Wright. The NEF was comprised of evangelicals from the mainline Methodist, Presbyterian, and Northern Baptist denominations along with many from smaller evangelical and fundamentalist denominations. In other words, the organization contained both separatists and nonseparatists. It was

a diverse group consisting of intellectually sophisticated and socially prestigious mainliners as well as working-class evangelicals, some of whom were
Pentecostals.

In 1941, fundamentalist firebrand Carl McIntire, who had been a leader
in the group that split off from Westminster Seminary in 1937, started a separatist fundamentalist national organization called the American Council of
Christian Churches (ACCC). One of the stipulations of McIntire's organization was that individual members and member churches had to separate
from mainline denominational bodies and the Federal Council of Churches,
of which most mainline churches were members. There were clearly two
groups of fundamentalists, those represented by McIntire and the ACCC
who insisted on separatism as a badge of honor and a test of truth, and the
NEF and like-minded evangelicals who wanted a more irenic and inclusive
brand of fundamentalism. In other words, there was a difference between separatist fundamentalists and inclusive evangelicals.[30]

Wright and the NEF took the lead in developing an alternative to both
the liberal FCC and McIntire's fundamentalist ACCC. In 1941, Wright
barnstormed the country raising support for a national organization that
would include all cooperating evangelicals. At a meeting in St. Louis in
1942, representatives from many evangelical and fundamentalist denominations convened to hear impassioned pleas for a united front of evangelicals
across denominational lines that could confront the secular cultural forces
that were opposed to the gospel. Harold John Ockenga, pastor of Park Street
Church in Boston, gave a speech in which he cited the perceived "disinte-
gration of Christianity" and the "break-up of the moral fiber of the American people."[31] Rather than calling for separation from such a culture, however, Ockenga and the others at the St. Louis meeting rallied many
fundamentalists to the idea of a national organization that would be culturally involved in an effort to stem the tide of decay. In the spirit of eighteenth-
and nineteenth-century revivalist evangelicalism, Ockenga predicted that
the remnant of evangelicals in America would be used by God to revive true
Christianity within the nation. He believed the meeting in St. Louis could
be the start of a "new era in evangelical Christianity."[32]

McIntire was also present at the St. Louis meeting, but not to promote a
new organization. Rather, he spoke in favor of the separatist course and urged
those present to join his ACCC. He was rebuffed, and the representatives
voted to start the NAE and scheduled a constitutional convention meeting
for the following May. Wright's desire seemed to represent the will of those
present at the 1942 and 1943 meetings. He wanted the NAE to steer a middle course between modernism on the left and separatist fundamentalism like

that promoted by McIntire and Norris on the right. Membership in the NAE was open to denominations, individual congregations, various religious agencies, and even individuals. The NAE represented most white evangelical organizations in one way or another.[33]

The NAE became the most important development in what one historian has called "an evangelical united front," which brought about the rebirth of evangelicalism after the fundamentalist period (1925–1950) that followed the fundamentalist-modernist controversy.[34] Other organizations that would aid in the growth of neoevangelicalism were World Vision, a food relief organization, and Youth for Christ, a campus ministry to high school and college students. The NAE and other groups helped forge a Christian identity by which it was possible to be an evangelical without being branded a fundamentalist, although many in the larger culture, both then and now, could not tell the difference. This united front consisted of organizations, radio broadcasts, revival campaigns, periodicals, and colleges that gave evangelicals across different denominations common experiences and venues for Christian activism. The NAE was part of a larger trend in twentieth-century America that saw Christians divided less along various denominational lines—Catholic, Episcopalian, Methodist, Presbyterian, Baptist, and so forth—and more according to whether one was conservative or liberal. This "restructuring of American religion," some scholars argue, has resulted in the liberals across denominational lines having more in common with each other than with the conservatives in their own denominations and vice versa, as conservatives across denominational lines have more in common with each other than with the liberals in their own denominations.[35]

A second development that fostered the rise of neoevangelicalism was the rise of a small cadre of evangelical scholars led by Carl F. H. Henry. Henry was part of the neoevangelical vanguard who studied for doctoral degrees at prestigious and respectable universities such as Harvard, Yale, Princeton, and the University of Chicago. Henry completed a doctorate in philosophy at Boston University in 1949. Highly educated neoevangelicals such as Henry studied with liberal professors and could not help but be impressed with their ethical vision. They realized that separatist fundamentalism had no such concern for the culture at large, and they acknowledged this as a deficiency. Henry also realized that other than Machen's book *Christianity and Liberalism*, there was no other fundamentalist intellectual work that was taken seriously at liberal universities or theological schools.[36] One of the neoevangelicals, Edward J. Carnell, went so far as to say that fundamentalism was becoming cultic, by which he meant that fundamentalists were concerned with purely individual sin to the exclusion of an interest in combating social evil. They were also obsessed with speculation about the end-times and the second coming of Christ with little concern for advancing the kingdom of God in the present age.[37]

Henry took the lead in fashioning a neoevangelical response to these fundamentalist deficiencies. In 1946, even before he completed his doctoral dissertation, he published *Remaking the Modern Mind*, in which he argued that the secular philosophies of the day were bankrupt and incapable of stemming the tide of cultural decay or preventing the collapse of Western civilization. Only a Christian worldview was coherent and capable of rescuing the culture, but the Christian worldview needed a fresh rearticulation that would avoid the excesses of modernism and the weaknesses of fundamentalism.[38] *Remaking the Modern Mind* was Henry's attempt to start a renaissance in evangelical scholarship that would be on par with Machen's work. Henry's second book would answer the ethical challenge posed by his liberal professors. Titled *The Uneasy Conscience of Modern Fundamentalism*, it appeared the year after *Remaking the Modern Mind*. Here Henry argued that fundamentalists, in their obsession with individual sin and end-times prophecy, were missing the opportunity to develop an ethical vision that would lead to social reform and cultural renewal. Henry's two books helped shape and define neoevangelicalism.

Christianity Today magazine began nine years after the publication of *The Uneasy Conscience of Modern Fundamentalism* and served as a third important component of neoevangelicalism. Evangelist Billy Graham and his father-in-law L. Nelson Bell were influential in starting the magazine, and Henry was the natural choice as the magazine's first editor. The *Christian Century*, founded in the early twentieth century, represented the mainline liberal denominations. Neoevangelicals saw a need for a periodical that would rival the *Christian Century* in influence and quality. This effort reflected the belief that evangelicalism could be articulated in an intellectually respectable way and that evangelical ideas could compete in the cultural marketplace. Founded in 1956, *Christianity Today* became the most influential organ for the vision of neoevangelical leaders.[39] It fairly quickly eclipsed *Christian Century* as the religious periodical most widely quoted in the secular press, and it quickly outran *Christian Century* in subscribers as well, which says something about the size of the fundamentalist/evangelical subculture. That subculture was much larger than the secular press and liberal academic community believed. Secular commentators who believed that fundamentalism would die out following the Scopes trial had been mistaken, but the extent of fundamentalist and evangelical influence would not be fully known until the 1980s. Initially geared for pastors, theologians, and educated laypeople,

Christianity Today over time evolved into a more popular yet respectable articulation of evangelical theological, cultural, and political concerns. Several other smaller periodicals with more focused audience appeal would eventually spin off from *Christianity Today*.[40]

In addition to the NAE, Carl Henry's books, and *Christianity Today*, a fourth important development in the rise of neoevangelicalism was the founding of Fuller Seminary in 1947 in Pasadena, California. The seminary was named for radio preacher Charles Fuller, largely because the initial idea was his. In 1946, Fuller contacted Ockenga at Park Street Church in Boston, lobbying the influential neoevangelical pastor to assist in the development of a new Christian college that would train evangelicals in the practical preaching of the gospel. Ockenga responded saying that neoevangelicalism really did not need yet another college but rather a more scholarly institution. Ockenga envisioned a seminary where the faculty would not just train preachers but also publish regularly in theological journals and write books that would compel the attention of the academic community, particularly liberal theologians. Ockenga's idea caught on with Fuller, and the two agreed that Ockenga would be responsible for organizing the new seminary and recruiting its first faculty. Among the original four professors at Fuller was Carl Henry, who was a natural choice given his books *Remaking the Modern Mind* and *The Uneasy Conscience of Modern Fundamentalism*. By 1950, the original four faculty members had added three new neoevangelical professors, all of whom had been trained at Harvard. The seminary opened in the fall of 1947 with a convocation that marked the occasion as "the beginning of a new age for evangelicalism." Those present, students and faculty alike, believed the seminary's founding would be instrumental in pushing evangelicalism to the forefront of intellectual life in America. In his convocation speech, Ockenga argued that only the Christian gospel articulated by evangelicals could save American culture from its imminent demise, virtually the same message he had delivered at the founding of the NAE five years earlier.[41]

While this was all pretty heady stuff for people who were emerging from a fundamentalist movement that had been thoroughly discredited slightly more than twenty years earlier in the Scopes trial, one must keep in mind the post–World War II context. Germany, the birthplace of theological modernism, had turned from the militarism of the World War I to the fascism that led to World War II. Russia turned to Marxist-Leninist communism in the revolution of 1917 and was in the process of taking over Eastern Europe. The early Cold War was just beginning as the Fuller faculty convened. In America, theological liberalism had proven by the measure of even many liberals to be a dry well, offering little that was distinct from America's secular ideologies. Moreover, the modernist belief that God was being revealed in the progress of civilization was no longer tenable after two world wars. It was hard to argue in the mid-twentieth century that things were getting better and better. In the view of the neoevangelicals, most of whom were moderate Republicans, secular philosophies such as pragmatism and the political ideology of the New Deal seemed to be ushering in an America where the state dominated people's lives and defined moral values according to what was expedient. The only hope was a reinstitution of the values of the Protestant Reformation that had laid the groundwork for Western democracy and religious freedom. As Ockenga said at Fuller's opening convocation:

> Here comes the message to America—America, which is experiencing today that inner rupture of its character and culture, that inner division with vast multitudes of our people following that secularist, rationalist lie of "scientific naturalism" in the repudiation of God and God's law. I tell you on the authority of the Word of God and with the full sweep of history behind us that in the proportion that America does that, and the church has to withdraw itself to a separated community again, and there enters a time of hostility of the world and the persecution of the anti-Christian forces, in that percentage we will open ourselves up to the kind of judgment that God brought upon Europe from which we escaped almost unscathed as a nation.[42]

Fuller Seminary would not quite live up to the lofty dreams of its founders, but the school remains to this day a solid source of evangelical cultural engagement and a vibrant center of Christian intellectual life. It seems fitting that an intellectual scholar-pastor, Harold John Ockenga, founded the seminary with a popular evangelistic radio preacher, Charles Fuller. The school represented the two primary aspects of evangelicalism that had been alive since the eighteenth century: the elite intellectualism of Jonathan Edwards as well as the populist and pragmatic evangelistic emphases of George Whitefield. The dream of saving American culture for the gospel, however, was up against the historical reality that in America no particular religious ideology would ever dominate the country again as evangelical Protestantism had from the days of Edwards and Whitefield through the nineteenth century. That era was gone forever as cultural and religious pluralism became facts. Moreover, it was not initially clear that the neoevangelicals could even persuade most fundamentalists to get onboard. Separatist fundamentalists such as Carl McIntire lambasted the neoevangelical cultural program as a sellout to theological liberalism. For true fundamentalists, separatism was a nonnegotiable element of the faith, and by 1960 or so, only those who were separatists and who were devotees of the end-times prophecy called dispensational premillennialism would continue to call themselves fundamentalists.

Along with the NAE, Carl Henry, *Christianity Today*, and Fuller Seminary, a fifth and final factor in the emergence of neoevangelicalism was not a development but a person—Billy Graham. Throughout its history, from the days of Edwards and Whitefield forward, evangelicalism had been organized around popular individual leaders more than formal institutions or denominations, and Graham was certainly one of these popular personalities. William Franklin (Billy) Graham was born on a prosperous dairy farm near Charlotte, North Carolina, in 1918. His parents were evangelical Presbyterians but not separatist fundamentalists. Later in life, he remembered growing up liking fast cars, girls, and baseball. As a boy, he once met the great baseball Hall of Fame homerun champion Babe Ruth. Graham said that after shaking hands with the Babe, he did not wash his hands for three days. He experienced conversion at the age of sixteen under the preaching of a fundamentalist evangelist Mordecai Ham. Contemplating the ministry, Graham enrolled at Bob Jones College in 1936, but he stayed only briefly and chafed under the strict rules of the college. Bob Jones College would soon become a bastion of separatist fundamentalism, while Graham gravitated instead toward neoevangelicalism. Graham attended the Florida Bible Institute from 1937–1940 then Wheaton College, where he graduated in 1943. At Wheaton he met and married Ruth Bell, the daughter of L. Nelson Bell, a missionary to China.

Following graduation, Graham pastored briefly, but his real love was traveling evangelism, which he had started while at Florida Bible Institute. In 1945, he became an evangelist with Youth for Christ (YFC). Like the NAE, YFC was one of the organizations in the evangelical united front. YFC, as its name indicates, was designed to reach young people in high school, college, and the military. As in the days of Edwards, Whitefield, and Wesley, evangelicalism had always been a transatlantic phenomenon, and Graham not only traveled the United States but also preached across the European continent and in Great Britain at YFC rallies. He developed a reputation in evangelical circles as one of the most gifted young preachers of the era. Graham's fame skyrocketed through the national media attention surrounding his Los Angeles crusade of 1949. The revival lasted roughly two months, and the total attendance was about 350,000. During the Los Angeles crusade, newspaper publisher William Randolph Hearst took a liking to Graham's message and allegedly told his newspapers across the country to "puff Graham"—that is, give him prominent coverage. Starting in 1950, on the heels of the Los Angeles success, Graham's crusades in major cities such as Boston, Charleston, and elsewhere routinely drew hundreds of thousands of people over the course of several weeks. In 1954, Graham preached a revival in London where 2 million people attended in three months. On the continent of Europe the next year, an estimated 4 million attended his crusades. This became standard for Graham over the next five decades. By the end of the twentieth century he had preached live to an estimated 210 million people in more than 150 nations, and this is to say nothing of the millions more who heard him on television, radio, and films. He has preached to more people than any evangelist in the history of Christianity. Among Christians only Mother Teresa and Pope John Paul II rivaled him in worldwide acclaim and affection.[43]

Graham became the most visible symbol of neoevangelicalism's emergence out of fundamentalism, but he was also a key player in the movement. Eschewing fundamentalism's separatist stance, he cooperated with any Christian group that would support his revivals, including the mainline liberals. By the late fifties, separatist fundamentalists such as Carl McIntire and Bob Jones consistently repudiated Graham, accusing him of selling out to liberals and disobeying God. More than any other person, however, Graham helped keep neoevangelicalism in the mainstream of American life. Personally charming and always above scandal, he was covered by television and major magazines, often appearing on their covers. He was beloved around the globe and voted consistently among the Ten Most Admired Men in the World. From the 1950s through the end of the century, he was a friend and confidante of U.S. presidents, being particularly close to Dwight Eisenhower (1953–1961) and Richard Nixon (1969–1974). His friendship with Nixon hurt Graham's popularity briefly when Nixon was forced to resign in 1974 because of corruption associated with the infamous Watergate scandal. Graham realized that he had been used by his politician friend, and he determined to better maintain a critical distance from partisan politics in the future. Still, Graham, like evangelicalism itself, proved resilient in the face of challenges. He was a central part of most evangelical developments before the rise of the Christian Right political movement of the 1980s. In addition to being a cofounder of *Christianity Today*, he also served on the board at Fuller. He sided with the neoevangelicals when they began to distance themselves from separatist fundamentalism, and he became the best, popular face of evangelicalism in the world. It is sometimes joked that the definition of an evangelical is "anyone who really likes Billy Graham."

Neoevangelicals were not being cranks to stress the failings of the West, as Ockenga did in his founding Fuller address and as Graham did in many 1950s sermons. The era from World War I through World War II had put

Western civilization through a severe strain that appeared to be nothing other than collapse. A group of former theological modernists even developed theological responses known as Neo-Orthodoxy and Crisis Theology because they believed liberalism had harmonized so much with secular science and modern political ideologies that it no longer had anything distinct to offer. Neo-Orthodox and Crisis theologians were less Biblicist and conversionist than fundamentalists and neoevangelicals, but they still sought to recapture the transcendence of God, the sinfulness of humankind, the chasm that separated God from humanity, and the need for a supernatural work of God's grace to bridge that chasm. The Neo-Orthodox Protestants had little use for the idea of an immanent God who was revealed in the evolutionary progress of civilization. Theological liberalism was on the defensive by 1960, with many critics in both the evangelical and Neo-Orthodox communities.

Along with the secular ideologies Ockenga criticized in his Fuller convocation speech, he also cited the threat of Roman Catholicism. This was part of a long tradition of Protestant anti-Catholicism that still existed in both liberal and fundamentalist camps. "[W]e have allowed Romanism to step in with a social program that will make Romanism the challenging religious factor in western civilization, and in particular the United States."[44] Ockenga was here referring to the belief that the Roman Catholic Church desired ultimately to transform America into a Catholic country where the church would be preferred and supported by the U.S. government. Liberals and fundamentalists and even some Catholic theologians and popes believed that this was the church's ultimate goal. Not until the 1960s, when America had its first Catholic president in the person of John F. Kennedy and the church had its revolutionary Vatican II council did Protestants begin to rest easier with the large Catholic presence in the country. Ironically, in the 1980s, as we shall see in a later chapter, evangelicals in the Christian Right began to see traditional Catholics as allies in the cultural war against secularism.

Conclusion

In the second half of the twentieth century and into the twenty-first, evangelicals were a diverse and loose coalition representing many different Protestant denominations. Many evangelicals are still in the mainline Presbyterian, Methodist, Episcopalian, and Baptist denominations, while many more inhabit the myriad of smaller, more obscure denominations and sects. There are evangelicals who virtually equate their faith with an American patriotism that supports all U.S. military endeavors, and there are evangelicals who are pacifists. There are charismatic and Pentecostal evangelicals who speak in tongues and engage in faith healing and other evangelicals who believe the gift of tongues and faith healing ceased after the first generation of Christian history. Many evangelicals and nearly all fundamentalists are deeply concerned about end-times prophecy and the Second Coming of Christ, while other evangelicals rarely think about these issues. There are evangelicals and fundamentalists deeply involved in American politics, and many more evangelicals and fundamentalists whose political activity does not extend beyond occasional voting. While most evangelicals who are politically engaged are conservative and Republican, there are evangelicals who are politically liberal and who identify with the Democratic Party. Some evangelicals believe higher education and the intellectual life should be a necessary part of the Christian walk, while others, especially in fundamentalist quarters, are virtually anti-intellectual.

Interpreting evangelicalism, some scholars use metaphors such as kaleidoscope, mosaic, or feudal kingdom, while others even question whether the term evangelical is useful.[45] Some historians would object to the way this chapter has portrayed Protestants as either evangelical or liberal and argue instead that there is a large center inhabited by most serious Christians who are not part of theological liberalism or neoevangelicalism. These critics would also want to say, as should be acknowledged, that the neoevangelicals were merely the most visible of the evangelicals in some quarters during the mid-to-late twentieth century. The vast majority of common people within evangelicalism could not have cared less about the founding of Fuller Seminary, if they even knew about it, and most have never subscribed to *Christianity Today* or been to a Billy Graham Crusade, although they have watched him on television and care very much that his ministry succeed in bringing people to Christ.

Only about 15 percent of Americans are likely to describe themselves as "evangelical," while 28.5 percent describe themselves as "born again," which is often used as a synonym for evangelical. Just over 47 percent of Americans describe themselves as "Bible believing," but one can believe the Bible is true while still living in rebellion against its teachings.[46] Other studies suggest that when all types of evangelicals are counted—self-identified evangelicals, self-identified fundamentalists, self-identified charismatics, members of Pentecostal denominations, and members of other conservative Protestant denominations—and when all the overlaps are statistically accounted for, conservative Protestants, another synonym for evangelical, make up about 29 percent of the American population.[47] Clearly, therefore, there are many more evangelicals in America than are likely to say, "I'm an evangelical." So, how can one know an evangelical when one sees one?

This takes us back to Bebbington's four components of evangelicalism from chapter one—Biblicism, crucicentrism, conversionism, and activism. When asked how one decides what is right and wrong, an evangelical is likely to mention the Bible pretty early in the conversation. He or she may do so in a sophisticated way or be simple and literal, but seriousness about scripture is the hallmark of evangelicalism. When asked how a person finds one's way to God, an evangelical will lead with Jesus and His crucifixion (crucicentrism). As for conversionism, when asked how one became a Christian, most evangelicals can pinpoint the time and place when they experienced the new birth. In doing so, evangelicals often but not always use terms such as "saved," "converted," or "born again" to label the experience. While some will not remember exactly when or how they experienced conversion, all evangelicals will attest to its having happened personally in their lives. Finally, with regard to activism, when encountering an evangelical, one is likely to find a person who leads an active life in which he or she is striving to do something for God that will make society better. This may be straightforward evangelism, where the evangelical attempts to lead others to a crucicentric conversion. Activism, however, may be political or civic, including support for pro-life causes or efforts to stem the tide of poverty, racism, and war. Whether left, right, middle, or apolitical, evangelicals tend toward an active life where they seek to put their faith to work in society.

As diverse, fractured, and disorganized as they are, when taken together, evangelicals as defined by Bebbington's quadrilateral rubric comprise the largest religious grouping in America, slightly larger than Roman Catholicism. We have discussed in this chapter what evangelicals believe and how this varied and diverse movement of theologically conservative Christians developed in the twentieth century. In the next chapter I analyze what evangelicals think about science.

Notes

1. William R. Hutchison, *The Modernist Impulse in American Protestantism* (Durham, North Carolina: Duke University Press, 1992), 2.

2. See Diana Butler, *Standing against the Whirlwind: Evangelical Episcopalians in Nineteenth-Century America* (New York: Oxford University Press, 1995).

3. Quoted in Gillis J. Harp, *Brahmin Prophet: Phillips Brooks and the Path of Liberal Protestantism* (Lanham, Maryland: Rowman and Littlefield, 2003), 26.

4. Harp, *Brahmin Prophet*, 33.

5. Quoted in Harp, *Brahmin Prophet*, 33–34.

6. David Bebbington, *The Dominance of Evangelicalism: The Age of Spurgeon and Moody* (Downers Grove, Illinois: InterVarsity Press, 2005).

7. Quoted in Hutchison, *The Modernist Impulse in American Protestantism*, 81. The quote is from British theologian Frederick Denison Maurice.

8. Quoted in George Marsden, *Fundamentalism and American Culture* (New York: Oxford University Press, 1980), 25.

9. Quoted in Mark Noll, *Between Faith and Criticism: Evangelicals, Scholarship, and the Bible in America* (Grand Rapids, Michigan: Baker Book House, 1986), 30.

10. Noll, *Between Faith and Criticism*, 11.

11. Quoted in Hutchison, *The Modernist Impulse in American Protestantism*, 120.

12. Quoted in Hutchison, *The Modernist Impulse in American Protestantism*, 120.

13. Quoted in Hutchison, *The Modernist Impulse in American Protestantism*, 217.

14. Hutchison, *The Modernist Impulse in American Protestantism*, 113–15.

15. Bebbington, *The Dominance of Evangelicalism*, 46–47.

16. Dwight L. Moody, *The New Sermons of Dwight Lyman Moody* (New York: H. S. Goodspeed and Co., 1880), 535.

17. W. V. Trollinger, "Northfield Conferences," *Dictionary of Christianity in America*, Daniel G. Reid, Robert D. Linder, Bruce L. Shelley, and Harry S. Stout, eds. (Downers Grove, Illinois: InterVarsity Press, 1991), 830.

18. G. A. Getz, "Moody Bible Institute," *Dictionary of Christianity in America*, Daniel G. Reid, Robert D. Linder, Bruce L. Shelley, and Harry S. Stout, eds. (Downers Grove, Illinois: InterVarsity Press, 1991), 769; Virginia Brereton, *Training God's Army: The American Bible School, 1880–1940* (Bloomington: Indiana University Press, 1990).

19. Marsden, *Fundamentalism and American Culture*, 117.

20. Marsden, *Fundamentalism and American Culture*, 117.

21. Marsden, *Fundamentalism and American Culture*, 119.

22. George Marsden argued this standard interpretation in 1980, and his point remains widely accepted among historians today. See Marsden, *Fundamentalism and American Culture*, 149. A twenty-fifth anniversary edition with a new final chapter appeared in 2005. See George Marsden, *Fundamentalism and American Culture* (New York: Oxford University Press, 2005). In the new edition, Marsden uses his last chapter to introduce the term "fundamentalistic evangelicals," which he applies to some conservative evangelicals today. I am applying the term to early fundamentalists before the term was used commonly, beginning in 1920.

23. Quoted in Marsden, *Fundamentalism and American Culture*, 159.

24. Marsden, *Fundamentalism and American Culture*, 4.

25. Hutchison, *The Modernist Impulse in American Protestantism*, 264.

26. Quoted in Hutchison, *The Modernist Impulse in American Protestantism*, 273.

27. Quoted in D. G. Hart, *Defending the Faith: J. Gresham Machen and the Crisis of Conservative Protestantism in Modern America* (Baltimore, Maryland: Johns Hopkins University Press, 1994), 79.

28. Hart, *Defending the Faith*, 133–35.

29. Barry Hankins, *God's Rascal: J. Frank Norris and the Beginnings of Southern Fundamentalism* (Lexington: University Press of Kentucky), 118–120.

30. Joel Carpenter, *Revive Us Again: The Reawakening of American Fundamentalism* (New York: Oxford University Press, 1997), 145–47.

31. Quoted in Carpenter, *Revive Us Again*, 147.

32. Quoted in Carpenter, *Revive Us Again*, 147.

33. Carpenter, *Revive Us Again*, 148–49.

34. Carpenter, *Revive Us Again*, 160.

35. Robert Wuthnow, *The Restructuring of American Religion: Society and Faith Since World War II* (Princeton, New Jersey: Princeton University Press, 1988).

36. Carpenter, *Revive Us Again*, 193.

37. Carpenter, *Revive Us Again*, 200.

38. Carpenter, *Revive Us Again*, 200.

39. Carpenter, *Revive Us Again*, 204.

40. D. G. Tinder, "Christianity Today," *Dictionary of Christianity in America*, Daniel G. Reid, Robert D. Linder, Bruce L. Shelley, and Harry S. Stout, eds. (Downers Grove, Illinois: InterVarsity Press, 1990), 262.

41. George Marsden, *Reforming Fundamentalism: Fuller Seminary and the New Evangelicalism* (Grand Rapids, Michigan: Eerdmans, 1987), 60–63, quote on 60. See also Carpenter, *Revive Us Again*, 194–95.

42. Quoted in Marsden, *Reforming Fundamentalism*, 63.

43. William Martin, *A Prophet with Honor: The Billy Graham Story* (New York: William Morrow and Co., 1991); L. W. Dorsett, "William Franklin 'Billy' Graham," *Biographical Dictionary of Evangelicals*, Timothy T. Larsen, David W. Bebbington, and Mark A. Noll, eds. (Downers Grove, Illinois: InterVarsity Press, 2003), 259–62.

44. Quoted in Marsden, *Reforming Fundamentalism*, 63.

45. See Darryl Hart's *Deconstructing Evangelicalism: Conservative Protestantism in the Age of Billy Graham* (Grand Rapids, Michigan: Baker Academic, 2004).

46. "American Piety in the 21st Century," Baylor Institute for Studies of Religion, 2006, p. 16.

47. Christian Smith, *Christian America?: What Evangelicals Really Want* (Berkeley: University of California Press, 2000), 16–17.

CHAPTER THREE

~

Battling with Science

From Antievolution to Intelligent Design

There is a persistent myth that the relationship between orthodox religion and science in the West has been dominated by warfare. This model for interpreting science and religion goes back to the infamous story of Galileo in the seventeenth century. Galileo confirmed Copernicus's theory that the sun, not the Earth, was the center of our solar system. The Copernican theory, argued in Copernicus's *On the Revolutions of Heavenly Spheres* (1542), was a threat to theology and philosophy because it seemed to rob human beings of their centrality in the universe. The Roman Catholic Church of the Middle Ages taught that human beings were God's ultimate creation. It followed naturally that the Earth as the home of human beings had to be the center of the universe. This geocentric astronomical theory harkened from the days of Greek philosopher Aristotle in the fourth century B.C.E. as rearticulated by Ptolemy in the second century C.E., then by medieval theologians. Copernicus's theory posited a heliocentric view that the sun, not the Earth, was the center of the universe, which was a direct challenge to the theology of the times. When Galileo (d. 1543) confirmed the theory in the early seventeenth century, he was hauled before the Inquisition and tried for heresy, an event that looms large in the story of warfare between Christianity and science. Found guilty, Galileo recanted and continued his scientific pursuits quietly for the rest of his life. As the story goes, the Galileo controversy shows the hostility of religion to modern science, and, as the myth continues, the same sort of hostility existed in the nineteenth century among evangelical Protestants

49

who rose up in opposition to Darwin's theory of evolution—opposition that led eventually to the Scopes trial.

As with most myths, there is some truth to this one, but there is also much historical data that has to be ignored to keep the myth intact, and in the past two decades historians have been correcting the history of the relationship between science and religion. There were perhaps several reasons why Galileo was tried and not Copernicus before him or the many scientists in between the two. For starters, Galileo lived in Italy where the Roman Inquisition, as an arm of the Counter Reformation, was active. The Counter Reformation of the sixteenth and seventeenth centuries was a conservative Catholic response to the challenges of Protestantism. In the face of this conservatism, Galileo offered not only evidence to confirm Copernicus but also a more liberal way of interpreting scripture. He believed that the Bible and nature were books given us by God and that God intended that the two books be read together. Neither could contradict the other, which for Galileo meant that when the scientific study of nature resulted in conclusions that contradicted older readings of the Bible, those readings should be reassessed and revised. As historians David Lindberg and Ronald Numbers argue, Galileo's problem with the church was not so much an example of Christianity waging war on science, but a struggle "between opposing theories of biblical interpretation: a conservative theory issuing from the Council of Trent versus Galileo's more liberal alternative."[1]

Whatever can be said about the warfare model, Galileo did not believe in it. Rather, he believed that some truths can be known best by studying the Bible, while others can be known best by studying nature. Nature and the Bible should be studied in light of each other so that true knowledge will be in harmony with both. As Galileo wrote:

It is most pious to say and most prudent to take for granted that Holy Scripture can never lie, as long as its true meaning has been grasped; . . . I think that in disputes about natural phenomena one must begin not with the authority of scriptural passages but with sensory experience and necessary demonstrations. For the holy Scripture and nature derive equally from the godhead, the former as the dictation of the Holy Spirit and the latter as the most obedient executrix of God's orders. . . . However, by this I do not wish to imply that one should not have the highest regard for passages of Holy Scripture; indeed, after becoming certain of some physical conclusions, we should use these as very appropriate aids to the correct interpretation of Scripture and to the investigation of the truths they must contain, for they are most true and agree with demonstrated truths. . . . I do not think one has to believe that the same God who has given us senses, language, and intellect would want to set aside the use of these and give us by other means the information we can acquire with them, so that we would deny our senses and reason even in the case of those physical conclusions which are placed before our eyes and intellect by our sensory experiences or by necessary demonstrations.[2]

This model for the relationship of science and religion was fairly typical of Christians from Galileo's day until the end of the nineteenth century. For a generation after the appearance of Darwin's theory of evolution, the best evangelical thinkers often resisted some of the implications of Darwin's theory while at the same time attempting to reconcile evolution with the Bible and theology. In other words, evangelicals did not accept the warfare model in large part until the Scopes trial of 1925.

Nineteenth-Century Evangelicals and Science

Long before evangelicals and fundamentalists of the twentieth century turned substantially against efforts to reconcile evolution and religion, key figures in the secular scientific community were already insisting that religion and science were irreconcilable. In particular, two books appeared in the late nineteenth century promoting the warfare model—John William Draper's *History of the Conflict between Religion and Science* and Andrew Dickson White's *A History of the Warfare of Science with Theology in Christendom*. White was the president of Cornell. His book started as an 1869 New York lecture entitled "The Battle-Fields of Science," was published in one volume in 1876 as *The Warfare of Science*, then grew into a two-volume work in 1897. Draper's book appeared first in 1874.[3] A growing body of scholarship in the past twenty-five years has forged a consensus that White and Draper were "anti-Christian polemicists" who overplayed the initial evangelical resistance to evolution while ignoring the fact that many of the debates in the history of science were among Christians, not between Christians and non-Christians.[4] As Lindberg and Numbers write, "Although it is not difficult to find instances of conflict and controversy in the annals of Christianity and science, recent scholarship has shown the warfare metaphor to be neither useful nor tenable in describing the relationship between science and religion." Concerning *A History of the Warfare of Science with Theology in Christendom*, Lindberg and Numbers add that there is "mounting evidence that White read the past through battle-scarred glasses, and that he and his imitators have distorted history to serve ideological ends of their own."[5]

Draper and White were part of a growing group of scientists called positivists, who followed the social scientific views of Auguste Compte. Compte and the positivists believed that only measureable, scientifically verifiable, or rationally demonstrable data should count as real knowledge. Moreover, they believed that science should be freed from metaphysical or philosophical thinking, especially from religion. White, Draper, and others had an agenda to discredit religion as a credible source of knowledge. As Neal Gillespie wrote in his book *Charles Darwin and the Problem of Creation*, "[T]he very existence of a rival science or of an alternate mode of knowledge was intolerable to the positivist. His emotional attachment to science as the pursuit of truth . . . made him intolerant of all other claims to scientific knowledge."[6] In short, in the late nineteenth century, the secular scientific community shifted from a paradigm that allowed for theological and metaphysical considerations to one that was positivist in nature. As positivists redefined science, they believed it necessary to rout the older views and those who held them from the field of inquiry. Any thinker who held the old view of science that allowed for special creation by a supernatural deity was, in Gillespie's words, viewed as "a charlatan, an imposter" by the devotees of the new science. The new paradigm consisted of antireligious prophets of a new scientific order who promoted the warfare model as a way of redefining knowledge. T. H. Huxley, who has been called "Darwin's bulldog," said it well: "Warfare has been my business and duty."[7]

Some fundamentalists in the twentieth century adopted the warfare model for themselves, but in the late nineteenth century there was a significant group of evangelical thinkers who have been called "Darwin's forgotten defenders."[8] The attempt to reconcile evangelical Christianity with science was part of a long tradition that historian George Marsden has described as the "Evangelical Love Affair with Enlightenment Science." While for some evangelicals the Enlightenment meant antireligious rationalism, for most evangelicals, especially through the nineteenth century, Enlightenment science was viewed as an ally of true religion. The Princeton school of evangelicals, for example, believed that theology was a science and that Christian truths could be shown to be true in much the same way that natural phenomenon could be demonstrated scientifically.

The evangelical love affair with Enlightenment science was possible because in America the type of the Enlightenment thinking that was most influential was the moderate Scottish school of thought known as Common Sense Realism. Common Sense Realism started with notions such as the existence of oneself and the reality of cause and effect. These things did not need to be proven or even demonstrated. They could be taken for granted and were the building blocks for other knowledge. Evangelical intellectuals joined Common Sense Realism with Baconian science. Baconian science was not theoretical, as was Darwinism, but instead emphasized careful observation and categorization of the facts of nature. When Common Sense and Baconianism were synthesized, the result was an evangelical approach to knowledge in which observation of nature would lead one toward truth that was embedded in creation, just as reading the Bible in straightforward Baconian fashion would result in knowledge of truth. Like Galileo, many evangelical thinkers believed that the two "books," nature and the Bible, should be read together and would always be in harmony. As Marsden puts it, the belief of nineteenth-century evangelicals was, "Scripture and rational moral science operating independently will reveal completely harmonious principles."[9]

Before surveying some of the nineteenth-century evangelicals who responded to Darwin, it is important to clear up a couple of popular misconceptions. First, Darwin did not invent the idea of evolution. The theory that species had developed over time had been around since the late eighteenth century. Darwin contributed the theory of natural selection that explained how organisms evolved. Darwin's natural selection taught that the mutations in organisms were first random. This posed a challenge to the idea that all that happened in nature had a divine purpose behind it. Darwin said that some of the most important changes in nature happened without purpose. As will be discussed below, some evangelical scientists and theologians attempted to modify this aspect of Darwin while retaining the theory of evolution. A second misconception is that after *Origin of Species* appeared, the lines of battle divided with religious people on one side and the nonreligious on the other—in other words, the warfare model kicked in again just as it had in the time of Galileo. Actually, one of the great champions of evolution in America was Asa Gray, an evangelical who worked hard to ensure that Darwin's views received a fair and open hearing. On the other side, the great opponent of Darwin was Harvard's Louis Agassiz, who was not an orthodox Christian. Agassiz, like many others, opposed Darwin on purely scientific grounds.[10]

Agassiz was originally from Switzerland and studied in Germany before coming to America permanently in 1848 as a professor at Harvard. Prior to coming to America, he studied the glaciers of Europe and Britain and developed the continental Ice Age theory. Agassiz was a Unitarian liberal in religious belief, and he did not adhere to the Biblicism of evangelicals. He saw no need to take the creation accounts of Genesis seriously, although he did believe that God created the universe. Scientifically, he never accepted the transmutation of species. Rather, he believed in the constancy of species owed to God's creation of each individually. He believed that there had been multiple creations of humans, each human type created for a particular geographic region. This belief fueled his racism, leading to his defense of slavery. God, he believed, had created the darker races to be slaves. Beyond racism, he simply did not want to associate with African Americans in restaurants and elsewhere, and he opposed intermarriage as a violation of the created order in which the races were intended to be separate geographically.[11] It should be noted that many evangelicals in America had racial ideas similar to Agassiz's, and his views were social orthodoxy in the South. That is part of the point, however. Such racial views, like Agassiz's scientific views, were not confined to any particular religious party, liberal or evangelical.

Asa Gray converted to evangelical Christianity in 1835, by which time he was already a medical doctor and scientist. He took a position as professor of botany at Harvard six years before Agassiz arrived on campus. Eschewing the Unitarianism that dominated the university, Gray attended church in Boston at Park Street Congregational, the church pastored a century later by Harold Ockenga, the first president of Fuller Seminary. At Park Street he taught a Sunday school class for black children. Scientifically, Gray's evangelicalism helped keep him in the empiricist camp. Like almost all Calvinist evangelicals, he rejected the sort of mysticism and idealism that led many New England intellectuals into a transcendentalist religious experience. Initially opposed to the evolutionary idea of transmutation of species, he was won over by empirical observation in the 1850s, even before Origin of Species appeared. When Darwin published his book, Gray worked to ensure that it received a fair hearing in the American scientific community.[12]

It was no great surprise that Gray was able to accommodate evolutionary theory. For a generation before him evangelicals had already been finding ways to harmonize scripture with the view that Earth was ancient. In surveying evangelicals involved in science during the first half of the nineteenth century, before Darwin's Origin of Species appeared, historian David Livingstone concludes that with a few exceptions, evangelical intellectuals had little trouble accepting the ancient age of the earth or the slow and uniform development of the earth, two ideas that had been argued in science before Darwin came along. There were ways of reading Genesis that were within the realm of evangelical Biblicism but did not rule out an ancient earth and a long period of time for creation to take place. Gray was merely working within that tradition.[13]

Of course, Gray could not accept all of Darwin's theory, but his reservations had nothing to do with Biblicism. In other words, he had already worked through Charles Lyell's geological theory that the earth was of ancient origin and had accommodated his reading of Genesis accordingly.

Moreover, Gray saw little need to harmonize science with scripture because he did not believe the Bible was a scientific textbook. He also saw the moral value of evolution and took a shot at Agassiz's racism when he pointed out that "the very first step backward makes the Negro and the Hottentot our blood relations;—not that reason or Scripture objects to that though pride may."[14] Where Gray took issue with Darwin was on the idea of design in the universe. Rather than attacking and rejecting Darwinism, however, he worked to show scientifically that evolution and transmutation of species did not rule out design.

Like many scientists of his day, Gray was a follower of the ideas of the eighteenth-century scientist William Paley (d. 1805), who had argued that the complexity of the universe was evidence of its having been designed by a creator, just as the complexity of a clock was evidence of a clockmaker. It should be emphasized that Gray did not reject or even attack Darwin over this disagreement. Rather, through scientific argument he attempted to modify Darwinism. He did this by pointing out that there was a vital piece missing in Darwin's theory. While natural selection explained why certain changes or variations in species survived, Darwin had no way to explain why the changes occurred in the first place; blind chance simply would not do. Gray believed that Darwin and Paley should be synthesized and that the two were in no way incompatible. Paley's God of design was the cause of Darwin's adaptation of species. Darwin appreciated Gray's work and arranged to have some of Gray's essays published in Britain; however, Darwin would eventually reject Gray's views, as would many evangelicals. Among the latter were many evangelicals who believed that evolution was part of God's creative design but that God did not directly control all adaptations, as Gray thought.[15]

Inspired by Gray, George Frederick Wright went on to a much longer and more influential career as an evangelical who sought to reconcile and harmonize Darwinism and evangelical Christianity. From his post at Oberlin College, which he took in 1881, he argued that the best of science confirmed rather than contradicted true religion. As Livingstone writes, "For over forty years Wright labored to present a Christian Darwinism that was more faithful both to Darwin and to Christianity than was the speculative evolutionism of the liberal theologians."[16] Wright took the evangelical side in the fundamentalist-modernist controversy and even wrote for *The Fundamentals*.

As with Gray and Wright, so it was with many other evangelical thinkers. They accepted evolution and the broad outlines of Darwinism, but they believed that Darwin had unnecessarily rejected Paley and the concept of design. The best evangelical theologians argued this way, and it is important to remember that in the nineteenth century the distinction we draw between a scientist and a theologian was much less developed. Theology was still considered the queen of the sciences. One of the leading theologians in America in the late nineteenth century was Charles Hodge (d. 1878). He was part of the Princetonian school of theology that made up the most important element of evangelical intellectual life in America. In 1874, just a year after he had published his multivolume systematic theology, Hodge published *What Is Darwinism?*. He had taken up the issue in the systematic theology and spun the book out of the larger work. Like most evangelical intellectuals, Hodge was devoted to Scottish Common Sense Realism and Baconian science. He had little patience for theories. Utilizing the Baconian emphasis on the categorization of plain facts, the first strike against Darwinism was that it was a theory. This criticism was echoed far and wide in the popular antievolution movement that led eventually to the Scopes trial. Hodge, however, was not hostile to evolution, nor was he hostile to Darwin himself. He believed that Darwin was a fine naturalist and a fair-minded thinker. Moreover, Hodge was open to the ancient age of the earth, and he was delighted when a colleague argued conclusively that dating the age of the earth using the Old Testament chronologies was not sound biblical scholarship.

Hodge still rejected Darwinism, however. For him, Darwinism consisted of three elements: evolution, natural selection, and an ateleological explanation. The third was the problem. Teleology is the idea that things are moving toward an end goal; in other words, toward their natural end or design. Applied to the origins of species, teleology was what Paley, Gray, and all Christian evolutionists believed. The end goal toward which evolution moved was the universe as God wanted it to exist. God was creating the universe through evolution. Darwin's later work, at least as interpreted by Hodge and most others, denied that there was any such purpose to evolution. Not only did natural selection happen in random fashion but also the entire process was simply one of chance. It was meaningless. As Hodge put it, "It is . . . neither evolution nor natural selection, which give Darwinism its peculiar character and importance. It is that Darwin rejects all teleology, or the doctrine of final causes. He denies design in any of the organisms in the vegetable or animal world." For this reason, Hodge believed a person "may be an evolutionist without being a Darwinian."[17] Hodge believed that Gray and other Christians who defended Darwinism actually were in this non-Darwinian evolutionist category. In the final analysis, therefore, Hodge believed that the theory of evolution by chance completely devoid of design was atheism even while the evolution of species with design could be Christian. As he wrote, "[T]here may be a theistic interpretation of the Darwinian theory."[18]

Beyond the mere question of Darwinism, Hodge always believed that science and evangelical Biblicism should go hand in hand. Like Galileo before him, he wrote, "Nature is as truly a revelation of God as the Bible; and we only interpret the Word of God by the Word of God when we interpret the Bible by science." In the same essay he wrote, "If the Bible cannot contradict science, neither can science contradict the Bible."[19] The belief that science could not contradict the Bible was precisely the idea that John William Draper, Andrew Dickson White, T. H. Huxley, and other secular thinkers reacted against when they promoted the science-religion warfare model. As said above, they wanted to free science from religion. Hodge and nearly all other evangelical intellectuals of his day believed religion and science were two forms of God's revelation to humankind and should be pursued together.

Other leaders of the Princeton school of theology were even less antagonistic to Darwinism than Hodge had been. James McCosh (d. 1894), who was president of Princeton University, and B. B. Warfield (d. 1921) at Princeton Seminary were open not only to evolution but also natural selection. They believed that even natural selection could be harmonized with teleology or design in the universe. Warfield believed that Darwin assumed that natural selection eliminated teleology because he lacked theological sophistication and became increasingly antagonistic to religion, art, music, and literature as he grew older.[20] Contrary to Darwin's view, natural selection confirmed God's design. This was because natural selection worked like natural law. Organisms and species did naturally, without recourse to miracle, what they were intended by natural law to do, and God was the creator of natural law. Natural selection meant that God set up the evolution process to work naturally; there was no need for supernatural intervention at several points along the way. Warfield did reserve a place for some supernatural intervention, for example, in the creation of the human soul, and he continued to believe in miracles, but for the most part evolution was natural because God was the author of nature. Warfield wrote in his lecture notes, "The upshot of the whole matter is that there is no necessary antagonism of Xty to evolution. . . . [I]f we condition the theory by allowing the constant oversight of God in the whole process, & his occasional supernatural interference for the production of new beginnings . . . we may hold to the modified theory of evolution & be Xians in the ordinary orthodox sense."[21]

Clearly, for Warfield, Hodge, and others, Christians could accept evolution. Whether they ought to or not was another question, one that should be settled by the scientific evidence. As for evolution and the Bible, Warfield was not only an evangelical Biblicist, he forcefully articulated the modern notion of biblical inerrancy. Yet, he said clearly that he saw hardly a passage of scripture, including the creation stories of Genesis 1 and 2, which could not be reconciled with evolution. For him, the six days of creation were six long periods or ages. Holding to the pre-higher critical view that Moses wrote the Pentateuch, Warfield said further that when Moses wrote the creation accounts he was not attempting to be exhaustive. Moreover, the prophet accommodated his language to the needs of his readers and thus spoke of six days of creation, not in a literal twenty-four-hour sense of days. Warfield also argued, like Hodge, that the age of the earth was of no theological significance, and like Gray, but not Agassiz, Warfield rejected the idea of multiple creations. Warfield believed that this so-called polygenesis view was simply a means for advancing racism, as it was for Agassiz. For Warfield, evolution confirmed the biblical view that human beings of all races came originally from one human source and were all therefore related and equal.[22]

These examples are fairly typical of the response to Darwin by the Reformed (Calvinist) tradition of evangelicals in America. As Livingstone writes, "American evangelicals in the Reformed mold absorbed the Darwinian shock waves fairly easily."[23] Livingstone acknowledges that many American evangelicals were not from the Reformed wing of Protestantism, but his research has convinced him that many non-Reformed evangelicals also took the middle ground on the question of Darwinism. There was some outright opposition to evolution, to be sure, especially in the South. Some of the early antievolutionists were popular writers and preachers who made a connection between the battles against modernism and the fight against evolution. One such antievolutionist, for example, portrayed Darwinism as a virtual conspiracy to eliminate the supernatural from religion, which of course would eliminate miracles. Others saw evolution as an attack on the Bible, especially the book of Genesis, which was connected to the higher critical view that Moses did not write the Pentateuch. One of the titles from this critic's books was *The Mosaic Record and Modern Science*, which appeared in 1881.[24] It is understandable that some critics would make the connection between modern biblical criticism and modern science.

The primary point is that for about a half century after the appearance of *Origin of Species* there was no uniform evangelical response to evolution or Darwinism. A minority of evangelical thinkers opposed evolution in any form, others accepted evolution while rejecting Darwin's interpretation, and still others went a good distance toward accepting a slightly adjusted form of Darwinism. Such ambiguity was represented as late as 1915 and the appearance of *The Fundamentals* discussed in the previous chapter. This multivolume tour de force of early fundamentalism contained essays that were open to evolution, one of them by George Frederick Wright, as well as two stridently antievolution essays.[25] The warfare model that John William Draper and Andrew Dickson White portrayed as the norm was in fact not the norm. Rather, they promoted the warfare model because they were convinced that real science had to be extricated from religion. This was not the view of the religious thinkers of the second half of the nineteenth century, either modernist or evangelical. We are left with this question, therefore: If so many evangelical intellectuals were open to evolution and even an adjusted Darwinism, why and how did some evangelical attitudes harden into the sort of fierce antievolution movement that led to the Scopes trial in 1925?

The Scopes "Monkey" Trial

For many popular fundamentalists in the twentieth century, evolution became a symbol of modernism. Just as the more sophisticated theologians attacked modernism in the denominations and seminaries, at the popular level fundamentalists attacked the teaching of evolution in the public schools, believing that Darwinism would corrupt the youth of America and ruin American culture. Many Americans believed that the demise of Germany in World War I was connected to the rise of theological modernism and evolutionary science. For America to avoid the fate of Germany, the nation would need to purge its culture of all vestiges of modernism. These early decades of the twentieth century also saw more and more young people actually attending high school, which raised the stakes of the debate, as did developments in the sciences. By 1925, the ground for accommodation between traditional religion and evolution had shrunk considerably because of the defeat of neo-Lamarckian views of evolution. Lamarckian evolution, dating from the late eighteenth century, had room for teleology, an end toward which evolution was moving. This meant that evangelical thinkers could view evolution as a purposeful activity of nature directed by God. When the neo-Darwinian synthesis won out over neo-Lamarckian views, this meant that natural selection was the driving force of evolution. Natural selection, as we have seen, meant a lack of purpose or teleology in favor of chance or accident. It was tougher to keep a purposeful God in the equation, and this led to the Scopes trial.

The Scopes trial is one of the most infamous incidents in modern American history: America's version of Galileo's trial, some believe. As a result of the antievolution crusade of the early 1920s, several states considered antievolution bills in their state legislatures. In February 1925, Tennessee passed the Butler Act, which was one of the first such antievolution bills. The American Civil Liberties Union (ACLU) believed such laws were unconstitutional and wanted a test case, so the organization placed an advertisement in newspapers across Tennessee offering to help any schoolteacher in the state challenge the Butler Act. George Rappleyea was a thirty-one-year-old from New York who managed mines in the small town of Dayton (population 1,800), situated between Knoxville and Chattanooga. He had already written a letter to the editor of the *Chattanooga Times* opposing the Butler Act, and when he read one of the ACLU ads, he seized the opportunity. At the local drugstore, where men of the community often met, Rappleyea tried to drum up support for a case. There was a mixture of motives among those who supported the idea. Some believed that a trial would help boost Dayton's public exposure and local tourism. They were correct on both counts.[26]

The group that decided to test the Butler Act recruited John Thomas Scopes to serve as the teacher to be arrested. Scopes was a twenty-four-year-old science teacher and part-time football coach at the local high school. He was single and living in Dayton temporarily and so had little at stake in terms of losing his job or experiencing local hostility. He agreed to participate as the victim, with a two-brother team of young city prosecutors agreeing to try him. One of the brothers was Scopes's close friend. The group wired the ACLU that they had a test case for the Butler Act. Through a somewhat convoluted set of circumstances, the case took on epic proportions when William Jennings Bryan joined the prosecution and famous attorney Clarence Darrow joined the defense.

Bryan had been for much of his career the leading progressive politician in America. He burst onto the national political scene in 1896 with his "Cross of Gold" speech at the Democratic National Convention, where he was chosen as the party's nominee for president. Because he supported the Populist farmers' movement, the People's Party also nominated him as their candidate. Bryan lost the election in 1896, ran and lost again in 1900, then a third time in 1908, making him the only major party presidential candidate in American political history to lose three elections. Still, through the three losses and for another decade thereafter, he was one of the most well-known politicians in the country, and he served as secretary of state in the Woodrow Wilson administration from 1913 to 1915.

The essence of Bryan's political theory was populist majoritarianism—the belief that in a democracy the people know best and that their will should be followed. In the 1890s, the hot issue among the farmers' populist movement was free silver. Free silver referred to a proposed policy whereby the government would increase the money supply by producing more silver coins. This would cause inflation, resulting in higher prices for farm produce and allowing farmers to get out of debt. Bryan was a young Nebraska congressional representative in the early 1890s when he allegedly remarked, "The people of

Nebraska are for free silver, so I am for free silver; I'll look up the arguments later." Beginning with free silver, Bryan moved on to champion a variety of progressive issues all intended to place more power in the hands of the people—direct election of senators (senators were still being chosen by state legislatures), women's suffrage, a graduated income tax, regulation of big business, anti-imperialism, and prohibition. Prohibition, while often viewed today as a reactionary or even fundamentalist movement, was actually championed by many progressives as a reform that would improve the country.

Bryan joined the antievolution crusade in 1919, and by 1921 had written a speech titled "The Menace of Darwinism," which he gave widely thereafter. Although his antievolution efforts would end up making him appear to be a reactionary fundamentalist, he saw the opposition to Darwin as one more progressive crusade. There were two reasons for this. First, antievolution laws were supported by the majorities of several states. Bryan believed that as such they were constitutional. This was related to Bryan's populism and was manifested in his views of education and academic freedom. For him the issue was simple: The people of these states did not want evolution taught in their schools, so it should not be taught. This was doubly so because the people paid for the public schools with their tax dollars. As he said famously on many occasions, "The hand that writes the check rules the school."[27] The public schools belonged to and were paid for by the people, so the people's will should reign supreme. Moreover, Bryan believed the people had good reason to oppose evolution; it was not scientific. "Science to be truly science is classified knowledge," he said in good Baconian fashion. "Tested by this definition, Darwinism is not science at all; it is guesses strung together."[28] This was a typical fundamentalist criticism that Bryan made in hundreds of speeches in the five years leading up to the trial. Bryan's majoritarian views represented the dominant populist and progressive cry of American politics in the late nineteenth and early twentieth centuries—power to the people. The landscape was shifting, however, from power to the people as a majority to the rights of individuals in their quest for freedom and autonomy. The ACLU, like a significant segment of the legal and academic communities, was moving toward the defense of individual rights against the power of majorities. This development was almost incomprehensible to Bryan.

Second, Bryan viewed evolution as a menace to progressive reform. The era before World War I was one of progressive optimism. Intellectuals, business leaders, politicians, and most others in the knowledge class believed that the techniques and knowledge produced by the modern age could be used to make society better. Converted at a revival meeting when he was fourteen years old, Bryan was an evangelical who believed that through Christian reform efforts the kingdom of God could be substantially realized on earth. For much of his career he even believed that war would eventually be outlawed. Many secular progressives had similar views about the potential for reforming society. In Europe, the Great War killed off most of this progressive optimism. Given that the best technology the modern world produced was used for wartime destruction on a scale never before contemplated, many were led to a sense of despair over the prospects for improving society. America was relatively unscathed by the war, however, so the optimism continued in some quarters, and this is where Bryan's critique of evolution came into play. Like many others, he interpreted Darwin through the lens of social philosopher Herbert Spencer, who had popularized the term "survival of the fittest." For Bryan, the idea of survival of the fittest was the law of hate. It meant that human beings had evolved to their present state by exhibiting power and ruthlessness, not love and justice. Two intellectuals had written books exploring the connection between evolution and German militarism that was exhibited during the war, and another academic had done a survey of college students showing that as they progressed through their four years of college, belief in God dropped significantly. Bryan concluded from these studies that the teaching of evolution as fact would produce a generation of amoral atheists who had no foundation from which to push society toward greater justice. For Bryan, the logical conclusion of evolution was a complete lack of a moral basis for reform. If evolution were true, human beings were just the highest form of animals, and there was no standard to which they could be held accountable.

Many popular fundamentalists by the 1920s fought evolution because they believed it violated a literal reading of the book of Genesis, but this was not Bryan's primary concern. As his testimony in the trial revealed, he was comfortable with the interpretation of Genesis that allowed a long period of time for God's creation. In short, like Hodge and Warfield, he did not believe that the "days" of Genesis had to be interpreted as twenty-four-hour days. Neither did he oppose teaching evolution as a theory. He was confident that if presented as a theory, Darwinism would lose out to creationist views. Nevertheless, Bryan was able to make common cause with antievolutionists of many stripes, and this led to his volunteering to help prosecute Scopes in 1925.

In his younger years, Scopes's defense attorney Clarence Darrow had much in common with Bryan politically. From rural Ohio, Darrow was nominated by the Democratic Party for Congress in 1896, the same year Bryan received his first presidential nomination, and Darrow probably spent more time campaigning for Bryan than he did for his own congressional seat, which he lost in a close election. As a lawyer, Darrow then pressed his talents into the cause of labor unions, at one time defending the famous socialist Eugene V. Debs. Over time, Darrow took on more high-profile criminal cases, the most famous being the Leopold-Loeb case where he defended two Chicago teenagers who had murdered a classmate merely to see if they could get away with the crime. Darrow had long employed social science to argue against free will, and he was able to convince the jury that the murderers were merely the products of their society and not responsible for their actions. Loeb and Leopold were convicted but spared the death penalty.

Obviously, as the Leopold-Loeb trial showed, by the twenties Bryan and Darrow were completely different in their moral views. In fact, Bryan and other antievolutionists had used the Leopold-Loeb murder as evidence of what happened when young people were led to believe that human beings were merely more highly evolved animals with no basis for morality. Religiously, Bryan and Darrow were also opposites. Darrow's father had been something of a village atheist. The son merely took the act onto a national stage. Darrow said frequently that Christianity was a "slave religion" because it taught people to be complacent concerning injustice and mediocrity. In articles, books, speeches, and courtroom arguments he had spent his life ridiculing traditional Christian beliefs. The Calvinist idea that all people were guilty of original sin but only some chosen by God to be saved was in his view "a dangerous doctrine . . . silly, impossible and wicked." "The origin of what we call civilization," he said on other occasions, "is not due to religion but to skepticism. . . . The modern world is the child of doubt and inquiry, as the ancient world was the child of fear and faith."[29] As historian Edward Larson puts it in his Pulitzer Prize–winning history of the Scopes trial, "Darrow's social views shaped his scientific views rather than the other way around, and the theory of evolution proved most helpful in his efforts to debunk the biblical notion of creation, design, and purpose in nature."[30] In short, Darrow went to Dayton to battle Bryan and evangelical religion, not to defend Scopes and individual rights. Some on the ACLU's team of lawyers who wanted the case to be about individual rights and academic freedom feared correctly that Darrow's presence would damage their cause.

The trial took on all the trappings of a circus. The media descended on Dayton, and so many people attended the trial that the proceedings had to be moved outside into the sweltering heat of the Tennessee summer. Bryan and the defense were able to show quite easily that Scopes had violated the Butler Act, which would have been fine with the ACLU attorneys because they wanted a conviction so they could appeal. They hoped to take the case all the way to the Supreme Court to have all antievolution laws overturned. Darrow and the defense wanted to establish the scientific truth of evolution and had called a team of expert witnesses for that purpose. When the judge ruled such expert testimony inadmissible, however, Darrow called Bryan to testify as a Bible expert. Bryan, of course, could have declined, and some of his associates encouraged him to do so. Instead, he accepted, and Darrow examined him for two hours.

Bryan did very poorly as Darrow peppered him with inconsistencies between science and the Bible and inconsistencies in the Bible itself. Darrow asked about the prophet Jonah being swallowed by a whale, to which Bryan could merely say he believed the event was a miracle like any other miracle. Darrow slyly got Bryan to suggest that perhaps God had extended the day of battle for Joshua by stopping the earth rather than making the sun stand still as the Old Testament actually reads, a nonliteralist interpretation and a concession to modern astronomy. Worse still was that Bryan seemed to have no idea what the scientific consequences would be if the earth actually did stand still for several hours. Darrow extracted a similar admission from Bryan that the days of Genesis were not twenty-four-hour days but perhaps long periods of time, another concession to figurative interpretation and modern science. Darrow followed with a query as to where Cain, the son of Adam and Eve, got his wife. Darrow's questions were indeed the stuff of a street corner atheist, but Bryan's answers were worse. At one point, the two men stood facing each other waving their fists and shouting, Darrow yelling, "I am examining your fool ideas that no intelligent Christian on earth believes."[31] In short, the examination of Bryan was a quite unflattering event for both individuals.

As expected, the jury found Scopes guilty and let the judge set the fine. Bryan offered to pay it; he had always opposed an actual penalty for violation of antievolution laws. The ACLU appealed the conviction to the Tennessee Supreme Court, which found the Butler Act constitutional but overturned Scopes's conviction on the technicality that the judge had set the amount of the fine instead of the jury as stipulated by state law. Because they had now effectively won the case, the decision robbed the ACLU lawyers of the ability to appeal the case to the U.S. Supreme Court. Bryan traveled locally for a week making a few speeches, including his closing argument, which he had been unable to deliver at the trial itself. He returned to Dayton the Sunday following the trial and died suddenly while taking a nap. When a reporter suggested to Darrow that Bryan had died of a broken heart, Darrow referred to Bryan's legendary eating habits by remarking, "Broken heart nothing; he died of a busted belly." Nationally renowned journalist H. L.

Mencken wrote in the *Baltimore Sun*, "God aimed at Darrow, missed, and hit Bryan instead," then gloated privately, "We killed the son-of-bitch."[32]

Not until the thirties was there a widespread notion that the fundamentalists had suffered a humiliating defeat in the Scopes trial. Immediately following the event, newspapers were ambivalent about who had fared worse, and hardly anyone had a sense that what had happened at Dayton was of lasting importance. Historian Ronald Numbers surveyed the coverage of five newspapers all in different regions of the country and over a dozen national magazines and reported, "I discovered not a single declaration of victory by the opponents of anti-evolutionism, in the sense of their claiming that the crusade was at an end."[33] What happened to make the Scopes trial seem so decisive in modern American history? Edward Larson argues persuasively that the image of the trial was transformed in a thirty-year period that began with the publication of a popular book in 1931 and ended with the appearance of the film version of *Inherit the Wind* in 1960.[34]

In 1931 journalist Frederick Lewis Allen published *Only Yesterday: An Informal History of the 1920s*, which surprisingly became a best-seller, selling over 1 million copies. Allen grossly oversimplified what happened at the trial. As Larson puts it, "Allen reduced fundamentalism to antievolutionism and antievolutionism to Bryan."[35] In doing so he became the first commentator to turn the trial into a decisive defeat for fundamentalism, which conveniently disregarded all the mediating positions on evolution that were covered earlier in this chapter. Moreover, Allen's book had some outright errors. For example, in Allen's words, "Bryan [on the witness stand] affirmed his belief that the world was created in 4004 B.C."[36] Actually, as we have seen, Bryan admitted to believing that the days of Genesis could be long periods of time, which had led to Darrow's claim that Bryan had denied his own faith by not interpreting the Bible literally. Allen acknowledged that there was no statistical evidence for the decline in religion following Scopes, but he dismissed statistics of continued healthy church attendance by saying, "In congregations, and especially among the younger men and women, there was an undeniable weakening of loyalty to the church and an undeniable vagueness as to what it had to offer them." Allen's evidence for this assertion was "the tone of discussions which accompanied the abandonment of compulsory chapel in a number of colleges."[37] As Larson writes, "This had been true in [Allen's] own life, but to extrapolate it to all Americans—and to suggest that the Scopes trial contributed to the process—was sheer speculation."[38] Nevertheless, other writers picked up Allen's interpretation, and by the end of the decade, it was commonplace. In 1939, William Warren Sweet, in his standard textbook on religion in America, said flatly concerning the trial, "It was Fundamentalism's last stand."[39]

If Allen's book began the process of reinterpreting the Scopes trial as fundamentalism's last stand, *Inherit the Wind* provided a caricature of the movement and its alleged great danger to society. First published in 1955 as a play by Jerome Lawrence and Robert E. Lee, the film version appeared in 1960 starring Spencer Tracy, Fredric March, and Gene Kelly. *Inherit the Wind* injected into the Scopes trial the ominous McCarthyism of the fifties, where Joseph McCarthy's U.S. Senate committee cast aspersions of communism on Americans far and wide, leading to, among other things, the blacklisting of actors in Hollywood who were suspected of Communist connections. Larson points out three ways the play and film fundamentally altered the story. First, the town becomes a mob and the atmosphere is that of a witch hunt. Joseph Wood Krutch, who had been a trial correspondent in Dayton in 1925, recalled in 1967 that on the whole the townspeople of Dayton had behaved well. By contrast, he wrote, "The authors of *Inherit the Wind* made it chiefly sinister, a witch hunt of the sort we are now all too familiar with." In reality, he continued, "The atmosphere was so far from being sinister that it suggested a circus day."[40] In the film, however, things are different. In one scene the townspeople march through the streets singing, "We'll hang Bert Cates (John Scopes) from the old apple tree; our God is marching on" to the tune of the "Battle Hymn of the Republic." When they reach the jail where Cates is confined throughout the trial (the real Scopes was never in jail), someone throws a bottle at Cates. It smashes against the bars of the cell, inches from Cates's face.[41]

The second alteration in the film concerns Bryan. Known as Brady in the play and film, he starts as a mindless reactionary and ends a raving lunatic. Along the way he is a dishonest charlatan as he tricks Cates's fiancée, who is also the local minister's daughter, then brutalizes her on the witness stand. When he takes the stand himself to be questioned by Drummond, Darrow's character, Brady insists that the earth was created in 4004 B.C., on October 23, at 9:00 a.m. The real Bryan made no such claim. Drummond gets Brady to call sex the original sin and to agree that he receives divine revelation. Then, in the film's final scene, Brady attempts to give his closing oration after the judge has already adjourned the trial. No one pays any attention as he rants and raves. In the play the crowd laughs at him, and Brady exclaims to his wife, "Mother. They're laughing at me, Mother. I can't stand it when they laugh at me." Then, he falls over dead in the courtroom.[42] At a Broadway production of the play, a constitutional scholar became so disgusted that he walked out, the only time he had ever walked out of a play. As he said later,

"I ended up actually sympathizing with Bryan, even though I was and continue to be opposed to his ideas in the case, simply because the playwrights had drawn the character in such comic strip terms."[43]

The third change cited by Larson is that just as the Brady-Bryan character is a mindless reactionary, Drummond-Darrow is a hero of open-mindedness. In the play, when another character in the trial mocks Brady's religion, Drummond actually stands up for him, saying, "You smartaleck. You have no more right to spit on his religion than you have a right to spit on my religion. Or lack of it."[44] In the film this scene becomes an exchange between Drummond and newspaper reporter E. K. Hornbeck of the *Baltimore Herald.* Drummond dresses down the cynical Hornbeck for not acknowledging Brady's tragic humanity. Hornbeck, who represents the real-life *Baltimore Sun* editor H. L. Mencken, comes off as a cynic, which Mencken was, while Drummond comes off as an idealist, which Darrow was not. The Drummond character has strong but vague religious principles; he is a friendly religious modernist who believes in freedom. Darrow, as said above, was a biological and environmental determinist who was hostile to religion. In the final scene of both the play and the film, Drummond picks up a copy of *Origin of Species* and the Bible, one in his right hand the other in his left, weighs them in the balance as if his hands were a scale, puts them together, and walks out of the empty courtroom.

These alterations were acknowledged and criticized when the film first appeared. As the *Time* magazine review said, "The script wildly and unjustly caricatures the fundamentalists as vicious and narrow-minded hypocrites, [and] just as wildly and unjustly idealizes their opponents, as personified by Darrow." The *Time* reviewer concluded that the fundamentalist position, even in its extreme form, was only slightly more absurd than "the shallow scientism that the picture offers as a substitute for religious faith and experience."[45] Other reviews in major magazines and newspapers said similar things. A liberal reviewer in the *The New Republic* wrote, "This film seems designed to make the liberal feel satisfied with his enlightened state."[46] Still, what most people know about the Scopes trial comes from the film more than a history of the actual event, such as Larson's fine book *Summer for the Gods.* The film was even recommended as a teaching tool in 1994 by the National Center for History in Schools, which suggested that teachers show the film as a way to get students to analyze the different views of Darrow and Bryan.[47]

The Rise of Creation Science

In 1983, Harvard paleontologist and evolution defender Stephen Jay Gould summarized *Inherit the Wind* as follows: "John Scopes was persecuted, Darrow rose to Scopes's defense and smite the antediluvian Bryan, and the antievolution movement then dwindled or ground to at least a temporary halt. All three parts of this story are false."[48] Gould criticized this caricature largely because it lulled the evolution establishment into believing that the forces of antievolution were part of a bygone era. "[S]adly, any hope that the issues of the Scopes trial had been banished to the realm of nostalgic Americana have been swept aside by our current creationist resurgence," he lamented.[49] Gould was referring to the Arkansas Creation Science case *McLean v. Arkansas* (1982), where a district judge struck down as unconstitutional a state law mandating the teaching of Creation Science in public schools wherever evolution was taught. Five years later a similar case from Louisiana went all the way to the U.S. Supreme Court. As in Arkansas, the Supreme Court ruled that Creation Science was religion masquerading as science. Mandating that it be taught in public schools, therefore, was an unconstitutional establishment of religion.

The shift from antievolution to equal time for Creation Science took place in response to a Supreme Court case that came out of Arkansas in 1967. In *Epperson v. Arkansas* the Supreme Court struck down all antievolution laws as unconstitutional, exactly what the ACLU had hoped the Scopes trial would accomplish. By 1967 when the Epperson case took place, there were few states even attempting to enforce the antievolution statutes that were still on their books. Even in Arkansas the law was unenforced. The lawyers for Susan Epperson, therefore, had to argue a hypothetical case because neither she nor anyone else was ever punished for teaching evolution. The attorneys argued that when the state required her to use the state-authorized science textbook with its section on evolution, the state was requiring her to break its own antievolution law. After the Epperson case made it clear that antievolution was a dead letter legally, fundamentalists shifted their strategy from trying to block the teaching of evolution to attempting to get Creation Science taught alongside evolution. The development of Creation Science, however, had started decades before.

Readers will recall from chapter two that after the Scopes trial, when elites in the media and academia believed fundamentalism had been vanquished, what actually took place was a period of realignment. In other words, fundamentalists withdrew from mainstream culture and began building their own denominations, Bible institutes, magazines, and so forth. In conjunction with this realignment, they largely abandoned efforts to banish evolution from schools, just as fundamentalists after Scopes gave up on the effort to recapture the mainline Protestant denominations from the modernists. Antievolutionism continued, but mostly to inculcate fundamentalists themselves, and especially their children, with an alternative to mainstream evolutionary science. Separatism from modernist theology corresponded with separatism from mainstream intellectual life.

The second quarter of the twentieth century was a low point for evangelical evolutionism. In other words, it was difficult after the Scopes trial to be an evangelical and publicly acknowledge that evolution was true. The real contenders among creationist views were 1) the day-age theory; 2) the gap theory; and 3) flood geology. The day-age theory had been around since at least the late nineteenth century and was espoused by Bryan when he was questioned by Darrow at the Scopes trial. Those holding this view interpret the "days" of Genesis not as twenty-four-hour days but as ages or epochs. From that basic idea, fundamentalists diverged as to just how God created the world, and it is possible for a day-age adherent to be a theistic evolutionist. The central points of the day-age theory were that the creation process could have taken a long time, the earth could be very old, and evolution could have been one of God's means for creating species. That said, the vast majority of evangelicals after Scopes, if they believed in evolution at all, exempted humankind from the evolutionary process at least as far as evolution from lower species was concerned.

Those holding to the gap theory attempt to retain a more literal interpretation of the six-day creation recorded in Genesis, but they posited a gap between Genesis 1:1–2 and the rest of the creation story. In Genesis 1:1–2 the heavens and the earth were created and were without form or void. As this theory goes, there was then a long gap before God completed the rest of his creation in six literal days. The gap theory helps explain why the geological strata give the appearance of being millions of years old, while at the same time the theory retains the view that humankind was created only about 4004 B.C.E. The idea of such a short period of time from Adam to modern humans was popularized by Bishop Ussher's chronology, which he devised in the seventeenth century by using the genealogies of the Old Testament to calculate the date of the creation. The gap position was sometimes called the "ruin and restoration" view because of the belief that a catastrophe took place at the end of the gap, necessitating the re-creation that is recorded in Genesis 1:3 and following. Some gap theorists even believed there had been life during the pregap era, although not human life. Still, the creation of plants, animals, and humans as we know them today is fairly recent, allowing for little, if any, evolution of species and certainly no evolution of humans from lower forms. The gap theory was promoted by the immensely popular *Scofield Reference Bible*, which sold millions of copies after its first appearance in 1909. After the Scopes trial popular scientist and debater Harry Rimmer was the leading creationist holding the gap view.

Both the day-age and gap theories continued throughout the twentieth century within evangelicalism and fundamentalism, and one can find many today who still hold these positions. Flood geology, however, would eclipse both the day-age and gap theories and become the dominant view of fundamentalists and some evangelicals in the second half of the twentieth century. Flood geology became known as Creation Science. The history of flood geology has been tied intimately to the Seventh-day Adventist denomination, which began in the mid-nineteenth century. In the 1840s, a Seventh-day Baptist preacher named William Miller predicted the return of Christ. Hundreds of people joined his movement only to experience the "Great Disappointment" when Christ did not return in 1844 as predicted. While most left the movement, a remnant pressed on and eventually came under the leadership of prophet Ellen White. She and her associates turned the fledgling and disappointed Millerites into the Seventh-day Adventist Church, which continues to this day as an evangelical denomination. Marked by an intense interest in end-times prophecy that characterized the Millerite movement, White and the Adventists also developed distinct views of the beginning of time as well.

Adventists' views of creation are tied to their belief in the literal seventh-day Sabbath, the observance of which is commanded in the fourth of the Ten Commandments. The sacredness of the Sabbath is tied to its having been the day that God rested after six days of heavy-lifting creation work. White would have no part in the day-age view because the idea of turning the days of creation into long, indefinite periods struck at the heart of the literal Sabbath. In one of her many visions, recorded in her nine volumes of writing, she was "carried back to the creation and was shown that the first week, in which God performed the work of creation in six days and rested on the seventh day, was just like every other week."[50] She also revived and tweaked an old view that the Genesis flood was responsible for the fossil record and the earth's present geological strata. After the flood, with dead carcasses and debris everywhere, God buried it all by causing a "powerful wind to pass over the earth . . . in some instances carrying away the tops of mountains like mighty avalanches, forming huge hills and high mountains where there were none to be seen before, and burying the dead bodies with trees, stones, and earth."[51]

White's views came in the form of prophecy, and the Adventists to this day have a special reverence for her writings. The first significant amateur scientist to take White's views and develop them into the science of flood geology was George McCready Price (1870–1963). During the Scopes trial when Darrow asked Bryan to name scientists whose views Bryan respected, Price was one of the two Bryan named. Bryan had even invited Price to attend the trial, but Price was in England and unable to make the trip. Price was from New Brunswick, Canada. His father died when he was twelve, leaving Price and his brother to run the family farm. After a few years the two Price boys and their mother joined the Seventh-day Adventists. In between stints peddling Ellen White's books as a door-to-door sales person, Price attended an Adventist college in Battle Creek, Michigan, for two years and a school back in New Brunswick for another year. He studied science at the latter, which was the only formal training he would ever have. Through his own study, Price concluded that the theory of evolution "all turned on its view of geology, and that if its geology were true, the rest would seem more or less reasonable."[52] He, therefore, set himself on a lifetime course of disproving evolution by proving flood geology.

For years, Price struggled financially, often working at maintenance jobs at Adventist colleges, but he still managed to study and write books. Whereas modern evolutionists believed that the fossils found in geologic formation gave evidence of progressive evolution, Price and other flood geologists argued that the Genesis flood was responsible for the order in which the fossils appeared in the strata. The reason that lower forms of life were found further down in the strata was not that these forms had existed earlier than more highly evolved forms. Instead, those lower forms were the first to be buried in the catastrophic flood, whereas higher forms of life could flee to the hills and mountains in an attempt to escape the rising waters. Following White's prophecy, Price posited a miraculous cosmic storm following the flood to cover the dead animals and humans that were left rotting on land when the floodwaters receded. As historian Ronald Numbers puts it concerning Price's view, "Thus to the discerning eye, the fossil record revealed not a temporal succession of life but simply a sorting out of contemporaneous antediluvian life-forms. Or, in other words, the universally accepted geological column was nothing but a cunningly devised fable."[53] Price tended to attribute geological wonders such as the Grand Canyon to rushing water rather than glaciers, although he did not completely rule out postflood glaciers in some instances. Deposits from the flood formed mountain ranges, such as the Alps.

Price outlined these basic views in his first book *Outlines of Modern Christianity and Modern Science* (1902). His second book was *Illogical Geology: The Weakest Point in the Evolution Theory* (1906). In 1923 he published his massive, 726-page college text titled *The New Geology*, which was no doubt the book Bryan had in mind when he cited Price at the Scopes trial. The text was used at many fundamentalist colleges for decades thereafter. Although it is tempting to write Price off as a crank, and at times he surely was, his tireless efforts on behalf of a battle he believed was of cosmic proportions gained the notice of many inside and outside fundamentalist circles. Within fundamentalism he became the central figure with which those holding other views had to contend, while outside fundamentalism some mainstream scientists took time to refute him. In particular, Stanford president David Starr Jordan, the leading American authority on fossil fishes, sparred with Price off and on for more than twenty years, trying to get him to see that his views were "based on scattering mistakes, omissions and exceptions against general truths that anybody familiar with the facts in a general way can not possibly dispute."[54] Far from causing Price to doubt his views, critics such as Jordan gave the flood geologist the sense that he was making headway by getting mainstream scientists to take him seriously enough to refute him.

While Price advocated the Baconian practice of simple observation of facts with as little theorizing as possible, he was wise enough to know that all facts have to be interpreted in some sense and that the interpreters all work from a particular perspective. Mainstream scientists interpreted the facts from the perspective of Darwin and geologist Charles Lyell, while he interpreted the facts from the lens of scripture. "The value of a theory," he wrote, "was not based on the pedigree of the theorizer, but on the theory's ability to give a reasonable explanation of the facts of nature."[55] He even admitted that the general direction of flood geology was suggested by the Bible and could never be arrived at through the study of nature alone. In a rather remarkable anticipation of later postmodern views, he seemed to believe that all science was done from a particular perspective. Like Bryan, he opposed the teaching of evolution in public schools primarily because he thought it un-American to compel parents to pay for the teaching of something they did not want their children to learn. Price also opposed teaching Genesis in schools, however, because this would be an unconstitutional violation of the Establishment clause of the First Amendment. This view was a reflection of the long-standing Seventh-day Adventist advocacy of religious liberty and the separation of church and state.

By the midthirties, Price was one of the two most popular creationists within fundamentalism. Attempts in the 1930s and 1940s to bring all fundamentalist creationists together usually faltered because of disagreements among flood geologists, day-agers, and gap theorists. The militant fighting within organizations such as the Religious and Science Association (RSA) and the Deluge Geology Society (DGS) were part of the bitter fundamentalist battles that took place in theological circles as well. As some of those who became disillusioned with fundamentalism put it later, "In the Fundamentalist movement we were usually in a fight of some kind. If we were not fighting Southern Baptists, Northern Baptists, the National Council of Churches, the Catholics, communism, or modernism, we fought each other."[56] These organizations were often top heavy with Seventh-day Adventists, and the fighting often pitted the Adventists against fundamentalists who thought Adventism was cultish with its reverence for prophet Ellen White. Sometimes Adventists with differing views were pitted against each other and ended up calling each other heretics. Still, the upshot was that creationism/antievolutionism became an article of faith for many fundamentalists.

In 1941, more moderate fundamentalists formed the American Scientific Affiliation (ASA), which became a forum for discussing the pros and cons of evolution and for critiquing the views of flood geologists such as Price and gap men such as Rimmer. Many in the ASA attempted to return to the non-warfare model that had prevailed among evangelicals in the late nineteenth century before the rise of fundamentalism. They rejected what has been called "the Bible only" approach to the study of nature that called for the rejection of mainstream science. Instead, they wanted to reassert the older evangelical way of doing science that dated back through Charles Hodge in the nineteenth century to Galileo in the seventeenth. Like those two, some members of the ASA believed that the study of nature and the study of scripture should be mutually reinforcing ways of knowing God and God's word. As the ASA creed read in part, "I cannot conceive of discrepancies between statements in the Bible and the real facts of science."[57]

The leading critic of flood geology in the ASA was Laurence Kulp (b. 1921). After graduating from Wheaton College, he took a Ph.D. in physical chemistry at Princeton in 1945 and within a few years was invited to be on the faculty of Columbia University to develop the new field of geochemistry. At Columbia he set up the second carbon-14 laboratory in the country and soon became an evangelical critic of young-earth flood geology. Other evangelicals with scientific training joined Kulp in his attempted rapprochement with mainstream science, but a conservative reaction followed their efforts, and the ASA experienced division between fundamentalists and evangelicals that mirrored the larger split between fundamentalists and neoevangelicals discussed in the previous chapter.

The fundamentalist backlash against the ASA opened the way for the further dispersion and acceptance of flood geology under the name Creation Science. This was precisely the opposite of what Kulp and others in the ASA wanted. Greater acceptance of Creation Science among fundamentalists and evangelicals was a harbinger of things to come and was largely a result of the work of John Whitcomb Jr. and Henry Morris. Whitcomb graduated from Princeton in 1948 with a degree in history then completed a theological degree at Grace Theological Seminary in Indiana in 1951. Morris was from Houston, Texas, and graduated from Rice Institute, the fledgling forerunner to present-day Rice University. In 1950, he completed a Ph.D. in hydraulics at the University of Minnesota. The year before, the same year that Kulp attempted to refute flood geology, Morris joined the ASA, hoping to push the organization in the opposite direction Kulp wanted. After teaching at his alma mater, Rice, Morris took a teaching position at the present-day University of Louisiana-Lafayette then moved to Virginia Tech in 1957.

Both Whitcomb and Morris were zealous for flood geology and young earth doctrine. Having met at an ASA meeting in 1953, Whitcomb began to lobby Morris to help on a book Whitcomb had written that attempted to refute the ASA view that evangelical biblical interpretation could be harmonized with evolution, the ancient age of the earth, and uniformitarian geology. Whitcomb needed someone with scientific training to strengthen the book and give it legitimacy. Morris signed on, and over time the book became more his than Whitcomb's. It was published in 1961 as *The Genesis Flood: The Biblical Record and Its Scientific Implications*. While they were writing the book, Whitcomb and Morris recognized that Price's name had fallen into scientific disrepute just as Price's Seventh-day Adventist theology had always been looked at askance by fundamentalists and other evangelicals. Believing they needed to downplay reference to the old DGS founder, even as they used many of his views, the book contained very few references to Price. Moreover, Whitcomb and Morris were in search of a name for their movement that would replace "flood geology." This opened the door for the term Creation Science. Nevertheless, the argument of *The Genesis Flood* was very similar to Price's. Essentially, the Creation Science argument goes, the geological strata and the species artifacts found in that strata may give the appearance that the earth and its species evolved slowly over a long period of time. The truth, however, is that the strata and species artifacts result from the settling that took place after the worldwide flood associated with the Old Testament story of Noah. Whitcomb and Morris's views were but an updating of flood geology.[58]

As historian Numbers puts it humorously, the new flood geology of Whitcomb and Morris would "flood the world" under the name Creation Science. Creation Science eclipsed the moderate evangelical views of the ASA and became the dominant scientific view of evangelicals and fundamentalists, but it must be remembered that a large and significant minority of evangelicals, including most faculty in evangelical colleges today, reject Creation Science. The difference between the two camps is largely between Creation Science adherents who insist on a young earth, or at least recent life, and those who are willing to accept an ancient earth and evolution. The Creation Science adherents believe the Bible teaches clearly that the earth was created no more than 10,000 years ago and pretty much in its present form. All scientific data must be interpreted in light of this view of scripture. Evangelicals who oppose Creation Science and flood geology believe that the Bible should be interpreted and sometimes reinterpreted in light of science. Some on this side of the debate are theistic evolutionists who believe that God created nature with the ability to evolve naturally, while others are "progressive creationists," who believe that God has taken a more active part in a long evolutionary creation that follows the broad outlines of the Genesis stories. Like earlier Christian views going back at least to Galileo, many who oppose Creation Science believe God has given humankind two books, not the Bible only, and both must be read in light of each other. Both sides in the debate, the Creation Science adherents and those who oppose Creation Science, believe they hold to the authority of scripture, but they disagree over how to interpret scripture and to what extent the Bible should be interpreted by the study of God's other "book," the book of nature as understood through science. Theistic evolutionists and progressive creationists, by and large, do not believe the Bible makes outright scientific claims; Creation Science adherents believe it does.

Whitcomb, Morris, and the Creation Science institutes and centers that were created in the 1970s skillfully promoted Creation Science and flood geology. They were successful in part because nearly all fundamentalists and a large swath of evangelicals by the 1960s were "fed up with articles and books which tried to make scripture conform to the latest theory."[59] The same secularizing forces that led fundamentalists and many evangelicals to see themselves in opposition to culture by the 1960s and 1970s led them to see themselves in opposition to mainstream science. They rejected mainstream science much as they rejected mainstream culture and its secularizing forces. At the popular level, this pro–Creation Science movement replaced evangelical antievolution, especially after the Epperson case. In *Edwards v. Aguillard* (1987), Creation Science experienced the same fate as antievolution; it was struck down as an unconstitutional establishment of religion when taught in public schools. By that time, some evangelicals were developing a new challenge to evolution known as Intelligent Design (ID).

Intelligent Design

There is a sense in which ID arguments go back at least two centuries. The aforementioned naturalist William Paley popularized a form of ID in the late eighteenth century, arguing that just as the intricate workings of a watch give evidence of a watchmaker, so the workings and beauty of nature give evidence of a designer/creator. The recent expression of ID began in the 1980s with the publication of *The Mystery of Life's Origin: Reassessing Current Theories* (1984), a book coauthored by chemist Charles Thaxton, mechanical engineer Walter Bradley, and geochemist Roger L. Olsen.[60] Dean H. Kenyon, a biology professor at San Francisco State University, wrote the book's foreword. Kenyon announced that like the authors, he no longer believed that naturalistic evolution was sufficient to explain the development of the cosmos. A few years later English physician and geneticist Michael Denton wrote *Evolution: A Theory in Crisis* (1986) in which he questioned the neo-Darwinian synthesis and argued that evidence of design existed in nature. As historian Ronald Numbers writes, these books were little noticed at the time they appeared, but they became the foundation on which the ID movement of the 1990s would be built.

The first book to explicitly promote ID as an alternative to evolutionary science was *Of Pandas and People: The Central Question of Biological Origins* (1989), written by Kenyon and Percival Davis. Davis was a community-college biology instructor and coauthor of a widely used biology textbook. While admitting later that his motives in coauthoring *Of Pandas and People* were religious, not scientific, Davis tried to put distance between ID and fundamentalism by pointing out that ID implied none of the typical components of Creation Science. There was no insistence on a young earth, six-day creation, or universal flood. Virtually all ID proponents argue that the nature of the designer, whether it be the God of scripture or something else, is a question outside the realm of ID and outside the purview of science. They have tried to portray the movement as primarily, if not exclusively, scientific, but with limited success. Such disclaimers notwithstanding, ID is viewed almost everywhere in the academic world as having religious implications and motivations.

To the extent that ID is the newest form of antievolution, one of the key players has been University of California, Berkeley law professor Phillip Johnson. Johnson's specialty in law is the analysis of the logical consistency of arguments. Putting that expertise to work in science, he wrote *Darwin on Trial*, in which he attempted to show that the evidence for naturalistic evolution only makes sense when one starts with materialistic assumptions. In other words, Johnson argues, evolution starts with the materialistic assumption that nature is all there is, looks at the evidence for naturalistic evolution, and concludes that nature is all there is. The end results are really the presuppositions of naturalistic science masquerading as conclusions, in short, a circular argument.

With Johnson leading the macro argument, attempting to unmask evolutionary science as materialistic philosophy in disguise, a handful of scientists and mathematicians have attempted to demonstrate ID in the small workings of the universe. Among the leaders in this area are biologist Michael Behe and mathematician/philosopher William Dembski. Behe wrote the 1996 book *Darwin's Black Box: The Biochemical Challenge to Evolution,* in which he argued that there are cellular structures so complex that they could not have developed through the evolutionary process of natural selection. He uses the analogy of a mousetrap, arguing that if one starts with the platform of a mousetrap, adding a spring does not improve the trap's performance. The trap has no performance and is in fact not a trap at all until all the parts are assembled. So it is with many cellular structures. They could not have evolved through natural selection because they are irreducibly complex—that is, they are worthless until completely assembled. Behe and other ID proponents believe such structures give evidence of design rather than random evolution accomplished through natural selection. *Darwin's Black Box* was the first ID book published by a major secular trade or academic press.[61]

While Behe works in biology as a professor at Lehigh University, Dembski has a Ph.D. in mathematics from the University of Chicago and a Ph.D. in philosophy from the University of Illinois, Chicago. Cambridge University Press published his book *The Design Inference: Eliminating Chance through Small Probabilities* in 1998. He also edited a collection of essays with the agnostic philosopher of science Michael Ruse, entitled *Debating Design: From Darwin to DNA* (2004). Dembski has written or edited roughly ten other books as well. Putting his expertise in probability theory to work, he has argued through mathematical models that it is highly unlikely, virtually impossible, that organisms with specific and valuable functions can arise randomly by accident and chance. Beyond this technical argument, however, he maintains that "The ground rules of science have to be changed."[62] Specifically, Dembski and other ID proponents believe that the rules of science should be rewritten to allow for supernatural explanations.

Recently, ID proponents have encouraged school districts to "teach the controversy." In other words, they argue, wherever evolution is taught, students should learn that there is debate over whether naturalistic evolution is sufficient to explain the origins of the universe and all living things. This is part of the "wedge" strategy developed by Johnson, whereby ID proponents hope to split open the solid hold that evolution has in the biological sciences, allowing ID to compete. The Discovery Institute in Seattle has funded and promoted much of the ID activity and advocacy. In 1999, the Kansas School Board went beyond teaching the controversy and actually deleted evolution, the Big Bang theory, and long geological ages from the state's teaching standards in the sciences. After being roundly criticized, a new board rescinded the 1999 action, but in 2004 conservatives won control of the board again and instituted standards that were essentially the wedge strategy of teaching the controversy and redefining science to include the possibility of supernatural explanations. Ohio and Wisconsin have also experienced controversy over ID and the wedge strategy of teaching the controversy, but the first ID court case took place in Dover, Pennsylvania.

In Dover the local school board voted not only to teach the controversy but also to make students aware of alternatives to evolution, including, but not limited to, ID. The board wrote a disclaimer and required that it be read in science classes whenever evolution was to be taught. The disclaimer read in part, "Because Darwin's theory is a theory, it is still being tested as new evidence is discovered. The Theory is not a fact. Gaps in the Theory exist for which there is no evidence."[63] The statement went on to recommend ID as an alternative to Darwinism and to inform students that the book *Of Pandas and People* was available in the school library for their perusal. A group of parents challenged the board's action, and the ACLU agreed to represent them. The defendants retained free counsel from the Thomas More Law Center, a public interest law firm founded by Catholic activist and Domino's Pizza baron Thomas Monaghan. The two-month long trial included testimony from Behe and the revelation that purchases of the book *Of Pandas and People* for the high school library had been funded by Grove Community Church, which billed itself as "an Independent, Fundamental, Bible Believing Church." Dembski and other Discovery Institute fellows initially agreed to appear in the trial, but then pulled out.

Although defending ID, Behe acknowledged that some statements in *Of Pandas and People* were problematic. Meanwhile, a left-wing postmodern critic of science from the University of Warwick, England, testified that there was no reason to confine the rules of science to naturalistic explanations and, therefore, ID was not unscientific. The trial ended with the judge ruling otherwise. He said that ID was unscientific because it invoked "supernatural causation" and failed "to meet the essential ground rules that limit science to testable, natural explanations."[64] Responses ranged from the apocalyptic to the more sober, with the Discovery Institute leader furious that the judge had ruled on the scientific status of ID itself instead of confining his judgment to the more narrowly legal question. Four days after the trial, the citizens of Dover voted the pro-ID school board out of office. Although the case applies legally only to the middle district of Pennsylvania, it may be a bellwether of things to come for ID, at least on the legal front. As some ID proponents would prefer, ID may need to win victories in the court of science through peer-reviewed publications instead of short-circuiting academic procedures by legal measures to mandate the teaching of ID in public schools. In other words, as this argument goes, if ID is eventually accepted as science by the scientific community, rather than by a school board led by fundamentalists, there will be no constitutional question over its being taught in science classes.

Conclusion

Clearly, the twentieth and twenty-first centuries have not been good for the relationship of evangelicals and science. In 1994, Mark Noll made this argument in his book *The Scandal of the Evangelical Mind*. Noll is one of the leading historians of American religion and is himself an evangelical. In this book, he lamented the fact that having once been at the center of mainstream intellectual life in Europe and America, twentieth-century evangelicalism experienced what he called "The Intellectual Disaster of Fundamentalism." Chief among the culprits for this disaster was Creation Science. Preferring the older, nineteenth-century attempts to find harmony rather than warfare between science and religion, Noll viewed the twentieth century as a time when evangelicals for the first time opted out of mainstream intellectual life in America. The ID movement can be interpreted either as a continuation of Noll's scandal or as an attempt to once again find harmony between religion and science. It all depends on one's point of view and on how ID is being handled. Some ID proponents attempt to return to the two-books approach of Galileo, starting with observations of nature and reading scripture with those in mind. Others seem determined primarily to extend the warfare model by battling and hopefully overturning Darwinism. All this headline-grabbing activity, especially when it lands in a courtroom in Dover or Dayton, combined with evidence from polls that show consistently that a majority of the American people believe creationism and evolution should both be taught in public schools, seems to suggest that in American culture religion and science have much in common. In both areas a majority of the American people believe the expert elites can be challenged by the notions of the common people as represented by school boards and legislatures.

Notes

1. David C. Lindberg and Ronald Numbers, "Beyond War and Peace: A Reappraisal of the Encounter between Christianity and Science," *Church History* 55:3 (September 1986): 347.

2. Quoted in Mark Noll, *The Scandal of the Evangelical Mind* (Grand Rapids, Michigan: Eerdmans, 1994), 205–6.

3. John William Draper, *History of the Conflict between Religion and Science* (New York: D. Appleton and Co., 1898). While the first edition appeared in 1874, the earliest I was able to locate and use was the 1898 edition. Andrew Dickson White, *A History of the Warfare of Science with Theology in Christendom* (New York: D. Appleton and Co., 1897).

4. George Marsden, *Understanding Fundamentalism and Evangelicalism* (Grand Rapids, Michigan: Eerdmans, 1991), 140. See also David Lindberg and Ronald Numbers, eds., *God and Nature: Historical Essays on the Encounter between Christianity and Science* (Berkeley: University of California Press, 1986).

5. Lindberg and Numbers, "Beyond War and Peace," 340.

6. Neal Gillespie, *Charles Darwin and the Problem of Creation* (Chicago: University of Chicago Press, 1979), 152. Gillespie is quoted in Marsden, *Understanding Fundamentalism and Evangelicalism*, 140.

7. Quoted in Marsden, *Understanding Fundamentalism and Evangelicalism*, 140.

8. David N. Livingstone, *Darwin's Forgotten Defenders: The Encounter between Evangelical Theology and Evolutionary Thought* (Grand Rapids, Michigan: Eerdmans, 1987).

9. Marsden, *Understanding Fundamentalism and Evangelicalism*, 132.

10. Livingstone, *Darwin's Forgotten Defenders*, xi.

11. Livingstone, *Darwin's Forgotten Defenders*, 57–60.

12. Livingstone, *Darwin's Forgotten Defenders*, 60–62.

13. Livingstone, *Darwin's Forgotten Defenders*, 27.

14. Quoted in Livingstone, *Darwin's Forgotten Defenders*, 63.

15. Livingstone, *Darwin's Forgotten Defenders*, 63–64.

16. Livingstone, *Darwin's Forgotten Defenders*, 70.

17. Charles Hodge, *What Is Darwinism?* (New York: Scrivener, Armstrong, and Co., 1874), 52.

18. Quoted in Livingstone, *Darwin's Forgotten Defenders*, 105.

19. Quoted in Noll, *The Scandal of the Evangelical Mind*, 183. The essay in which Hodge wrote these words was "The Bible in Science," *New York Observer* (March 26, 1863): 98–99. Noll points out that he said much the same thing in his *Systematic Theology*, 3 vols. (New York: Charles Scribner's Sons, 1872–1873), 1:59, 170–71, and 573–74. Hodge wrote repeatedly in these passages that there are times when scripture must be interpreted and reinterpreted in light of science.

20. Livingstone, *Darwin's Forgotten Defenders*, 118.

21. Quoted in Livingstone, *Darwin's Forgotten Defenders*, 118.

22. Livingstone, *Darwin's Forgotten Defenders*, 120–21.

23. Livingstone, *Darwin's Forgotten Defenders*, 131.

24. Livingstone, *Darwin's Forgotten Defenders*, 132.

25. Livingstone, *Darwin's Forgotten Defenders*, 145. For essays open to evolution see: James Orr, "Science and the Christian Faith," *The Fundamentals: A Testimony to the Truth*, vol. 1 (Grand Rapids, Michigan: Baker Book House, reprinted 1970), 334–47; and George Frederick Wright, "The Passing of Evolution," *The Fundamentals: A Testimony to the Truth*, vol. 4 (Grand Rapids, Michigan: Baker Book House, reprinted 1970), 72–87. For an antievolution tract see: Henry Beach, "Decadence and Darwinism," *The Fundamentals: A Testimony to the Truth*, vol. 4 (Grand Rapids, Michigan: Baker Book House, reprinted 1970), 59–71. *The Fundamentals* were originally published in twelve paperback volumes. The 1917 version and the Baker Book House 1970 edition are collected into four volumes.

26. Unless otherwise noted, the following outline of the trial comes from Edward Larson, *Summer for the Gods: The Scopes Trial and America's Continuing Debate over Science and Religion* (New York: Basic Books, 1997).

27. Quoted in Larson, *The Scopes Trial*, 44.

28. Quoted in Larson, *The Scopes Trial*, 42.

29. Quoted in Larson, *The Scopes Trial*, 71.

30. Larson, *The Scopes Trial*, 72.

31. Quoted in Larson, *The Scopes Trial*, 190.

32. Quoted in Larson, *The Scopes Trial*, 200.

33. Quoted in Larson, *The Scopes Trial*, 206.

34. Larson, *The Scopes Trial*, 225.

35. Larson, *The Scopes Trial*, 226.

36. Frederick Lewis Allen, *Only Yesterday: An Informal History of the 1920s* (New York: Harper and Brothers, 1931), 204.

37. Allen, *Only Yesterday*, 197.

38. Larson, *The Scopes Trial*, 227.

39. Quoted in Larson, *The Scopes Trial*, 229.

40. Joseph Wood Krutch, "The Monkey Trial," *Commentary* 43:5 (May 1967): 83.

41. *Inherit the Wind*, United Artists Pictures, Inc., 1960; MGM Home Entertainment Inc., 2001, scene 11.

42. Quoted in Larson, *The Scopes Trial*, 242.

43. Quoted in Larson, *The Scopes Trial*, 242.

44. Quoted in Larson, *The Scopes Trial*, 242–43.

45. "Inherit the Wind," *Time* (October 17, 1960): 95. The first quote is in Larson, *The Scopes Trial*, 243.

46. Stanley Kauffmann, "O Come, All Ye Faithful," *The New Republic* (October 31, 1960): 30.

47. Larson, *The Scopes Trial*, 244.

48. Stephen Jay Gould, *Hen's Teeth and Horse's Toes* (New York: Norton, 1983), 270.

49. Gould, *Hen's Teeth*, 273. Quoted in Larson, *The Scopes Trial*, 245.

50. Quoted in Ronald Numbers, *The Creationists: The Evolution of Scientific Creationism* (Berkeley: University of California Press, 1992), 74. Unless otherwise noted, the history of Creation Science discussed below comes from Numbers.

51. Quoted in Numbers, *The Creationists*, 74.

52. Quoted in Numbers, *The Creationists*, 75.

53. Numbers, *The Creationists*, 77.

54. Quoted in Numbers, *The Creationists*, 89.

55. Quoted in Numbers, *The Creationists*, 91.

56. Luther Peak, "Why We Left Fundamentalism to Work with Southern Baptists," *Baptist Standard* (April 7, 1956): 6.

57. Quoted in Numbers, *The Creationists*, 159.

58. This discussion of Whitcomb and Morris comes from Numbers, *The Creationists*, 184–213.

59. Quoted in Numbers, *The Creationists*, 228.

60. This section on ID comes from the expanded edition of Ronald Numbers's *The Creationists: From Scientific Creationism to Intelligent Design* (Cambridge, Massachusetts: Harvard University Press, 2006), 373–98.

61. Michael Behe, *Darwin's Black Box: The Biochemical Challenge to Evolution* (New York: Free Press, 1996).

62. Quoted in Numbers, *The Creationists*, Expanded Edition, 385.

63. Quoted in Numbers, *The Creationists*, Expanded Edition, 391. For the whole story of the Dover case see Edward Humes, *Monkey Girl: Evolution, Education, Religion, and the Battle for America's Soul* (New York: HarperCollins, 2007).

64. Quoted in Numbers, *The Creationists*, Expanded Edition, 394.

CHAPTER FOUR

~

Millennialism

Folk Religion and the Career of End-Times Prophecy

In 2004, a reporter called to ask about the wildly popular *Left Behind* series of books by Jerry Jenkins and Tim LaHaye. The reporter thought the extraordinary sales of these novels about end-times prophecy must mean something significant about evangelicals in America. Apparently thinking this was a new phenomenon in American religion, she wanted to know what such a fascination with the end of time and the Second Coming of Christ might mean, what new turning point the books indicated for evangelicals. With a feeling that I was spoiling the thesis of a good story, I explained to the reporter that the *Left Behind* phenomenon was neither new nor ominous. A significant percentage of American evangelicals and others have had deep interest in end-times prophecy for well over a century, and books and pamphlets on prophecy belief have been appearing regularly in great numbers throughout this period. In 1992, when cultural historian Paul Boyer wrote *When Time Shall Be No More: Prophecy Belief in Modern American Culture*, he reported having read over 300 books on prophecy, 100 of them published before 1945. In addition to this vast literature there were eight major prophecy conferences held between 1870 and the 1970s, all but one in America, and more than twenty-five periodicals and newsletters dedicated to prophecy belief.[1] While the *Left Behind* novels are the most popular and best-selling books in this genre of popular evangelical literature, the only new aspect to the story this reporter was covering was that the media was paying attention.

What is prophecy belief, and why is it so popular with evangelicals and fundamentalists and even with many Americans who are not otherwise particularly religious? Boyer says that the key to the popularity of prophecy belief is that "It gives a grand, overarching shape to history, and thus ultimate meaning to the lives of individuals caught up in history's stream."[2]

Millennialism in America

American Protestants have generally held to one of three views of the end times—postmillennialism, premillennialism, or amillennialism. Postmillennialists generally believe that God is working through history, preparing the earth for the millennium, which is the 1,000-year reign of Christ on earth. Premillennialism, the subject of this chapter, is the belief that the earth will get worse and worse until Christ returns. Only then, with His supernatural Second Coming, will the millennium dawn. Amillennialism is the belief that apocalyptic scriptural passages discussing a millennial reign of Christ on earth are not to be taken literally. Amillennialists, therefore, are not given to speculation or even much interest in the end times. I once had a professor who said there was a fourth position, aha millennialism. This position, he said in jest, means that when the end times take place, people will say, "Aha, that's what the Bible meant."

The best scholars of Protestant millennialism generally view the Puritans of colonial America as being premillennialists, but by the mid-eighteenth century, a shift occurred to postmillennialism, which then dominated the Protestant landscape throughout most of the nineteenth century. The revivals discussed in chapter one were often cited as evidence of God's work in the world, and they often engendered in believers a sense that the kingdom of God was about to dawn. Jonathan Edwards seems to have believed that the events taking place in the American colonies might lay the foundation for Christ's millennial reign. Such a position grew in intensity when the revivals gave way to the American Revolution. In what some scholars call "civic millennialism," American preachers saw the hand of God advancing freedom through the political events of the Revolution. This idea that the march of democracy and freedom was part of the coming Kingdom of God grew throughout the nineteenth century. During the Second Great Awakening, most revivalists believed that individuals would be saved from sin by the revivals, while the reform efforts that went hand in hand with the revivals would transform America, leading the world toward the millennium. In the second half of the nineteenth century, ideas about the advance of God's kingdom became entwined with the notion that America had a manifest destiny to spread Christianity and democracy throughout the world as part of God's kingdom work. Postmillennialists generally believed that God's kingdom would be inaugurated before Christ's return, hence his Second Coming would be *post* millennial—that is, after the 1,000-year reign of the kingdom on earth.

During the second half of the nineteenth century, premillennialism began to challenge postmillennialism as the dominant end-times belief among evangelicals. Put simply, premillennialists do not believe history is progressing toward the kingdom but rather that conditions are declining. Only the Second Coming of Christ will stem the tide of degeneration and inaugurate the millennium. The exchange between Henry Ward Beecher and Dwight Moody epitomizes the difference between post- and premillennialists. Recall from chapter two that Moody said, "I look upon this world as a wrecked vessel. God has given me a lifeboat and said to me, 'Moody, save all you can.'" In reply, Beecher said, "Mr. Moody thinks this is a lost world, and is trying to save as many as possible from the wreck; I think Jesus Christ has come to save the world, and I am trying to help him save it." When Moody and Beecher had this exchange in the late nineteenth century, premillennialism was making inroads within conservative evangelicalism, while liberal evangelicals and modernists held onto postmillennialism. This was in keeping with the modernist view that Christianity was more natural than supernatural. Postmillennialists believed that through the natural processes of reform, the world can be transformed into the kingdom.

During the heyday of postmillennialism, there was always a remnant of premillennialists, but at times they seemed to contribute to the unpopularity of their own beliefs. This was certainly the case with the prophet William Miller discussed in the previous chapter. Miller used what scholars refer to as historicist premillennialism to calculate the exact date in 1843 (then revised to 1844) that Christ would return. Historicist premilliennialists attempt to correlate biblical prophecy with actual historical events in the past or present. For example, when the pope was exiled from Rome by French forces in 1798, historicist premillennialists interpreted this event as a fulfillment of the prophecies of Daniel 7 and Revelation 13, which speak of the "beast" or "Antichrist." In the tradition of Protestant anti-Catholicism, historicists such as Miller associated the beast with the pope. The book of Daniel predicted that the reign of the beast would last for 1,260 days. Miller and others converted the days to years, dated the beginning of the papacy at 585, and concluded that the 1798 exile of the pope was the prophesied end of the reign of the Antichrist. The next major prophesied event was the Second Coming of Christ. Daniel 8:14 says that the Messiah would come 2,300 days after the desolation of the sanctuary. Dating the Babylonian King Nebuchadnezzar's profanation of the Jewish Temple at 457 B.C.E., once again converting days to years, Miller predicted that Christ would return to earth 2,300 years after 457 B.C.E., or 1843. Miller amassed over 50,000 hard-core followers in the Northeast who readied themselves by selling their possessions, leaving crops unplanted, and boarding up their businesses in order to wander about spreading the news of Christ's imminent return. In addition to those who took radical action in preparation for the Second Coming, there may have been as many as a million who believed Miller's prediction. When the day of Christ's predicted return passed uneventfully, Miller recalculated that the return would be the next year, 1844. This second prediction bought him a little more time with some followers, but when the second date passed, the movement began to break up. Many postmillennialists believed that the Millerite fiasco would be the death knell of premillennialism.[3]

The Rise of Dispensational Premillennialism

Nothing could have been further from the truth, for after the Civil War a new kind of premillennialism flourished and by Moody's death in 1899 was established within evangelical circles. This new movement was called dispensational premillennialism, and rather than being historicist, it was futurist. Futurist premillennialists believe that biblical prophecy predicts future events. Futurists, therefore, watch the news to see if current events might be preparing the way for the fulfillment of ancient prophecy. Dispensationalism is a form of futurist premillennialism that divides all of history into dispensations, or periods. In each of these dispensations, it is believed, God has related to humankind in a different way. In its most developed form, there are seven dispensations. The first five all occurred in the Old Testament: (1) the dispensation of innocence that reigned when Adam and Eve were in the Garden of Eden before the Fall into sin; (2) the dispensation of conscience, which lasted from the Fall until Noah's flood; (3) the dispensation of human government, which lasted from Noah to Abraham; (4) the dispensation of promise, which was God's covenant with Abraham and the Hebrew people; and (5) the dispensation of law, which began with Moses and lasted until the coming of Christ. Christ's life, death, and resurrection started the sixth dispensation, which is the dispensation of grace, also known as the "Church Age," which will be in force until Christ's Second Coming. Christ's Second Coming will inaugurate the seventh and final dispensation, the dispensation of the kingdom.

Dispensationalism flourished in Great Britain before coming to America. The founder, or at least popularizer, was the British evangelical John Nelson Darby (1800–1882). Darby was born in London in 1800 and educated at

Trinity College in Dublin, Ireland. He was trained in law, but after a conversion experience in 1820 he decided to seek ordination in the Church of Ireland, which was the Protestant state church imposed on Ireland by the British government. Darby was appointed to a rural district, but after a second profound religious experience in 1828, he spent much of his time as an itinerant (traveling) preacher, not unlike John Wesley in the previous century. He later described his 1828 experience as the time when he became convinced that the Bible was the divine link between God and humankind. In his travels he eventually joined with a group of religious dissenters known as the Brethren, and when they divided, he became the leading light of the faction known as the Plymouth Brethren. He spent the rest of his life traveling throughout Europe, North America, Australia, and New Zealand promoting the Brethren faith.[4]

Darby began devising his dispensational theory in the 1830s. While Darby identified the seven distinct dispensations already mentioned, the most important feature of his theory was the clear distinction between God's dealing with his chosen people, the Jews, and with gentile Christians. As dispensationalists teach, Christ came to be king of the Jews, but they rejected him. Instead of being placed on a kingly throne, Christ died on a cross. God then turned to the gentiles, and the Christian Church was established. The church age interrupted God's covenant with the Jews. As a result of this interruption all of history from the establishment of the church at the Day of Pentecost in the book of Acts until Christ's Second Coming serves as a historical parenthesis. In other words, there has been a pause in God's relationship with the Jews. Whereas historicist premillennialists such as Miller believed that biblical prophecy applied to the church, futurist dispensationalists believe almost the opposite. The church age is an interlude when the prophecy clock is stopped and God's covenant with the Jews is suspended in favor of the building up of the church. All prophecy pertaining to the Jews must be literally fulfilled, however, which necessitates the restarting of the prophecy clock. But God does not exercise two covenants at once, so before his covenant with the Jews can become operational again, the church must be removed. What event will remove the church and restart the prophecy clock, resulting in the resumption of God's dealings with the Jews? The answer was a new and unique feature of dispensationalism known as the rapture.

Beginning with Darby and the Plymouth Brethren, dispensationalists taught that at any moment of history, Christians may be raptured out of the world to meet Christ in the air. Following the rapture, the tribulation will ensue. The tribulation is a seven-year period of chaos that will see the Antichrist come to power as the leader of the revived Roman Empire. This Antichrist will make a pact with the restored nation of Israel, allowing the Jews to re-build their temple and reinstitute their sacrificial system. Eventually, however, the Antichrist will turn on the Jews, enter the temple, and demand to be wor-shipped as God. Those who refuse the Antichrist and turn instead to the true God will be severely persecuted. In retaliation for the persecution of former Jews who have converted to Christ, God will pour out His wrath on earth in accordance with the visions of the book of Revelation. This will result in more chaos, disorder, violence, and suffering. Powers from the north, consist-ing of a confederation headed by Russia, will join a confederation of southern nations, and together they will invade Israel, leading to the Battle of Ar-mageddon. Kings from the east who fear the power of the revived Roman Em-pire will also converge on Israel and join the battle, but in a major twist of plot these armies from the north, south, and east will unite with the Antichrist. The Battle of Armageddon then becomes an all-out war against God's people, the Jews. At the height of the battle, Christ will return with all the saints of history, including those taken in the rapture. The forces of the Antichrist and all those from the northern, southern, and eastern armies that joined him will be defeated, and Christ will inaugurate his millennial reign. Following the 1,000-year kingdom of Christ on earth, there will be one last victorious bat-tle against Satan followed by the resurrection of the dead and the last judg-ment of all humankind.[5]

Dispensationalism caught on among evangelicals for a variety of reasons in the context of the fundamentalist-modernist controversy. While mod-ernists downplayed the importance of the Bible, often teaching that the Christian faith had evolved since biblical times, dispensationalism was bib-licist. Dispensationalists believe the Bible has all the answers, even to things pertaining to what some would view as secular history. Believers need only to "rightly divide the word," which became a catch phrase for dis-pensationalist Bible study. Rightly dividing the word means knowing which prophecies pertain to which dispensation. For example, with regard to Old Testament prophecies that did not appear to be fulfilled, dispensationalists would answer that such prophecies were for the future and would only be fulfilled in a later dispensation. Or, with regard to the teaching of the Ser-mon on the Mount, where Christ advocated turning the other cheek in an apparent endorsement of pacifism, dispensationalists explain that such an admonition was intended for the kingdom age yet to come, not for the church age of the present. Likewise, apparent inconsistencies that mod-ernists cited were smoothed over by showing that one passage applied to one dispensation while a passage that seemed contradictory made perfect sense when viewed in light of a different dispensation. Dispensational premillennialists opposed higher criticism of scripture, arguing that one need not be a scholar to understand the Bible. Rather, when rightly divided, the Bible could be taken literally and at face value. Unlike modernists who were optimistic about the possibility of saving the world, recall again Beecher's famous saying to Moody, dispensationalism made better sense when things did not seem to be getting better and better, especially after the destruction of World War I. Finally, where modernists low rated the supernatural aspects of Christianity in favor of a naturally evolving faith, dispensationalism heightened supernaturalism. The end-times events would be just as supernaturally charged, if not more so, than biblical times. In short, future events were biblical times.[6]

In an era when evangelicals had to close ranks in their defense of orthodoxy against modernist revisions, postmillennial and amillennial evangelicals tolerated premillennialists in evangelical organizations. When the Bible conference movement began in the 1870s, dispensational premillennialists were the minority, but by the end of the century they had become dominant not only in the Bible conferences but also in the more than fifty Bible institutes as well. Although he was relatively unconcerned about the particularities of the seven dispensations, Moody did much to popularize premillennialism. He and many other revivalists not only believed the rapture was imminent, they also believed that premillennialism motivated evangelism and missions. It was important that as many people as possible be converted to the faith before the rapture occurred and God's attention shifted to the Jews.

Dispensational premillennialism received a huge boost after the turn of the century with the publication in 1909 of the *Scofield Reference Bible*. C. I. Scofield (d. 1921) was born in Michigan but raised in the slaveholding South in Tennessee. About the time he was ready to go to college, the Civil War broke out, and he served as a soldier rather than a student. He never received the formal education he desired. Following the war he clerked in a law office in St. Louis, and through self-study he learned enough to pass the bar in Kansas. There he practiced law and served briefly in the state legislature and then as an appointed U.S. attorney. He married, divorced, abandoned his wife and two young daughters, and headed back to St. Louis, where he landed in jail on forgery charges. He was also accused of stealing political contributions that were intended for Senator John Ingalls, with whom he had once been a partner. His troubles during this period of his life seem to be attributed partly to alcohol abuse. He converted while in jail and soon after his release began serving in Moody's revival campaigns. After the Congregational Church licensed him to preach, Scofield moved to Dallas and became pastor of the First Congregational Church in 1882.

In Dallas, Scofield came under the influence of Presbyterian preacher and Bible teacher James Brookes, who had organized the first major premillennial conference at Niagara Falls in 1875. Brookes introduced Scofield to the teachings of Darby. Soon, the entrepreneurial Scofield was offering his own Bible correspondence courses and in 1888 published his first book, *Rightly Dividing the Word of Truth*. At Moody's insistence, Scofield moved to Northfield, Massachusetts, to take a pastorate and become president of Moody's Northfield Bible Training School, which had grown out of Moody's Northfield Bible Conference. After 1903, Scofield took a lengthy sabbatical from his pastoral and educational duties in order to devote himself full time to the development of his reference Bible. Later he organized correspondence courses and operated a Bible night school in New York City before founding the Philadelphia School of the Bible with Lewis Sperry Chafer. The Philadelphia School flourishes to this day.

Scofield and a team of seven coeditors developed the prominent features of the *Scofield Reference Bible*. Taking the standard text of the Bible, they added definitions of terms, marginal notes explaining certain passages, Scofield's own paragraph divisions and headings, and an outline. These features, especially the notes and outline, highlighted the dispensational understanding of scripture. Between 1909 and 1967 the Reference Bible sold 5 to 10 million copies and helped standardize dispensationalism within American fundamentalism. Revised and updated in 1967, the dispensational framework remains a prominent feature. To this day many fundamentalist churches give a copy of the *Scofield Reference Bible* to the children of the congregation when they are old enough to start reading it themselves.[7] Readers will recall from the previous chapter that Scofield's Bible also popularized the gap theory for Genesis 1 and 2 and Bishop Ussher's dating of the creation at 4004 B.C.

Dispensationalism and the Two Wars

In addition to the *Scofield Reference Bible* and the general ways that dispensationalism stood opposed to modernism, World War I played a significant role in boosting the fortunes of premillennialism as the fundamentalist-modernist controversy began to intensify. In short, the events of the war years seemed to fit the prophetic outline that was already in place as a result of Darby's teachings and the refinements of others made since his death in 1882. While dispensationalists do not believe biblical prophecy applies to the current church age, they do believe in watching to see if world events might be laying the groundwork for the age when prophesied events will begin to unfold. World War I seemed to move things into place for the beginning of the end. First, the war fit the prophetic framework by redrawing the boundaries of Europe, making those boundaries conform more closely to the Roman Empire, which dispensationalists believe will be reconfigured and headed by the Antichrist during the end times. For example, the Austro-Hungarian Empire was broken apart, freeing Slavic peoples who had not been part of the Roman Empire. Second, Germany, most of which had not been part of the Roman Empire, seemed to play no part in biblical prophecy and would therefore have to be defeated, which of course happened. Moreover, Germany lost western territory to France that had been part of the Roman Empire. Third, the Ottoman Empire broke apart and the Turks lost control of Palestine, opening the possibility for the reestablishment of the nation of Israel. Obviously, if the Antichrist were to ever make a pact with Israel, and if the confederation of nations from the north, south, and east were ever to invade Israel, Israel had to exist again. Dispensationalists, therefore, believed that Israel had to be reestablished before the end times would begin. Fourth, Russia's experience in the war also seemed to fit the prophetic pattern. The Communist Revolution took place in conjunction with Russia's participation in the war, and the revolutionaries instituted a godless, atheistic government, preparing the way for Russia to lead the northern confederation into the Battle of Armageddon against God's people, the Jews.

While careful observers of European history were not surprised by these events and may well have predicted some of them, dispensational premillennialists had arrived at their predictions without careful study of history. Rather, they had predicted these things as a result of their study of scripture. As one leading dispensationalist said in 1916, "[T]he only thing a Christian can safely say about these unprecedented conditions among the nations is that these events fully confirm the characteristics of the age and its predicted end as revealed in the Bible and that all that is happening in a way prepares for the very end of the times of the Gentiles [i.e., the church age] and the coming of the king."[8]

The dispensational movement gained credibility among Protestants as a result of the war, so much so that modernists could no longer ignore premillennialism. Liberals began to attack premillennialist teachings. Shirley Jackson Case and Shailer Matthews, both of the University of Chicago, wrote caustically and sometimes outrageously about premillennialism. Like most American liberals, Matthews and Case bought into President Woodrow Wilson's battle cry that this was "a war to make the world safe for democracy." Premillenialists, while generally supportive of their country, rejected that the end goal of world history was democracy. Democracy, like all world government systems, was doomed. In a book edited by Matthews, Case wrote a chapter attacking this dispensationalist line of thinking. He accused premillennialists of disloyalty and of preferring a German victory. In another article, he suggested without evidence that German money was funding the dispensationalist cause. Premillennialists were quick to reply that while dispensationalism had no link to Germany, it was a well-known fact that the theology of modernists such as Matthews and Case had come directly from German theological schools in the nineteenth century. As historian Timothy Weber puts it, "The liberal attack demonstrated the growing credibility of the premillennialist movement. . . . It was obvious that as soon as the liberals began attacking it openly, premillennialism had arrived."[9]

None of the events of the Great War was more significant than the breakup of the Ottoman Empire and subsequent British policy toward Palestine. In the Balfour Declaration of November 1917, Britain announced a policy of support for Jewish immigration into Palestine for the purpose of establishing a national home for Jews. In early 1918, forces under General Edmund Allenby defeated the Turks, freeing Palestine and opening the way for the declaration to go into effect. Dispensational premillennialists were thrilled by these events and wrote widely of them in fundamentalist newspapers and magazines. There were a couple of hastily organized but well-attended prophecy conferences in Britain and the United States in 1918 that were given over to discussion of these momentous developments that turned many fundamentalists into supporters of Israel.

Some important dispensationalists had been supporters of the Zionist movement for two decades before the war. W. E. Blackstone (d. 1935), in particular, had become a leading evangelical voice for the reestablishment of Israel as a Jewish nation. His book *Jesus Is Coming: God's Hope for a Restless World* was perhaps the most popular premillennial book of its time, and he had earned the respect of important Jewish Zionists. Beginning in the 1890s, he organized conferences of Christians and Jews and secured signatures from major political figures on petitions of support for a Jewish nation. The petitions were then forwarded to U.S. presidents Benjamin Harrison and his Secretary of State James G. Blaine in 1881 and another to President Wilson in 1916, just before the Balfour Declaration. The first of these petitions was signed by the Chief Justice of the U.S. Supreme Court and by business magnates John D. Rockefeller and J. P. Morgan. Blackstone and other premillennialists attended Zionist conferences, and on one occasion Blackstone even chided a prominent Jewish Zionist for wavering in his support of a national homeland for Jews. In 1956, Jewish leaders commemorated the seventy-fifth anniversary of Blackstone's petition to President Harrison by dedicating a forest in his honor.

While World War I helped establish dispensationalism's credibility, events leading up to World War II proved initially more difficult to reconcile with prophetic teaching. In the 1920s, there was brief anticipation that Italian dictator Benito Mussolini might reestablish the Roman Empire and perhaps even be the Antichrist himself. One fundamentalist couple from Belgium secured an interview with Il Duce and asked him if this was his intention. When Mussolini replied that reestablishing the empire would be impossible, the Nortons told him it was prophesied in scripture. Mussolini reportedly replied, "Is that really described in the Bible? Where is it found?"[10]

Most dispensationalists found Mussolini deficient as the potential Antichrist, however, and instead suggested he was merely a prototype of the beast of prophecy. Likewise, some speculated that Adolph Hitler might be a type of the beast, but given that Germany was to be part of the northern alliance with Russia in the Battle of Armageddon, and not part of the revived Roman Empire, Hitler was out as the potential Antichrist. When Mussolini and Hitler joined forces in 1936 in the Rome-Berlin Axis, this seemed to eliminate both as potential beasts.

More ominous for dispensationalists, by the 1930s it looked like the Balfour Declaration was a dead letter. Largely because of violence stemming from Arab resistance to Jewish immigration to Palestine, the British abandoned their policy of aiding Jewish settlement. In 1939, however, when Germany and Russia entered into their alliance, premillennialists were sure that prophecy was about to be fulfilled. The standard interpretation of Ezekiel 38 has Gog and Magog referring to Russia and Gomer to Germany. This alliance could be the beginning of the great northern army that would square off with the Antichrist, then make a pact with him in order to make war on Israel. When Hitler broke the Nazi-Soviet Non-Aggression Pact and invaded Russia in 1941, that prediction was temporarily shelved. When the United States entered the war later that year, the puzzle became even more problematic as Russia and the United States were on the same side. For the most part, the United States plays no role as a nation in end-times prophecy, but the alliance with the great northern Gog was troubling nevertheless for premillennialists. Nothing seemed to be going right for premillennialist predictions. As Weber puts it, "One is struck by how forgiving and forgetful the premillennialist rank and file must have been during this period. . . . The leaders themselves seemed little deterred by their mistakes. Events were changing so quickly that they had little time for apologies." Weber argues that premillennialism might well have "undercut completely any claim to credibility had it not been for one thing." That one thing was the formation of Israel after the war. "That one fulfilled prophecy gave premillennialism a new lease on life and brought it more credibility and visibility than ever."[11]

With Israel restored, the godless Soviet Union locked in a Cold War with the West, and China as the great Communist power from the East, almost everything seemed to be in place for the end times. All that was needed was the appearance of the Antichrist who would revive the Roman Empire. As for the empire, fundamentalists and some evangelicals had been watching for years the development of the European common market. By the 1970s, they were counting how many nations had joined, anticipating the tenth member, the number of nations premillennialists believed would be part of the reconstituted empire. With so many events seeming to fall into place, dispensational premillennialism flourished, but it was still largely a subcultural movement. In other words, dispensationalism was a cottage industry that appealed to fundamentalists and some evangelicals but did not make much headway as a popular movement outside the evangelical subculture. This changed in the 1970s, largely because of Hal Lindsey's best-selling book *The Late Great Planet Earth*.

The Late Great Planet Earth

Lindsey was from Texas. He was educated at the University of Houston and worked at a variety of jobs before attending Dallas Theological Seminary, including at one point serving as a tugboat operator on the Mississippi River. Founded in 1924 by dispensationalist Lewis Sperry Chafer, Dallas Theological Seminary was perhaps the leading dispensationalist seminar in the country. While some evangelical seminaries and all fundamentalist seminaries teach dispensationalism, Dallas is known for its dispensational emphasis and its dispensational scholars. After seminary, Lindsey worked as campus minister for Campus Crusade for Christ at UCLA where he began to teach about the end times to packed lecture halls. During one particular week of prophecy teaching, a student raised his hand and asked, "Mr. Lindsey, when do you think these events might start?" Lindsey replied, "No one can be sure, but I think it might be before the end of the semester."[12]

There was almost nothing new theologically in Lindsey's book. Written with the help of author Carole Carlson, Lindsey published *The Late Great Planet Earth* in 1970. Lindsey's knack was not as an original thinker but rather in putting traditional dispensationalist theology, complete with the correlation between biblical prophecy and current events, into a language that made the book read like pulp fiction or a romance novel. When the book appeared, some of his old classmates at Dallas Theological Seminary complained that all he had done was repackage and popularize his class notes from Dallas Seminary. The book sold over 18 million copies in its first decade, and *The New York Times* listed Lindsey as the 1970's best-selling author.[13] Until the *Left Behind* series, Lindsey was easily the most widely read prophecy writer of all time.

As other prophecy writers since the Balfour Declaration had done, Lindsey kept Israel at the center of the story, and he was able to capitalize on events in the Middle East that more than ever before seemed to point to the end times. The Six Days War of 1967 saw Israel expand its borders and most importantly occupy Jerusalem. This led to speculation about the rebuilding of the Temple, where dispensationalists believe the Antichrist himself will eventually demand to be worshipped. With the United States firmly backing Israel and the Communist Soviet Union backing some of Israel's hostile neighbors, it looked like events were falling into place for the Battle of Armageddon. China, now a major Communist player in world events, seemed poised for an alliance with the Soviet Union for the war that really would end all wars. In a throwback to historicist premillennialism, Lindsey even hinted at when the end times might begin, just as he had as a campus minister at UCLA. Lindsey cited Jesus's words in Matthew 24:34: "Verily I say unto you, this generation shall not pass away till all these things be fulfilled." In this passage Jesus was telling the parable of the fig tree as an analogy for reading the end times. When the fig tree is ripe, we know that summer is coming. Lindsey interpreted the fig tree as being a symbol for the reestablishment of Israel, meaning that within a generation of 1948 the end-times events would begin: "What generation?," he asked rhetorically. "Obviously in context, the generation that would see the signs—chief among them the rebirth of Israel," Lindsey answered. Then, explaining that in the Bible a generation is about forty years, he wrote that "within forty years or so of 1948, all these things could take place. Many scholars who have studied Bible prophecy all their lives believe that this is so."[14] In Lindsey's scenario, the European Common Market would be the reconstituted Roman Empire, which would be ruled by the Antichrist, whom Lindsey and others believed was already alive.

The Late Great Planet Earth was so popular that its sales crossed over from Christian bookstores into secular bookstores and the paperback stands in supermarkets. This led to a dilemma over how to categorize the book. Did it go in the theology section or with the other popular books that appeared in the 1970s by secular prophets such as Jeane Dixon, who claimed to be able to tell the future, or with nonreligious predictions of an impending apocalypse resulting from environmental degradation, population explosion, or nuclear proliferation? In other words, Lindsey's book appeared at a time not only when the biblical prophecy clock seemed poised to restart but also at a time of increasing concern with humankind's potential for destroying the world. Add to this the beginning of religious experiences, known now as New Age religions, and the fascination with UFOs and other signs and wonders, and we can see that the time was ripe for *The Late Great Planet Earth* to lead a crossover of prophecy belief into a wider market, some of which was neither evangelical nor fundamentalist. In his next book *The 1980s: Countdown to Armageddon*, Lindsey seems to have tapped into these developments intentionally. He predicted that the so-called Jupiter effect would lead to an increase in earthquakes and argued that UFOs were real manifestations of evil. "It's my opinion that UFOs are real and that there will be a proved close encounter of the third kind soon," he wrote. Then, tying UFOs to the demonic, he continued, "I believe these demons will stage a spacecraft landing on Earth. They will claim to be from an advanced culture in another galaxy."[15] Lindsey also used his second book to tie end-times prophecy to the conservative politics of the Christian Right and the era of President Ronald Reagan.

Left Behind

As is the case in most premillennialist teaching including Lindsey's, Christians will escape the horrors of the tribulation because they will have been raptured away beforehand, only to return in victory with Christ at the end of the Battle of Armageddon.[16] This brings us to the *Left Behind* novels, twelve works of dispensational premillennialist fiction written by Tim LaHaye and Jerry Jenkins and published between 1995 and 2003. LaHaye is a longtime evangelical popular author and activist. Born in 1926, he is essentially a fundamentalist who left behind, so to speak, cultural separatism but retained the militant fighting spirit of twentieth-century fundamentalism. Historian George Marsden has dubbed such activists, "fundamentalistic evangelicals." They militantly defend the faith but do not eschew cultural and political engagement as fundamentalists before the 1980s did.[17] LaHaye has been a significant force in the Christian Right and has written a number of books, some coauthored with his wife Beverly, who founded Concerned Women of America. The LaHayes' books range from a Christian sex manual to calls for political action to Creation Science and antievolution to prophecy belief, and more. Exhibiting the militant spirit of fundamentalistic evangelicals, some of the LaHaye books have the word "battle" in the title—*The Battle for the Mind*, *The Battle for the Family*, and *The Battle for the Public Schools*. LaHaye was longtime pastor of Scott Memorial Baptist Church in San Diego and in 1970 founded a Bible college in La

Jolla, California, called Christian Heritage College. With the help of others he also set up the Creation Science Research Center in conjunction with the college.

Left Behind marked LaHaye's foray into fiction based on dispensational premillennial prophecy belief with his coauthor Jenkins, who had written a number of sports biographies. LaHaye and Jenkins did not invent the prophecy novel. The genre actually began in the 1930s with a book about a typical American city after the rapture. In that story a committee formed to investigate the sudden mass disappearance of so many people recalls a deceased mother and child recently buried together. The committee opens the grave to find the child is gone, leaving behind the mother's body and child's clothes. One member exclaims in somber wonder, "I guess the Bible is infallible," and another replies, "It looks that way." The 1930s book proceeds with the gruesome atrocities of the Antichrist and other assorted horrors leading to the Battle of Armageddon.[18]

By 1995, life on earth after the rapture was a well-worn prophecy novel theme that LaHaye and Jenkins reprised in the first of the *Left Behind* novels. The plot line of the books centers around four individuals who come together on a transatlantic flight during the rapture. Passengers aboard the flight are hysterical to find friends and family members have vanished, leaving behind clothes, jewelry, and all other earthly artifacts. The captain of the flight, Rayford Steele, head flight attendant Hattie Durham, and first-class passenger and Ivy-League trained journalist Buck Williams take charge. Steele returns to his hometown of Chicago only to find what he feared—his wife and young son have vanished with the others. Over the previous few years they had become active in the evangelical New Hope Village Church. He had been more than mildly annoyed with his wife's newfound faith and had been drifting toward an affair with his head flight attendant, Hattie. Chloe, Steele's college-age daughter at Stanford, has been left behind as well. Over the course of the next few weeks Steele, Chloe, and eventually Buck all convert, largely through the ministry of Bruce Barnes, the young associate pastor at New Hope who was also left behind. Utilizing a video cassette that the head pastor prepared for those who would miss the rapture, Steele, Chloe, Buck, and Bruce piece together what has happened. Realizing that the seven-year tribulation period is about to dawn and that the Antichrist will soon appear, they form the Tribulation Force and set out to win as many people as possible to the Christian faith in order to battle the Antichrist. In the chaos that follows the disappearance of millions of people in the rapture, a charismatic leader, Nicolae Carpathia, rises to power as the leader of Europe and the United Nations. As the first novel ends, Carpathia has ascended the world stage in New York

and the members of the fledgling Tribulation Force are in Chicago, virtually
the only people who know Carpathia is the Antichrist.[19] Readers are left in
anticipation of what the force will do. In the rest of the eleven novels, the
story unfolds.

LaHaye and Jenkins provide fast-paced action at the expense of character
development. While the books are interesting, they also contain their fair
share of banality and implausibility. In the words of scholar Glenn Shuck in
his book-length analysis of the *Left Behind* novels, characters on the Antichrist's side are often "humorous fools," given to bumbling errors and even
physical maladies such as the evil Leon Fortunato's painful hemorrhoids. Ordinary people are often gifted with implausible ability and knowledge. As
Shuck writes, "The characters LaHaye and Jenkins create resemble ordinary
churchgoers one might expect to meet at a bake sale or potluck dinner—except they fly transport aircraft and have knowledge of advanced weapons systems and complicated electronics that many governments would envy."[20] In
addition to excitement, the novels provide evangelicals with a wholesome
entertainment option, devoid of gratuitous sex, where morality and righteousness triumph in the end. Shuck believes there is more to their appeal,
however. He argues that the books present a struggle for evangelical identity.
The *Left Behind* novels, like other prophecy books, address the perceived
threat posed by a technological world and what Shuck and others call "the
network" culture. The novels highlight the "simplicity of a premodern world,
while gradually easing [evangelicals] into the multiplicity of postmodern
worlds, in which their identities as Christians are miraculously safeguarded,
and the complex economic and technological forces that threaten them are
nothing more than the latest of Satan's deceptive machinations."[21]

A good example of such safeguarding is the scene in the first novel where
Carpathia takes power as the Antichrist. Buck is credentialed by his high-
profile news weekly and present at the meeting. Having met with Pastor
Barnes, Steele, and Chloe, Buck is convinced that Carpathia might be the
Antichrist. Buck has also been brought to the brink of conversion, and just
before the meeting begins he commits his life to Christ. In the meeting,
Carpathia brings the others under his sway, commits cold-blooded murder of
two rivals, then in a sort of hypnotic spell convinces the others that the two
died in a rash and sudden suicide-murder pact. Not only do the others in the
room leave the meeting believing Carpathia's lie, they also have no recol-
lection of Buck having been there. He was miraculously protected from
Carpathia's spell. As Carpathia goes around the room quizzing each person
present as to what just happened, all say that one of the victims killed the
other, then himself. As the narration reads, "Buck's body felt like lead, know-

ing Carpathia would eventually get to him and that he was the only one in the room not under Nicolae's hypnotic power."[22]

No doubt many evangelical readers moved through the novels in anticipation of how the plot would unfold. For the fundamentalist and evangelical prophecy believer, however, there is never a doubt about who will emerge triumphant in the battle between the Tribulation Force and the Antichrist Nicolae Carpathia. An old joke makes it simple. There is a plain old country fellow reading the book of Revelation. A sophisticated liberal theologian asks him smugly, "Do you understand all that prophecy stuff?" "Yep," the man replies, "Jesus wins."

Evangelical Protestants shaped and dominated American culture from colonial times through the nineteenth century. In the twentieth century, however, things changed. From the fundamentalist-modernist controversy forward, fundamentalists and evangelicals have lived with the sense of being cultural outsiders. This world is not their home. Even in the late twentieth century, as evangelicals and some fundamentalists have reentered culture with an activist political agenda, they often feel as if the government, media, and educational systems are in the hands of Christianity's adversaries. Sociologist Christian Smith argues compellingly that evangelicals in America are "embattled and thriving," and that this sense of being embattled is important to their sense of identity, so much so that evangelicals highlight and sometimes create scenarios where they are the underdogs. Their identity requires a certain amount of tension between themselves and the mainstream. Too little tension will result in evangelicals losing their distinctive witness, much as they believe theological liberals have. A lack of tension means that evangelicals have become too much like the culture. On the other hand, too much tension results in their becoming irrelevant, which was the weakness of militant, separatistic fundamentalism during the twentieth century. Shuck sees the *Left Behind* novels functioning as a thermostat that helps evangelicals maintain the proper tension. Even while the culture seems to be degenerating quickly and they are becoming a discriminated-against minority, God is in control, and in the end all will be well. Moreover, in the meantime, before the return of Christ, there are many ways in which evangelicals are gaining influence and power. There are signs of hope.

At least one historian has made the case that being outsiders to the mainstream is not just an evangelical trait but part of the larger religious culture in American history. In his *Religious Outsiders and the Making of Americans*, R. Laurence Moore argues that evangelicals, Jews, Mormons, and Catholics all at one time or another portrayed themselves as religious outsiders and in doing so took on the distinctly American trait of being a dissenter.[23] The *Left*

Behind novels remind evangelicals that the present culture is not theirs, but in the end Jesus will win.

The novels have wider cultural significance. Through aggressive marketing the books have crossed over and sold well in Wal-Mart, K-Mart, and Costco stores, as well as in secular bookstores such as Borders and Barnes and Noble. Estimates in 2006 put total sales of the novels at more than 60 million, and there are plans in the works for spin-off action books for children and for a television series. Sales figures and future plans confirm what historian Paul Boyer argued in *When Time Shall Be No More*—that is, prophecy belief is a significant staple of American culture and has been for more than a century. The solution offered evangelicals in *Left Behind* and in all dispensational premillennialist literature is that eventually one's adversaries will be incinerated in the Battle of Armageddon, justly destroyed by God's vengeance. This, of course, is highly offensive to many who stand to be the victims. It is worth pointing out, however, that while many evangelicals and fundamentalists take comfort in the fact that they will be spared, they are also motivated by the portent of the end times to win their neighbors to the truth so they, too, can escape Armageddon.[24] This is what drives the Tribulation Force in the *Left Behind* series. Beyond this, being biblicists, evangelicals and fundamentalists see no alternative to believing the end-times scenario because it is based, they believe, on a plain reading of the Bible. It is God's doing, not theirs, and they are in no position to take issue with God.

Conclusion

There is something deeper going on as well. Scholars are increasingly coming to interpret prophecy belief throughout history as trembling "on the brink of major intellectual issues," to use the words of historian Christopher Hill, who has written on seventeenth-century English views of the Antichrist.[25] The major intellectual issue Hill, Boyer, and Shuck all address is how to make sense of the world and deal with the threats of complexity, diversity, technological sophistication, and rapid change. These forces and their challenges seem especially acute in the wake of 9/11. Shuck believes the events of 9/11 "created for many if not most Americans a palpable sense of apocalypse." While most of the novels were published before 9/11, much of their sales have included the post–9/11 period. As Shuck puts it, "The *Left Behind* novels both anticipate and reflect the anxieties that have become important in recent American culture, especially since 9/11."[26] Similarly, Hal Lindsey's *The Late Great Planet Earth* appeared in 1970 in the midst of the Vietnam War, campus radicalism, assassinations, alternative lifestyles, and racial unrest. Many people in America at that time thought this was "the unraveling of America," as Allen Matusow called it some years later in his history of the sixties.[27] Put another way, evangelicals are hardly alone in struggling to find their place in a complex and chaotic postmodern world. While evangelicals may be "living in the shadow of the second coming," many other Americans also have a foreboding sense that they, too, are living in the shadow of something ominous and possibly apocalyptic.

This brings us to another feature of the appeal of prophecy belief in general and prophecy novels in particular. In addition to its theological importance among evangelical and fundamentalist Bible scholars and teachers, prophecy belief functions as a folk religion for common people.[28] Folk religion exists alongside particularistic faiths and even among people who are not formally religious. It serves to answer certain questions and ease unspoken anxieties. As a folk religion, prophecy belief has apparently spilled over from the evangelical community into the wider culture. While roughly 30 percent of Americans are evangelicals, a *Time*/CNN poll conducted in 2002 indicated that 59 percent of Americans believe the events of Revelation will actually take place.[29]

All this should not lead one to assume that evangelicals, fundamentalists, or anyone else obsess about the end times on a daily basis. Some do, of course. There are those who attend prophecy conferences every year, and there are churches where pastors preach frequently about the end times. There are Sunday school classes and television programs in which prophecy teachers attempt to match up the weekly news with prophecies from the Bible. This is not the norm, however, and such intense interest in end-times prophecy is more common among fundamentalists than evangelicals. Much more commonly, end-times beliefs are one part of an overarching Christian worldview but not something that evangelicals think about daily. If the subject comes up, many evangelicals are willing to talk, while others are little interested or even puzzled by the various end-times scenarios. For most evangelicals it is the big picture that matters, and the big picutre is that sometime in the future Christ will return to bring an end to history. In the meantime, they need to be active agents of light in an often dark world.

Notes

1. Paul Boyer, *When Time Shall Be No More: Prophecy Belief in Modern American Culture* (Cambridge, Massachusetts: Belknap Press of Harvard University Press), xiii.

2. Boyer, *When Time Shall Be No More*, xi.

3. Timothy Weber, *Living in the Shadow of the Second Coming: American Premillennialism, 1875–1982*, enlarged edition (Grand Rapids, Michigan: Academie Books, 1983), 14–16.

4. See Neil Dickson, "Darby, John Nelson," *Biographical Dictionary of Evangelicals*, Timothy Larsen, David Bebbington, and Mark Noll, eds. (Downers Grove, Illinois: InterVarsity Press, 2003), 178–81.

5. Weber, *Living in the Shadow of the Second Coming*, 17–26.

6. Weber, *Living in the Shadow of the Second Coming*, 36–42.

7. Barry Hankins, "Scofield, Cyrus Ingerson," *Biographical Dictionary of Evangelicals*, Timothy Larsen, David Bebbington, and Mark Noll, eds. (Downers Grove, Illinois: InterVarsity Press, 2003), 589–91. See also C. G. Trumbull, *The Life Story of C. I. Scofield* (New York: Oxford University Press, 1920); and Boyer, *When Time Shall Be No More*, 97–98.

8. Arno Gaebelein as quoted in Weber, *Living in the Shadow of the Second Coming*, 115.

9. Weber, *Living in the Shadow of the Second Coming*, 119.

10. Quoted in Weber, *Living in the Shadow of the Second Coming*, 179.

11. Weber, *Living in the Shadow of the Second Coming*, 202–3.

12. Timothy Weber was a student at UCLA and present at these meetings. He related this story to me in a conversation.

13. Weber, *Living in the Shadow of the Second Coming*, 211.

14. Hal Lindsey with C. C. Carlson, *The Late Great Planet Earth* (Grand Rapids, Michigan: Zondervans, 1970), 54. Quoted in Weber, *Living in the Shadow of the Second Coming*, 212.

15. Quoted in Weber, *Living in the Shadow of the Second Coming*, 218.

16. There are some strands of premillennialism that teach that the rapture will occur either at the midpoint of the tribulation or even at the end. The three positions, therefore, are known as 1) pretribulation rapturist, which is the dominant position and the one held by Lindsey; 2) midtribulation rapturist; and 3) post-tribulation rapturist. All three are still premillennial because Christ must return before the millennium begins.

17. George Marsden, *Fundamentalism and American Culture*, 25th Anniversary Edition (New York: Oxford University Press, 2005).

18. Quoted in Boyer, *When Time Shall Be No More*, 106.

19. Tim LaHaye and Jerry B. Jenkins, *Left Behind: A Novel of the Earth's Last Days* (Wheaton, Illinois: Tyndale House, 1995).

20. Glenn W. Shuck, *Marks of the Beast: The Left Behind Novels and the Struggle for Evangelical Identity* (New York: New York University Press, 2005), 12–16, quote at 16.

21. Shuck, *Marks of the Beast*, 16.

22. LaHaye and Jenkins, *Left Behind*, 460.

23. R. Laurence Moore, *Religious Outsiders and the Making of Americans* (New York: Oxford University Press, 1986).

24. Amy Johnson Frykholm, *Rapture Culture: Left Behind in Evangelical America* (New York: Oxford University Press, 2004), 4

25. This quote is from Christopher Hill's study of seventeenth-century Antichrist literature and is quoted in Boyer, *When Time Shall Be No More*, 17 and Shuck, *Marks of the Beast*, 19. The quote comes from Christopher Hill, *Antichrist in Seventeenth-Century England* (London: Oxford University Press, 1971), 177.

26. Shuck, *Marks of the Beast*, 21.

27. Allen Matusow, *The Unraveling of America: A History of Liberalism in the 1960s* (New York: Harper and Row, 1984).

28. George Marsden, ed., *Evangelicalism and Modern America* (Grand Rapids, Michigan: Eerdmans, 1984), x.

29. Shuck, *Marks of the Beast*, 23.

CHAPTER FIVE

~

Considering Equality

The Tradition of Gender, Race, and Gay Rights

In 1998, the largest Protestant denomination in America, the Southern Baptist Convention, revised its confession of faith by adding the following statement: "A wife is to submit herself graciously to the servant leadership of her husband even as the church willingly submits to the headship of Christ. She, being in the image of God as is her husband and thus equal to him, has the God-given responsibility to respect her husband and to serve as his helper in managing the household and nurturing the next generation."[1] Known as the "submission statement," the revision of the confession received widespread coverage in the secular and religious media. *The New York Times* covered the story on the top half of its front page—above the fold, so to speak. Southern Baptist Seminary president Al Mohler appeared on CNN's program *Larry King Live* to defend the submission statement in a telecast that also featured evangelical political activist and preacher Jerry Falwell and the National Organization for Women president Patricia Ireland. Clearly, Southern Baptists and other evangelicals make big news when they take a position on gender that seems out of step with the wider culture.

While issues such as the Southern Baptist submission statement give the appearance that today's evangelicals are uniformly antifeminist, this not altogether accurate. Rather, evangelicals are deeply divided on the issue of gender and are in the midst of a serious debate over proper roles for men and women in the family, in churches, and in society. Moreover, this division has always existed. Throughout the eighteenth and nineteenth centuries, evangelical revivals usually generated an egalitarian atmosphere that opened avenues for the participation of women in public affairs, while at the same time there was always resistance to this egalitarian trend. There have been times when much of evangelicalism was more egalitarian than the wider culture and times more recently when evangelicals have been, on balance, less egalitarian.

Eighteenth- and Nineteenth-Century Gender Issues

Historian Susan Juster has argued that when eighteenth-century New England Baptists were the dissenting minority shaped by revivalistic conversion, their congregations were substantially egalitarian. Women participated fully, often wrangling with male members over correct doctrine and carrying full voting rights in electing and dismissing pastors. Juster follows other scholars in suggesting that revivalistic religion was itself a gendered experience that was substantially feminine. Not only was the emotion of conversion associated with the feminine but also the experience itself was a socially radical event that placed one on the margins of the more staid and conservative New England culture. Revival converts found themselves in a liminal, or in-between, state in the larger society. This liminal state was much like the status of women. In other words, Baptists and other sectarians, whether men or women, were not fully enfranchised members of New England society. Within their own congregations, however, the conversion experience was precisely what brought full-fledged membership. The result was that while all sectarians tended to be in a sort of feminine state on the margins of society, within their congregations they were full participants, and this was so whether they were men or women.[2]

All this changed as the evangelical Baptists moved from the periphery of society to the center in conjunction with their support of the American Revolution. As they did, Baptists traded their egalitarian approach to spiritual matters for more masculine and hierarchical societal norms. As Juster puts it, "A politically vigorous and socially respectable religious society needed a more masculine image, and hence we see the emergence of patriarchal language and structures in Baptist churches after 1780. As these Baptists became successful and moved closer to the mainstream, however, they took on the gender restrictions of the larger society."[3]

This transition from gender egalitarianism to a masculine hierarchy was tied substantially to notions of family hierarchy. For example, in 1803 in the Providence, Rhode Island, First Baptist Church, Joanna Gano brought heresy charges against her husband Stephen, who was an elder in the church. Most of the charges were in connection to Stephen's membership in the Masonic Order. Joanna accused him of "worshipping idols," "perverting the

Scriptures," and "holding himself in connection with a Society which in her view was the 'Mystery of Iniquity' and 'in Covenant with Death and agreement with Hell.'"[4] This was strong stuff, to be sure, but women had routinely brought such charges against men. Whereas the norm for much of the eighteenth century had allowed women to present their charges in person, in this trial Joanna Gano had to write her charges down so they could be read to the congregation because she was not allowed to speak before the assembly. Even more significantly, her husband read the charges for her, which made the trial a sham, the accused presenting his accuser's case. The trial ended with Stephen Gano being found innocent but also Joanna was found guilty of "disorderly conduct." Things had changed a good bit from the pre-Revolutionary norm of egalitarian gender status in New England's Baptist churches.

We do not want to overinterpret the gender egalitarianism of the eighteenth-century revivals, nor do we want to portray evangelical revivalism as monolithic with regard to gender. Not all revivals or revivalists were egalitarian, and very few men or women advocated that women should be ordained ministers of congregations. Even some of the most prolific women preachers believed that ordination was reserved for males, and women preachers were often treated as outsiders in the evangelical culture that was dominated by male personalities. Moreover, there were regional variations on the issue of gender egalitarianism. Women preachers were prolific in the North, but in much of the South, they were not even allowed to teach, let alone preach. One must also be careful not to equate secular feminism in the nineteenth century with the religious feminism that often accompanied the revivals of the Second Great Awakening. Women evangelical preachers were radical in the act of preaching yet traditional and conservative in their theology. Still, with all that said, there exist records of more than 100 evangelical women who preached in the period from the First Great Awakening through the Second Great Awakening, 1740–1845.[5] It was not so much that people advocated egalitarianism and thereby opened opportunities for women. Rather, the revivals as historical events were destabilizing phenomena, undercutting social distinctions with the crucicentrist idea that "all people are equal at the foot of the cross of Christ." In other words, all are equally sinners and in need of Christ's atoning work. Within some parts of evangelicalism, there was an egalitarianism that existed in few other places in the culture until the rise of the feminist movement of the 1840s and 1850s, and much of the energy and leadership of that first wave of feminism came from evangelical women.

While the evangelical revivals and the first wave of feminism opened some doors for women, in the latter half of the nineteenth century the Victorian view of the family dominated America. Gender roles within Victorian America were based largely on the view that women were inherently more moral than men and possessed a greater natural aptitude for religion. One might think that those holding this view would want women deeply involved in society in order to reform the culture. Ironically, the Victorian view held just the opposite. Rising in conjunction with industrialization, the standard belief was that because she was more moral, the woman was needed in the home nurturing children, not out in society where she might be corrupted. If women were allowed into the workforce, they might become morally degraded, leaving no one to nurture the children. Men were often viewed as inherently weaker morally, corrupted by the rough-and-tumble industrial world, and, therefore, unfit to play a primary role in the nurture of children. The well-being of society rested on preserving women in the home to properly inculcate morality.

Fundamentalism and Evangelical Gender Views

Moving into the twentieth century, we begin to see challenges to the Victorian image of family life and women, especially in the 1920s when the fundamentalist-modernist controversy was at a fever pitch. We might ask why it is that in the eighteenth and nineteenth centuries one was likely to find more gender equality in the evangelical subculture than in society as a whole, while in the twentieth century one was likely to find the most traditional, conservative, and nonegalitarian forces within evangelicalism. The short answer is that when evangelicals defended orthodoxy against the inroads of modernist theology, they were responding to what they believed were destabilizing changes wrought in the culture and within the churches. Among the destabilizing forces were changing gender norms. One historian has gone so far as to say, "Inherent in the fundamentalist attack on the current state of religion was an attack on the current state of morality. In these materials, 'morality' is often just a code word for conventional gender behavior and 'immorality' a code word for sexual and gender impropriety."[6] There is a debate over just how central issues of gender were in the rise of fundamentalism and the shaping of twentieth-century evangelicalism, but there is little doubt that these issues were significant.

Related to this view of destabilization was the evangelical desire to mark oneself off from the wider culture. From a conservative evangelical or fundamentalist viewpoint, capitulation to secular culture is a serious offense. Early twentieth-century fundamentalists argued that modernists had gone too far in accommodating secular culture by adjusting theology to fit modern science. This did not mean that fundamentalists uniformly held to a Victorian view of gender. Many early twentieth-century fundamentalists believed the Victorian view of woman's superiority was also part of the secular culture that they needed to resist. The Victorian view of the superiority of women, it seemed to some fundamentalists, was heresy because it exempted women from the original sin of Adam and Eve. As firebrand fundamentalist John R. Rice put it, "[It is] a lie out of hell . . . a wicked, hellish, ungodly, satanic teaching that by nature men are not as good, that by nature women are . . . [more] inclined toward God and morality."[7] In resisting the Victorian view, however, Rice and others did not move to the egalitarian position that saw men and women as equally sinful, equally forgiven, and, therefore, equal in the functions of the church. Rather, fundamentalism reversed the Victorian view and claimed that men were more naturally suited for religion than women were, not because they were less sinful but because they were tougher.[8]

Still, it took until the 1930s for this fundamentalist view of women to so-lidify. The fluidity and openness that existed in the first two decades of the century were largely the result of the continued fundamentalist and evangel-ical emphasis on revivalism. The evangelistic impulse of revivalism was one of the primary molding forces of twentieth-century evangelicalism and fun-damentalism. Recall that activism, one of the four basic components of evan-gelicalism, most often takes the form of evangelism—the spreading of the gospel message—and that the primary technique of evangelism is revivalism. Evangelicals are evangelistic and revivalistic for a couple of reasons. First, the Bible commands that the gospel be taken to all people, hence evangelical Biblicism is tied to evangelical revivalistic activism. In the Gospel of Matthew 28:18–20, Jesus's last recorded words on earth are known as "The Great Commission." "All authority in heaven and on earth has been given to me," Jesus is recorded as saying. "Therefore go and make disciples of all na-tions, baptizing them in the name of the Father and of the Son and of the Holy Spirit, and teaching them to obey everything I have commanded you."[9] The biblical command is enough to make evangelism and missions a primary focus of evangelical activism, but there is also a second motivation—the love and logic of evangelism associated with premillennialism. Simply put, if peo-ple are not converted before they die, they go to hell. Or, if they are uncon-verted when the rapture takes place, they are left behind to face the horrors of the Tribulation. People in secular culture often see evangelism as intoler-ant, especially when it is geared toward getting Jews and people of other re-ligions to renounce their present faith and become Christians. Lost in this view is that evangelicals believe they have the good news that Christ is the way to salvation and that out of love and concern they have an obligation to share this gospel. Premillennialism only fuels this evangelistic and revivalistic logic by holding that the rapture could occur at any moment. At their best, evangelicals and fundamentalists sense a loving urgency to evangelize. They do not want anyone to miss out.

Because of the premillennialist notion that time was short, Bible institutes in the early twentieth century trained both men and women for evangelism. There was simply no time to waste female human resources by worrying whether women should be active in spreading the gospel. Until the 1930s, there was openness toward women evangelists that resembled the Awakenings of the eighteenth and nineteenth centuries. William Bell Riley is a good example of this openness. Riley was the leading fundamentalist in the Midwest during the first half of the twentieth century. He led the fight against modernism in the Northern Baptist Convention (NBC) at the same time he helped promote a separatist fundamentalist denomination that would compete with the NBC. His Northwestern Bible Institute in Minneapolis trained a significant number of the pastors for both denominations. Until the thirties, Northwestern trained women not only as pastor's wives and church secretaries but also as evangelists and even pastors. Minnie S. Nelson, a Northwestern trained preacher, recorded in 1948 her experiences serving as pastor for several churches in Minnesota, Montana, and Michigan over a fourteen-year period following her graduation from Northwestern Bible Institute. In addition to these churches where she served full time, she also served temporarily in three other churches when those congregations needed a preacher to fill the pulpit. Two other Northwestern graduates, Alma Reiber and Irene Murray, comprised a renowned evangelistic team that traveled the Midwest for thirty years preaching the gospel. Using the same preacher/song-leader team concept employed by Dwight Moody and Ira Sankey before them and Billy Graham and George Beverly Shea after, Reiber was the preacher and Murray the song leader. Their work was covered positively in religious and secular newspapers and periodicals.[10]

By the 1930s, the attitude at Northwestern was changing. Writers in Riley's newspaper, *The Pilot*, began to argue that I Timothy 2:12 limited authority in the church to men. This passage, widely believed to be from the apostle Paul, reads, "I do not permit a woman to teach or to have authority over a man; she must be silent." Such authority included all preaching and Bible teaching. This was and still is the standard view of many evangelicals as we will see shortly. As one Northwestern professor put it in *The Pilot*, "This does not bar her from the Sunday School class, daily Vacation Bible School, etc., but certainly closes the door of the public ministry of the church. It is as plain as anything could possibly be that a woman is not to take the over-sight of the church, or publicly teach or preach in the man's appointed place."[11] By 1935, Riley himself seems to have concluded that since there were no women preachers mentioned in the Bible, "it is not our purpose to prepare women for that particular office."[12] This change in view led to a real irony in Riley's ministry, as practice lagged behind theology. The official po-sition of his newspaper seemed to be, as one Northwestern professor wrote, "[it is]not scriptural for women to preach and teach," yet as late as 1937 *The Pilot* announced that Northwestern would lead an evangelistic campaign across the upper Midwest that would include the school-sponsored evangel-ists and "eminently successful soul-winners—Miss Alma Reiber, and Miss Irene Murray."[13] Churches that wanted the services of these two women evangelists were instructed to contact *The Pilot*.

The conflicted and changing attitude toward women preachers exhibited by Riley and his Bible institute appear to have been part of a trend toward the eclipse of egalitarianism within a large segment of evangelicalism. There can be little doubt that this narrowing trend resulted from the development of fundamentalism. Scholar Janette Hassey has argued that the fundamentalist-modernist controversy that resulted in fundamentalism moving from the center to the margins of American culture resulted in the narrowing of views of women in ministry. As fundamentalists sought to separate from the cul-ture, one of the ways they did so was to reject the increased liberation of women that took place in the 1920s.[14]

If Hassey is correct, fundamentalists became less egalitarian for exactly the opposite reasons that New England Baptists in the late eighteenth century became less egalitarian. Eighteenth-century New England Baptists became less egalitarian as they moved from the periphery to the center of culture, while Hassey is saying that twentieth-century fundamentalists became less egalitarian when they moved from the center to the periphery. The two views are actually complementary, however, in that fundamentalists of the twentieth century wanted to avoid doing what the New England Baptists had done—that is, become more like the culture. In order to resist the culture, fundamentalists became less egalitarian as the culture became more egalitar-ian. This is not to say that resistance to culture was the only issue. Funda-mentalist theology, derived as it is from a literal and plain reading of scrip-ture, was very important, and there are biblical passages that seem to relegate women to secondary status within the churches. All Christians, however, read scripture within a cultural context. The Bible teaches Christians to be wary of the world and to avoid being seduced by the false prophets of the age. In the context of twentieth-century America, with theological modernism becoming dominant within the mainline Protestant denominations, the gender question was an area where fundamentalists could take a clear stand.

The aforementioned John R. Rice made the gender issue a semiregular feature in his magazine *The Sword of the Lord*. Rice was a southerner who ministered for years in Dallas, Texas. The Sunday School of his church in Dallas catered to masculine Christianity. One advertisement carried the message, "Most Sunday Schools are run by the women-folks and appeal primarily to women and children. We seek to care for the needs of children and give women her rightful place, but New Testament teaching and preaching was usually directed first of all to men, and we seek to have it so here."[15] In 1940, Rice moved his magazine and ministry to Wheaton, Illinois, which was in many ways the heart of American evangelicalism. From that perch he gained wider national exposure, often leading evangelistic crusades in the Chicago area. During these campaigns he started an afternoon series called, "Bobbed Hair, Bossy Wives, and Women Preachers." The series led to a book by the same title that was quite successful. Rice's work was part of a spate of similar books in the late 1940s and 1950s that have been characterized as sharing "a common air of exasperated authority at the confused state of gender relationships in postwar society."[16] A typical publication in 1950 by a Moody Bible Institute teacher rearticulated some of the Victorian views of the differences between the sexes, although steering clear of the Victorian theological notion that women were morally superior. The author argued that "man is organized to operate in the affairs of science, commerce, and the state. The woman is organized to regulate the home and family. . . . Differences of sex are not to be toned down and obliterated but to be accentuated and brought into moral harmony. . . . A masculine woman and a feminine man are monstrosities to be abhorred."

This author also spoke of the complementary nature of the sexes, a theme that is taken up below.[17] It should be noted that through the 1950s, attitudes like those expressed by the Moody Bible Institute teacher were typical of the larger society as well. Even as a few modernist theologians and secular voices called for gender equality, and fundamentalists responded with traditional biblical notions of gender differences, until after World War II most Americans were still living the Victorian model. Fundamentalists simply gave gender roles a theological gloss. They argued that in "the order of God's creation" God had created Adam first, then Eve, but in the Fall into sin, Eve was deceived first, then Adam. Women were second in creation, first in the Fall. Women's propensity toward sin was part of the modern view that they were licentious tempters, and this view pervaded fundamentalist and evangelical preaching. The pervasiveness of sin in society was often highlighted with examples of pinup girl posters and other references to the seductive, tempting nature of women.[18] The view of women as tempters of men goes back at least to the Middle Ages, if not to ancient times.

In the 1940s and 1950s, one might have expected that the rise of neo-evangelicalism would lead to a revival of the older evangelical egalitarianism, and over time in some quarters this was the case. Recall from chapter two that the neoevangelicals wanted to leave the militant and separatistic tendencies of fundamentalism behind in favor of a more culturally engaged evangelical faith. Initially, however, the attitude of neoevangelicals toward women in ministry differed little from the attitudes of fundamentalists such as Riley. If anything, neoevangelicals merely toned down the rhetoric of John R. Rice but retained his principles. As historian Margaret Bendroth argues, neoevangelicals were willing to dialogue with liberals about theological and cultural issues, but they "rarely, if ever, examined [their own] fundamentalist legacy of attitudes toward masculinity and feminity."[19] The view of fundamentalists and neoevangelicals was compounded by the fact that after World War II mainline denominations debated the ordination of women pastors. With a generation of practice in resisting changes that the modernist churches advocated, it was natural for fundamentalists and evangelicals to resist challenges to traditional views of gender once the mainline churches began to consider such reforms. In the sixties, when a new wave of secular feminism began to challenge Victorian gender norms in the wider society, there seemed even greater need to resist. While it took time to develop the argument, by the 1980s many evangelicals and nearly all fundamentalists grouped feminism with other components of the secularism they believed had swept over America in the radical 1960s. The high visibility of key politically active fundamentalists would give the impression that all of evangelicalism was virulently antifeminist and antiegalitarian.

Fundamentalist Gender Views as Flexible Absolutes

It is true that virtually all fundamentalists and many evangelicals ascribe to the view of male leadership and female submission described in the Southern Baptist confession quoted at the beginning of this chapter. In actual practice, however, evangelical and fundamentalist women often wield significant power in both families and churches. Scholar James Ault Jr. found this to be so in his ethnographic study of a fundamentalist congregation in Worcester, Massachusetts. A pastor who studied at Jerry Falwell's Liberty Baptist University led the Shawmut River Baptist Church in the 1980s. The church was part of the independent fundamentalist movement that Falwell and his school helped shape. As is the case with all fundamentalist and many evangelical churches, folks at Shawmut River interpreted Ephesians 5:22–23 as defining male headship and female submission. "Wives submit to your husbands as to the Lord. For the husband is the head of the wife as Christ is the head of the church, his body, of which he is the Savior."[20] Women at Shawmut River believed this passage meant that men should have the final say in decisions, but the women were quick to point out verse 25 that says men are to love their wives "as Christ loved the church." Moreover, verse 21 of the Ephesians passage calls on husbands and wives to "submit to one another out of reverence for Christ." Submission is a two-way street with husbands and wives submitting to one another. Ironically, egalitarian evangelicals who do not accept wifely submission as outlined in the Southern Baptist confession emphasize the view that men and women are to submit to one another. Most of the folks at Shawmut River would not have seen themselves as egalitarian evangelicals. Instead, they believed that even while there should be a two-way submission, submission was not the same for men and women. There was, in their view, a "chain of command" for the family with the male at the top and the female subservient.[21]

Holding this interpretation, the women at Shawmut River were very hostile to feminism. Feminism, in their view, destroyed the distinctions between male and female. Gender meant nothing. This led to women losing their status under God and becoming just like men. For this reason, Shawmut River women often lamented the decline in male social habits such as opening doors for women, not swearing in the presence of a woman, and the like. Women no longer needed to be treated like women because feminism had taken away their special status and brought them down a notch. They also objected to feminism because it denigrated domesticity. They charged that feminism was "knocking the housewife and mother," as one Shawmut River woman put it. "While God's word puts women on a pedestal, feminism brings women down to be walked on," another woman said emphatically. Even more telling, this woman said, "[Feminists] want everybody to be important individually. They don't want family units."[22]

The criticism that feminism denies the importance of the family starts to get at the differences Ault found between his fundamentalist subjects and those from the secular academic world he resided in as a scholar. Shawmut River Baptist Church was not merely a collection of individuals who believed that religion was their private concern. Rather, the congregation operated as a large extended family where all members had specific roles and obligations to one another. Ault wrote that the church had the feel of village life even though the members were drawn from all over the urban Worcester area.[23] From this point of view, women held significant power as they networked together and carried out their assigned roles in families and in the congregation. The women were in charge of nurturing the children of the congregation, an activity that made it necessary for them to know what was going on in their own families and also in the families of other women. This nurturing responsibility drew women together in a natural solidarity with one another, creating a power bloc within the congregation. By contrast, feminist liberation from these assigned roles would have left women isolated and powerless, mere individuals fending for themselves. As Ault wrote, "[T]he role of housewife and mother did not isolate the women of Shawmut River socially. Instead, it bound them in cooperative relations with women relatives— cross-generational groups in which their common identity as women was collectively fashioned. That identity emerged in a world separate from men's, in which women as well as men appeared as distinctly different creatures."[24]

One woman at Shawmut River spoke to the differences between men and women by calling them "fractions with different denominators," but she and some of the others did not learn about the differences between men and women from the Bible. Rather, they first learned these distinctions before they were Christians, when their marriages were failing because each partner pursued his or her inclinations in such a way that the two spouses had little to share in common. The men were often carousing and drinking with their buddies, while the women were left at home alone. The women then needled their husbands or gave them the silent treatment in an effort to get back at them for staying out too late and ignoring the family. Some of these couples were on the brink of divorce when they converted and joined Shawmut River. Fundamentalist Christianity gave them a rule book, the Bible, which allowed the differences between male and female to come together in harmony. As they matured in their faith, their marriages began to thrive. While mandating a chain of command and a specific role in the family for women, the rule book also outlined men's responsibilities. As the Ephesians passage reads, men were to love their wives as Christ loved the church. This meant the husband had a responsibility to help nurture his wife and even treat her as he would treat his own body, as verse 28 says. To trade this sort of male responsibility for feminist freedom would have been regressive from the point of view of Shawmut River women. As Ault summarized these women's view, "[Feminism] served to legitimatize men's unbridled detachment from family responsibilities and promised no end to the relentless conflict and chaos in marriages." In other words, feminist freedom meant each individual was free to pursue his or her own end. Fundamentalism at Shawmut River, by contrast, emphasized different but mutually reinforcing responsibilities for men and women toward each other. Not every marriage at Shawmut River thrived, to be sure, but acknowledging distinct differences between males and females, and then following literal interpretations of scripture as to how those differences are supposed to work together, was highly productive for most of the couples Ault studied.[25]

The power that women were able to fashion collectively was most apparent when the church went through a controversy that resulted in the pastor being dismissed. Men were the heads of the family and the church, but as one Shawmut River woman put it, "The woman [is] the neck that turns the head."[26] This was possible because fundamentalist churches are usually institutions "where the positions of formal authority are reserved . . . for men, while organizational strength is built through family ties sustained, by and large, by women."[27] Women carry out their roles of child rearing and nurture collectively in relationships that extend across family lines. These relationships are maintained through a powerful oral tradition. Men, on the other hand, tend to be more individualistic in their leadership. This means that when a husband and wife operate within the confines of their own home, the wife brings to the conversation a communal perspective that has been informed and shaped by her conversations with the other women in the church. The husband's viewpoint, by contrast, is merely his own. The wife speaks with the authority of the collective oral tradition, while the man carries only his own rather isolated opinions.

As Ault summarizes, "Within each family, then, as husband and wife face each other, collective meanings and the weight they naturally carry over and against individual opinion are more apt to be arrived at through women's relationships than men's."[28] In short, the woman knows a lot more of what is going on within the church because collectively women feel a responsibility to be involved in the lives of other church families. In many mainline churches, and certainly in the world of academics and business, this would be considered prying into the private lives of other families. Because fundamentalist churches tend to be organized more like villages, however, the private and public are arranged differently. There is a sense in which things that would be considered private in the larger culture can be viewed as the collective responsibility of all in a fundamentalist church. Ault, for example, found that at Shawmut River when one couple had marital problems it became public knowledge, and there were several people who intervened to see if they could get the couple to reconcile.

The pastor's dismissal at Shawmut River was a complicated event. The chain of command in fundamentalist and many evangelical families is mirrored by a chain of command within the church. God is the head of the pastor, and the pastor the head of the church. For this reason, troubles in the pastor's home often lead to questions such as, "If he can't lead his own household, how can he lead the church?" Something like this happened in conjunction with the Shawmut River pastor's daughter becoming pregnant as an unwed teenager, but there were many other complications as well. In the context of dissatisfaction with the pastor, key women in the church played decisive roles as "the neck that turns the head." The pastor's wife, Sharon, even complained to Ault at one point that the women were exerting too much power. "The women wouldn't come [to the deacon's meetings]," Sharon told Ault, "but they might as well have been there, because their husbands were mouthing what they felt. You would see guys coming in there confused—'Now, how am I supposed to think on this thing?' . . . And their wives would be at home: chip, chip, chip, chip. . . ."[29] The husbands, in short, had learned what to say in the church meetings from their conversations at home with their wives who knew more about what was going on in the church because they were part of the collective oral tradition.

All this is not to say that wifely submission is superior to other arrangements. As we will see, not even all evangelicals believe that wives are to submit to their husbands in the way outlined at Shawmut River or in the Southern Baptist confession. Moreover, many evangelicals and fundamentalists view male headship as a "trump card" that is only to be played when mutual submission and egalitarian arrangements break down. In other words, if the husband and wife cannot agree on something, the man has the final say, but he rarely actually plays his trump. In sociologist Christian Smith's far-reaching study of evangelicals, even his most ideologically rigid subjects had trouble coming up with an example where the male had to exert his headship to break a tie. One Massachusetts evangelical put it well: "In general, [my wife] and I reach agreement. If we had a major decision that we couldn't agree on, I think I would be responsible to make that decision. That's never happened. And I personally think that if both people are in the Holy Spirit, it's not going to happen."[30] This view helps explain why another study of evangelicals in the mid-1990s showed that 87.4 percent of evangelicals and 82.6 percent of fundamentalists agreed that marriage should be an equal partnership, while 90.4 percent of evangelicals and 82.8 percent of fundamentalists agreed that the husband should be the head of the family. As the author of this study put it, the evangelical ideology of family is quite hierarchical, but the practice of evangelical families tends to be much more egalitarian. This arrangement has been called "symbolic traditionalism and pragmatic egalitarianism."[31]

Most evangelicals see no contradiction between male headship and an equal partnership in marriage, and when they talk about male headship evangelicals usually talk about the burdens and responsibilities the male has more than about wifely submission. Where wifely submission is the accepted norm, research done by Ault, Smith, and others suggests that it functions in surprising ways that often defy the stereotype of male dominance. Scholar Brenda Brasher, for example, spent six months attending every women's event sponsored by two fundamentalist congregations in California. As she explained, "[T]o Christian fundamentalist women, the restrictive religious identity they embrace improves their ability to direct the course of their lives and empowers them in their relationship with others." Similarly, R. Marie Griffith's studied Women's Aglow, the largest women's interdenominational missions organization in the world. She found that the evangelical concept of submission operated in surprising ways in this charismatic organization of women. Griffith's study focused, in her words, "on the practices by which female participants improvise, resist, and continually reshape their own roles and relations" and on "the interplay between the repressive or disciplinary aspects of women's devotionalism and the ecstatic, liberatory potential of particular practices."[32] Both Brasher and Griffith found that evangelical wifely submission is more complex and less restrictive of women than often assumed by the wider public.

Certainly, this view of wifely submission can be abused. Recent research shows that rates of spousal abuse are higher in marriages where the view of wifely submission reigns supreme. However, there is an important variable to this statistic—church attendance. This research seems to show that higher rates of abuse do not correlate necessarily with views of wifely submission but rather with wifely submission combined with a lack of regular church attendance. Where wifely submission and regular church attendance coexist, as was the case at Shawmut River, the abuse rates are lower. Sociologist Mark Chaves has argued that the gender statements of Christian groups, liberal or evangelical, are best understood in cultural terms. He concluded in a 1997 study that, "A denomination's policy allowing (or prohibiting) women's ordination is better understood as a symbolic display of support for gender equality (or of resistance to gender equality) than as a policy either motivated by or intended to regulate the everyday reality of women inside the organization."[33] Applied to the Southern Baptist submission statement, this would mean that the policy serves more as an announcement to the world that Southern Baptists resist culture than it does as an indicator of Southern Baptists' desire for men to dominate, let alone abuse, women. This view jibes nicely with Ault's findings. While reiterating that when push came to shove the men made the decisions at Shawmut River, Ault acknowledged, "Yet on the face of it, the women of Shawmut River did not seem dominated by their husbands in any respect."[34]

Complementarian versus Egalitarian Evangelicals

The ideal undergirding the Southern Baptist submission statement, which was illustrated in practice in Ault's study of Shawmut River, is known as the complementarian view. The term refers to the idea that men and women are inherently different by nature and have different roles in families, churches, and societies. These differences are intended to complement one another, so that when men and women join together in marriage, they complete each other. In this view, the roles of women are circumscribed. Women are not to exercise spiritual authority over men in the church, and they are to submit to their husbands at home. While complementarians will acknowledge that men are also to submit to their wives, as verse 21 of Ephesians 5 says, they point out that the two kinds of submission are different. While the husband submits to his wife and loves his wife "as Christ loved the church," he is also head of the wife as Christ is head of the church. There is no sense in which the wife can be the head of the husband any more than the church can be the head of Christ. Christ and the church cannot submit to each other in the same way.

Wifely submission is not something that men can force on women, however. Rather, as Southern Baptist theologian Dorothy Patterson says, Christian women should of their own accord graciously submit to their husbands. This is their Christian duty, but it is not something that men have the prerogative to demand. Moreover, on the other side of the ledger, complementarians teach that men must be worthy of their role as leader of the family. This message of worthiness was prominent in the Promise Keepers movement of the 1990s. Founded by former University of Colorado football coach Bill McCartney, Promise Keepers rallies packed sports stadiums around the country with evangelical men seeking to become better fathers and husbands. The meetings were often cathartic events with men weeping as they confessed their sins to one another. The message of Promise Keepers was mostly that men needed to improve in their ability to fulfill their spiritual obligation to love, lead, and nurture their wives and children. At its best, Promise Keepers taught men to be worthy of their wives' submission by loving them as Christ loved the church, even laying down their lives for women and children if need be. At its height the organization was heavily evangelical but supported by many traditional Roman Catholics as well.

The principal complementarian organization among evangelicals is the Council on Biblical Manhood and Womanhood (CBMW). Several evangelical leaders convened in Danvers, Massachusetts, in 1987 and composed the Danvers Statement, which serves as the organization's mission statement. The statement cites a variety of cultural challenges to the biblical view of gender roles, including ambivalence about the role of motherhood and homemaking, growing claims of legitimacy for sexual relationships that are unbiblical, and the promotion of feminist egalitarianism that rejects scriptural roles outlined for men and women.

Directly challenging the egalitarian view, the Danvers Statement criticizes the "hermeneutical oddities devised to reinterpret apparently plain meanings of Biblical texts," resulting in roles of men and women in church leadership that do not conform to scripture. This quote is a reference to evangelicals who do not believe the Bible calls for restrictions on women preachers and Bible teachers. These egalitarian interpretations are cited as a threat to biblical authority, and the statement attributes such views to an "accommodation of some within the church to the spirit of the age."[35] In short, the statement accuses egalitarians of compromising scripture in an attempt to accommodate culture.

The Danvers Statement affirms that Adam and Eve were created equal but distinctly gendered. God ordains the distinctions between the roles of men and women. Adam's headship in marriage was established as part of the created order. Many egalitarian evangelicals teach that the subordination of women resulted from the Fall into sin, not from the creation. Complementarians reject this view vigorously. They believe that God intended males to lead and women to be submissive within marriage. Still, the Danvers Statement also mentions distortions of the roles of men and women that entered humankind as a result of sin. Among these distortions are male domination in the home replacing the husband's loving and humble leadership, a love of power within the church among men, and a desire to resist limitations on their roles in the church among women. The statement is careful to say that while women's roles are limited within the church, men and women are equally valued by their creator. In the home, husbands are admonished to be loving and caring leaders. On this issue the statement reads in part, "In the family, husbands should forsake harsh or selfish leadership and grow in love and care for their wives; wives should forsake resistance to their husbands' authority and grow in willing, joyful submission to their husbands' leadership." For each such statement scriptural references follow, such as Ephesians 5:21–33; Colossians 3:18–19; Titus 2:3–5; I Peter 3:1–7; and I Corinthians 11:7–9.[36]

Christians for Biblical Equality (CBE) is the primary evangelical egalitarian organization, and like the CBMW, it also began in 1987. CBE's Statement on Men, Women, and Biblical Equality is similar in length to the Danvers Statement of the CBMW and also contains many biblical references. To outsiders it may seem odd that while evangelicals in these two groups all affirm the authority of scripture, they differ so much on what the Bible actually teaches with regard to gender. The CBMW points to several passages of scripture that say clearly that women are to be submissive to their husbands. Some passages also seem to clearly indicate that women are not to take leadership positions of authority in churches. CBE interprets such passages in light of other verses of scripture that seem to outline equality. The CBE statement says, "We believe that Scripture is to be interpreted holistically and thematically." This statement allows for tension in scripture on the roles of men and women, and it acknowledges that passages must be interpreted in context. Examples of context have to do with passages in I Corinthians and I Timothy that instruct women to be silent in the church. The context, egalitarians say, was a group of women in the first-century church at Corinth and elsewhere who were troublemakers. Paul was instructing them to be silent, but he was not making a blanket prohibition on women speaking in church that was to be the norm for all time. The lesson taken from this passage of scripture is that troublemakers should be prohibited to speak in churches, not necessarily women. Evidence for this view is that in other passages of scripture Paul affirms the role of a woman deacon named Phoebe. This is an example of tension. In one passage Paul seems to relegate women to silence, while in another he praises a woman who is a deacon in a church. When these and many other examples are taken into consideration, egalitarians say, the teaching of the Bible on balance is complete equality. As Paul wrote in Galatians 3:28: "There is neither Jew nor Greek, slave nor free, male nor female, for you are all one in Christ Jesus." For egalitarians, this is a powerful theological principle that throws light on many other difficult passages of scripture. The Galatians passage appears in the first paragraph of the CBE home page Web site.[37]

Another contextual difference between CBE and CBMW has to do with the Ephesians passage discussed above. Whereas complementarians in the CBMW emphasize the differences between husbands and wives that result in her submission and his leadership, egalitarians in the CBE emphasize verse 21 of chapter 5 that calls on Christians to "submit to one another." This verse is interpreted as the overarching principle that governs the interpretation of verses 22–33, resulting in what egalitarians call "mutual submission." The CBE statement says, "The husband's function as 'head' (*kephale* [in the

Greek]) is to be understood as self-giving love and service within this relationship of mutual submission." The statement then cites Ephesians 5:21–33, Colossians 3:19, and I Peter 3:7. Egalitarians also reject the notion that Eve and, therefore, all women were implicated more severely in the Fall, emphasizing instead the equal culpability of both Adam and Eve in sin. Moreover, Adam's rule over Eve was, in the egalitarian view, a result of the Fall into sin and not part of God's original created intention. In Christ, therefore, God's created intention of equality should be restored as men and women function equally. Within the churches, egalitarians believe, "The Bible teaches that, in the New Testament economy, women as well as men exercise the prophetic, priestly and royal functions." The CBE statement then lists several biblical examples such as Acts 2:17–18, where both men and women prophesied on the Day of Pentecost, and I Corinthians 11:5 that mentions women praying and prophesying. The CBE statement then says, "Therefore, the few isolated texts that appear to restrict the full redemptive freedom of women must not be interpreted simplistically and in contradiction to the rest of Scripture, but their interpretation must take into account their relation to the broader teaching of Scripture and their total context."[38]

While the complementarians of the CBMW accuse egalitarians of capitulating to culture, egalitarians of the CBE charge that complementarians of the CBMW are overly simplistic in their interpretation of scripture. Some evangelical denominations have agreed to live with the tension and allow both viewpoints to be represented in their seminaries, churches, and denominational agencies, while many other denominations have taken a harder line. In the latter category are the Southern Baptist Convention and its 1998 confession of faith. Because the submission statement is part of the SBC's confession, egalitarians cannot serve in Southern Baptist seminaries, as missionaries, or in denominational boards or agencies. Individual Baptist congregations operate autonomously, however, and therefore can preach and practice whatever they like on the issue of gender. In diverging from the confession, however, they do risk having their representatives turned away at the annual Southern Baptist Convention meeting or at their state convention or local associational meetings.

Evangelicals and Race

To the extent that evangelicals and fundamentalists want to mark themselves off from the larger culture, gender is their best issue. With the exception of the egalitarians, who comprise a large minority of evangelicals, evangelicals and fundamentalists resist gender equality within churches and families at least so far as equality is understood to mean that women have access to the same positions of leadership as men. This sets them apart from the dominant rhetoric, even if not always the practice, of our time. The issue of race is more complicated because here evangelicals and fundamentalists are on the same side, at least rhetorically, as the secular progressive culture. In other words, on the issue of race it is difficult to say in what way evangelicals' stated views are different from the dominant views of the larger culture.

As with gender, the history of evangelical Protestantism and race is long and checkered. As discussed in chapter one, revivalism tended to promote an egalitarian spirit, especially in the area of the crucicentric plank of Bebbington's four-fold description. This led to the evangelical antislavery movement, much of which flowed out of Charles Finney's revivals in the 1830s. It must be said, however, that just as evangelicals along with transcendentalists in the North led the antislavery movement, so also did many evangelicals in the North and South defend slavery, developing an elaborate biblical argument favoring that peculiar institution, as slavery has been called. Historian Mark Noll argued in his 2006 book *The Civil War as a Theological Crisis* that as Protestants interpreted the Bible's view of slavery, the Civil War became a theological controversy. Moreover, it was precisely the way that evangelical Biblicism was carried out that made the debate intractable.

Evangelical Biblicism in the nineteenth century was intuitive, natural, commonsensical, individual, and, wherever possible, literal. Evangelicals read scripture in plain Baconian fashion. The Bible was a storehouse of theological facts that needed merely to be categorized properly to reveal the mind of God on any matter. Noll describes the way pro-slavery evangelicals read scripture as follows: First, just read the Bible for oneself and see what it says. Read Leviticus 25:45—"You may also buy some of the temporary residents living among you and members of their clans born in your country, and they will become your property." Or, even better read I Corinthians 7:20–21—"Each one of you should remain in the situation which he was in when God called him. Were you a slave when you were called? Don't let it trouble you—although if you can gain your freedom, do so." Second, do not rely on a priest or bishop to tell you what the passages mean, and certainly do not rely on a Yankee abolitionist. Third, look critically at the theological views of anyone who does not interpret such passages in a natural, commonsensical, and ordinary way. One will usually find unorthodox theology among those who say the Bible opposes slavery. In short, as Noll puts the case, those who interpreted scripture as opposing slavery were usually viewed as undercutting the very authority of the Bible.[39]

In a panel discussion of his book in January 2007, Noll suggested that if one interprets scripture as nineteenth-century evangelicals did, it is very difficult, if not impossible, to argue against slavery biblically. Taken at face value, the Bible seems at best to assume the existence of slavery. To be sure, there were evangelicals who carefully considered the whole teaching of scripture and concluded that at the least the type of slavery practiced in the American South was unbiblical. In particular, some of these biblical commentators pointed out that slavery in the Bible was colorblind—that is, it was not based on race, as was American slavery. Pro-slavery Biblicists rarely took this argument seriously, precisely because views of white racial superiority were so ingrained in the minds of Americans in the North and South. Even most abolitionists believed in the inferiority of African Americans.[40] In this sense the problem of race in America was distinct from the problem of slavery, even as the two were bound together until the Civil War. Once separated, as subsequent American history revealed, the race problem would take much longer to solve than the slavery issue. American evangelical Protestants tended to read American racial views into scripture, even as they claimed to be purely biblicist.

Because the slavery issue was biblically intractable and therefore was turned over to the generals to be settled by force of arms, Americans made an implicit pact to never again "base public policy of any consequence on interpretations of Scripture." "In other words," Noll writes, "even before there existed a secularization in the United States brought on by new immigrants, scientific acceptance of evolution, the higher criticism of Scripture, and urban industrialism, Protestants during the Civil War had marginalized themselves as bearers of a religious perspective in the body politic."[41] Whatever the result of such secularization, and Noll believes there are both negative and positive consequences, evangelical debates over the Bible and race would continue for at least another century, right into the modern Civil Rights movement. But, the nation's peace never again hinged on the outcome of evangelical wrangling over the Bible's teaching. Race would not be a central concern for the most influential political or religious leaders again until the Civil Rights era. Not a single, prominent white political reformer of the Progressive Era (1900–1920) made racial injustice a consistent theme. That was left to African American progressives such as W. E. B. DuBois. During the fundamentalist-modernist controversy, neither the liberal nor the conservative side said a thing about race. Early fundamentalist Bible colleges, in their zeal to train evangelists, often overlooked color barriers and trained African American preachers, just as they did women. When they rescinded their egalitarian gender views, however, so too early fundamentalists eventually conformed to the segregated culture around them. Not until the 1960s would the race question that lay smoldering beneath the surface of American culture explode into view.

In one of the most recent interpretations of the Civil Rights movement, historian David Chappell argues that the movement succeeded precisely because of the power of religion, not the power of modern liberalism. The religious force of the movement was African American evangelicalism, but a primary difference between the Civil War and the Civil Rights movement with regard to white southern evangelical Protestants is that in the former there was a vigorous biblical defense of the slave system. During the Civil Rights movement, by contrast, white southern churches offered only de facto support, and segregation needed more than that in order to endure. Segregationists needed the sort of cultural legitimacy the slave system received from religion, and such legitimation was not forthcoming. Vigorous support of segregation was left to constitutional scholars, who argued for states' rights, and desperate and violent public bigots. By contrast, black Civil Rights workers did receive cultural and political support from black churches. As Chappell puts the case: "[B]lack southern activists got strength from old-time religion, and white supremacists failed, at the same moment, to muster the cultural strength that conservatives traditionally get from religion."[43] This was one of the reasons the Civil Rights movement succeeded.

But what about white evangelicals during the Civil Rights movement? There had not been a systematic scholarly treatment of evangelicals in the 1960s, let alone a book on evangelicals and the Civil Rights movement. Evidence from a variety of studies that treat civil rights reveals a mixed impression. For example, America's most famous and influential evangelical, Billy Graham, integrated his crusades in the early fifties, long before secular southern universities and other public or private places of accommodation integrated. At the same time, the person Graham considered his pastor, Southern Baptist preacher W. A. Criswell, was an outspoken defender of segregation until the late sixties, while Graham's father-in-law, L. Nelson Bell, was a moderate on the segregation issue. Representatives to the Southern Baptist Convention meeting in 1955 passed overwhelmingly a resolution supporting the landmark *Brown v. Board of Education* (1954) desegregation Supreme Court case. Still, almost everyone agrees that the resolution was not representative of rank-and-file Southern Baptist preachers or laypeople, the vast majority of whom appear to have opposed the Court's decision. Southern Presbyterians passed a similar resolution.[43]

The southern Presbyterian Bell, who served as one of the founders of the evangelical flagship magazine *Christianity Today*, was probably representative of most evangelicals in the North or South in believing that while segregation could not be defended biblically, getting involved in the Civil Rights movement would divert attention away from the conversionist or evangelism plank of evangelicalism. If such an impression holds up under historical scrutiny, we will eventually end up with a picture that looks like this: Southern Protestant churches, the vast majority of which were evangelical, presented only de facto support for segregation, not the vigorous defense that southern evangelical Protestants afforded slavery a century earlier. Similarly, northern evangelicals neither supported segregation nor did much to support Civil Rights. White religious support of the movement was left to Protestant liberals who joined African American evangelicals to push the movement toward legislative success.

While there are these similarities and differences between Civil War–era responses to slavery and Civil Rights–era responses to segregation, there is also a major parallel between the evangelical debate over slavery in the nineteenth century and the debate over gender in the twentieth. In short, the debate over the Bible and slavery was repeated with regard to the Bible and gender. In the late twentieth century egalitarian evangelicals, as discussed above, argued that passages of scripture that seem on their face to disallow women leadership roles in churches and require them to be submissive to their husbands must be taken within the totality of biblical equality. This less literal and more holistic reading of the Bible is similar to the abolitionists' interpretation a century-and-a-half before. Meanwhile, complementarian evangelicals take scriptural passages at face value, arguing that the Bible disallows women pastors and deacons and requires wifely submission. Both sides can gain rhetorical advantage at different points in this debate. The complementarians can say that egalitarians avoid the plain meaning of scripture and therefore are not fully evangelical. Ephesians 5:22 says, "Wives submit to your husbands as to the Lord." Egalitarians answer that reading scripture consistently in such an intuitive, commonsensical, and simplistic way would result not only in the support of wifely submission but also slavery as well. In Ephesians 6:5, just sixteen verses after wives are exhorted to be submissive, the text reads, "Slaves obey your earthly masters."[44] In this sense, evangelical debates over slavery in the nineteenth century and over gender in the twentieth and twenty-first are also over what evangelical Biblicism means and how it should be practiced.

The most prominent progressive evangelicals in the last quarter of the twentieth century were sixties youths repulsed by evangelical conservatism on issues of race and poverty. Jim Wallis, who founded *Sojourners* magazine, for example, was ashamed that his evangelical church in Detroit preached Jesus while harboring overt racial prejudice, showing little concern for the poverty of the inner city, and supporting the Vietnam War. Well into the 1970s, the strain between conservative theology and conservative views on race and poverty put white evangelicals among the least likely segments of society to support racial justice. Evangelicalism in the 1960s also retained vestiges of fundamentalist separatism, which taught that the wider culture was to be avoided, not engaged. It was easy, therefore, to dismiss civil rights or the Vietnam War as political issues that have nothing to do with Christian faith.

With the exception of some on the radical fringe of fundamentalism today, most evangelicals and fundamentalists espouse racial equality, and it is worth noting that the radical fringe of racists in America is made up of both secular and religious groups. Various skinheads and other neo-Nazis sometimes speak with religious overtones, while at other times they are completely secular. Moreover, some of the religious racists blend Christianity and Nordic or other non-Christian religions in ways that are roundly condemned by evangelicals and fundamentalists. Through the 1960s and into the 1970s many southern evangelical churches gave de facto support to segregation, and there were those such as Sam Bowers in Mississippi who fashioned a Christian racist theology that was frightening, all the more so because it was so well developed.[45] By the 1990s even these fringe voices were muted, and today one can scan the world of television evangelicalism and even separatist fundamentalism and hear nary a word of support for racism. Many of the Pentecostal and Charismatic ministries are integrated, with people of color preaching regularly to mixed-race audiences. Even while 90 percent of those who call themselves evangelicals are white, most African American Christians would qualify as evangelicals under the four-fold Bebbington rubric we have been using in this book.[46]

The racial situation among evangelicals is still complicated, however. The question today is not so much whether evangelicals and fundamentalists preach racism; hardly any do. Rather, the more sophisticated analysis asks to what extent the overall theology of evangelicals and fundamentalists contributes to a racialized society. Whether America is a racist society may be open to question, but hardly anyone questions that our society is racialized. Sociologists define a racialized society as "one in which intermarriage rates are low, residential separation and socioeconomic inequality are the norm, our definitions of personal identity and our choices of intimate associations reveal racial distinctiveness, and where 'we are never unaware of the race of a person with whom we interact.'" In short, as Michael Emerson and Christian Smith write, the unchanging essence of a racialized society is "a society wherein race matters profoundly for differences in life experiences, life opportunities, and social relationships."[47] These three areas—life experiences, life opportunities, and social relationships—can be statistically measured. For example, every study shows that African Americans are less well off economically than whites. This includes lower average income, less personal wealth, and higher rates of poverty. Black people have significantly different life experiences than the average white person and significantly less opportunity to acquire valued social resources such as higher education.

In their 2000 book, *Divided by Faith: Evangelical Religion and the Problem of Race in America*, Emerson and Smith asked whether evangelical religion has an impact on a racialized society. Their answer, based on quantitative and qualitative sociological research, is that evangelical Christianity contributes to a racialized society by maintaining racial divides that already exist and sometimes by creating new ones. Emerson and Smith are quick to point out that the structure of religion in America "is conducive to freeing groups from the direct control of other groups, but not to addressing the fundamental divisions that exist in our current racialized society."[48] As said above, in the history of American evangelicalism, from the Great Awakening of the eighteenth century to the present, evangelicals have often interpreted the crucicentrist plank of Bebbington's four-fold definition of evangelicalism to mean that "everyone is equal at the foot of the cross." As we have seen, evangelical revivals from the First Great Awakening to the present have usually been socially destabilizing events that often throw both gender and racial distinctions aside in the quest to see sinners brought to Christ, hence Billy Graham's integrated crusades in the South in the 1950s. It should also be noted that the revival at Azuza Street in Los Angeles that launched the modern Pentecostal movement in the first decade of the twentieth century was fully integrated and led by a black preacher. The revivals of the Second Great Awakening (1800–1835) contributed significantly to the abolitionist movement. Theodore Dwight Weld, his wife Angelina Grimke, and her sister Sarah are classic examples. Converted in Finney revivals, they became three of the leading abolitionists of the era.

The evangelical story on race, therefore, has been checkered, but with the exception of the South, it is hard to claim that evangelicals have been more racist than society at large, and in some instances evangelicals have been at the forefront of freedom movements. Emerson and Smith acknowledge the times throughout American history when the moral force of evangelicalism has resulted in a push for freedom and equality, and the two sociologists include in their book an overview of the myriad evangelical racial reconciliation efforts that have come to life over the past quarter-century. These efforts include specific ministries of reconciliation, many books coauthored by white and black evangelicals, Christian rock and rap groups that make racial reconciliation a regular theme in their recorded music and live performances, and discussion of race issues in *Christianity Today*.

The most visible example of evangelical racial reconciliation in the 1990s was the Promise Keepers movement that we met earlier in this chapter. As the coach of the University of Colorado football team before founding the organization, Bill McCartney recruited many African American players and came face to face with the inequality and deprivation they had faced during their upbringing, let alone the discrimination they still faced in a culture that often stereotypes young African American men as having a high propensity for crime. In the late 1990s, McCartney began to emphasize racial reconciliation as a major component of Promise Keepers rallies, along with marital reconciliation. The rallies became increasingly interracial, and just as they were often cathartic events for men repenting of their inattention to their families, so too the rallies saw white and black men embracing each other in tears, often with whites apologizing for discrimination against blacks. Before long, however, attendance at Promise Keepers rallies began to decline. Mc-Cartney points to a 1996 Promise Keepers survey that showed that among attendees who had a complaint, 40 percent "reacted negatively to the reconciliation theme." McCartney attributes the decline in attendance at 1997 Promise Keepers rallies to the reconciliation message that was launched the year before. This belief was buttressed by his own experiences speaking in evangelical churches where he claimed that the wild enthusiasm that greeted his introduction turned to a "morgue-like chill" after he spoke of the need for structural changes to address racialization.[49] Why was this?

The problem evangelicals have in addressing race stems from three components of what Emerson and Smith call the evangelical tool kit—a tool kit being the moral and ideological resources a group uses to deal with social issues. The evangelical kit contains three primary tools for understanding culture—individualism, relationalism, and antistructuralism, all of which stem from the revivalist tradition that shapes evangelicalism.

Individualism stems directly from Bebbington's conversionism component of evangelicalism. Conversion, as we have seen in this book, is necessary because all humans are sinful and in need of forgiveness. Even though theologically evangelicals believe that everyone is sinful by nature, on a popular level the idea that a person will be held accountable for actually sinning is usually accompanied by the idea that one is free. In other words, if an individual did not freely choose to sin, he or she could not be held accountable for something in which there was no choice. The remedy for sin and guilt is found in the work of Christ, but most evangelicals believe that the choice as to whether or not to accept Christ is an individual decision made freely in response to revivalist preaching or some other type of evangelism. Individualism leads to relationalism, the second tool in the evangelical kit. The converted individual has been brought into a right relationship with Christ. One's sinful state was a result of the wrong type or the lack of a relationship with Christ. Evangelicals view most social problems to be like sin—the result of poor relationships. Individualism and relationalism lead to the third tool in the evangelical tool kit, antistructuralism. Because evangelicals believe that salvation is largely the result of a free and individual choice, and that sin is largely the result of poor relationships, it is very difficult for evangelicals to acknowledge the structural features of the race problem. Racism is an individual problem, the result of poor relationships between blacks and whites, not from the structures of society.[50]

White evangelicals often view racism as a problem stemming from the heart of individuals who have not been brought into a right relationship with Christ. For example, Emerson and Smith asked one white evangelical, "Now do you view this [racial problem] as mostly an attitudinal thing or do you view prejudice and discrimination as having affected the legal system and housing patterns?" The respondent answered, "I think it's individual attitude, but it affects larger areas." Emerson and Smith countered, "It affects the system?" The respondent replied, "I think it's within our government because our politicians are acting as individuals." In other words, as Emerson and Smith write, "This woman saw prejudice and discrimination in institutions, but only insofar as they contained individual bigots."[51] Often, when evangelicals did see structural aspects to racial problems, they identified government affirmative action programs as the culprit, not the solution. These programs, they believed, created or fueled white racism. In other words, while evangelicals in Emerson and Smith's study hardly ever acknowledged structural causes of racism against African Americans, they were quick to identify structural causes of reverse discrimination against whites.

Individualism, relationalism, and antistructuralism are born out statistically in many measures of the racial attitudes of white evangelicals. For example, nearly two-thirds of white Protestants attribute black poverty to an individual lack of initiative and motivation, while only about half of other Americans view the problem this way. Conversely, while almost half of other Americans explain black poverty as a result of lack of access to quality education, only about one-third of white conservative Protestants see things this way. By contrast, black evangelicals rate lack of ability and motivation as the least likely causes of black poverty; they were more likely than other Americans to see black poverty as stemming from structural forces. Not only are black evangelicals more likely than their white counterparts to see structural causes for racial injustice, black evangelicals are less individualistic and more structural than nonevangelical blacks. In other words, black evangelicals are less likely than other African Americans to cite lack of motivation as a cause of racial inequality and more likely to cite discrimination as the cause. While we are not sure why black and white evangelicals see things so differently, the evidence suggests that evangelicalism, rather than bringing blacks and whites together, actually seems to contribute to very different racial views that actually drive the groups apart and contribute to a racialized society.[52]

The good news is that the gap between the racial attitudes of white and black evangelicals seems to shrink significantly when there is increased contact between the races. Emerson and Smith compared data from "high interracial contact" white evangelicals and those who experienced "low interracial contact." High-contact evangelicals were those who say that African Americans live in their neighborhood and that someone in their family has had an African American over for dinner sometime in the past two years. High-contact white evangelicals were significantly less likely to attribute racial inequality to individual, nonstructural causes. For example, 73 percent of low-contact white evangelicals attributed racial inequality to a lack of motivation on the part of African Americans, which is a decidedly individualist explanation. Meanwhile, only 42 percent attributed racial inequality to a lack of educational opportunity, which is a structural explanation. The gap, therefore, was 31 percentage points. By contrast, the gap was just 4 percentage points for high-contact evangelicals—56 percent to 52 percent.

These statistics were explained in large part in the interviews Emerson and Smith conducted. For example, when a woman evangelical told the sociologists matter of factly that racial inequality was the result of discrimination against African Americans, a somewhat surprised Emerson and Smith asked her why she believed this. Her answer: "I have a black brother-in-law. I've heard some of his stories, know some of his experiences, and other family members of his."[53] Extended contact with African Americans clearly shaped her unusual sensitivity to discrimination against African Americans. Emerson and Smith are quick to point out, however, that limited contact with African Americans produces only sporadic changes in racial attitudes. In other words, having a black friend or two, some sociologists have argued, seems to give whites (all whites, not just white evangelicals) a license to believe whatever they want about African Americans, often leading whites to overgeneralize about the bad behavior of blacks. Comprehensive change, by contrast, seems to require a network of interracial relationships.[54]

Evangelicals and Gay Rights

Unlike gender and race, the gay rights debate is of recent vintage. Until the latter twentieth century evangelicals, like the rest of American society, took for granted the idea that homosexuality was a disorder, and this was the official view of the American Psychological Association until the last third of the century. Evangelicals merely added that homosexual practice was also a sin, but even here they were joined by their Roman Catholic and liberal Protestant rivals. This all changed when the progressive, secular segment of society decided that homosexuality was a preference, not a disorder. Evangelicals, liberal Protestants, and Roman Catholics have been struggling with the issue ever since. Many liberal Protestants and a few liberal Protestant denominations have become gay affirmative, while evangelicals and Roman Catholics have attempted to hold the line on the traditional view.

For evangelicals, there is much less diversity on gay and lesbian questions than on gender issues. Evangelicals and fundamentalists almost uniformly oppose the gay lifestyle, largely because the Bible is quite consistent in its condemnation of homosexual practice. As we have seen in this chapter, scriptural passages concerning the roles of husbands and wives in the home and men and women in religious leadership, even on slavery, are varied and subject to interpretation. Even many who proclaim themselves to be biblical inerrantists believe there is room for diverse interpretations of the Bible when it comes to gender. By contrast, there is no biblical equivocation or complexity with regard to homosexuality. The New Testament portrays all sexual practices outside of heterosexual marriage as sinful. This includes homosexuality. Evangelicals display diversity on this issue primarily in the intensity with which they condemn homosexuality, with progressive evangelicals calling for compassion for those who experience a homosexual orientation and in some cases calling for fair treatment and full civil rights for gay people. Only a very small fraction of evangelicals, however, believes that the gay lifestyle is acceptable for Christians. Disapproval of the gay lifestyle is so pronounced that in many quarters merely to entertain the legitimacy of homosexuality is to call one's evangelicalism into question because such an interpretation seems to defy even a sophisticated, nonliteral form of Biblicism.

Evangelicals who are politically active in the Christian Right (to be covered in the next chapter) have joined Roman Catholics in making opposition to gay rights and gay marriage a key issue in their political program. Generally, they believe that the traditional family is the basic unit on which a healthy society is built and that if the state equates gay marriage and traditional marriage, the state is contributing to the degeneration of society. Direct mail literature from Christian Right organizations is filled with references to the social dangers of gay rights and gay marriage. The gay marriage issue is so recent that there is very little reliable, long-term research on its effects. Some have suggested that in European countries where gay marriage has been legal for some time, the Netherlands for instance, marriage of any kind has become less common. One interpretation of this phenomenon is that when marriage can mean anything, it basically means nothing and therefore loses its value as a social institution. Christian Right activists are convinced this is the case.

At the core of the fight over gay rights and gay marriage, as well as many other issues in America's so-called culture wars, are different views of what constitutes morality. On one side of the culture wars are the orthodox or conservatives who believe that morality is a fixed and transcendent entity created by God. A good society will seek to discern and follow what is morally absolute. Evangelicals, of course, believe in a transcendent morality whether they are active in the culture wars or not. On the other side of the culture wars are the progressivists, who believe that morality is for the most part created by societies and subject to change and development over time. Only about 20 percent of Americans on each side are actively involved in these culture wars, leaving 60 percent of us somewhere in the middle.[55] While it would probably be going too far to say that America is in a culture war, it seems that there is a culture war in America, even if only a minority of the people are fighting. When one considers these two different views of morality, it becomes easier to see why evangelical culture warriors make such an issue of gay rights and gay marriage. In short, they believe that activists in the gay rights movement are attempting to use the power of government to foist their own morality on the rest of the population. Of course, this is exactly what gay rights activists believe evangelicals are attempting to do as well, and therein lays the intractable nature of the culture wars. People on both sides believe their opponents are coercive; both sides believe their opponents are attempting to use the power of government to support a particular moral position that they do not hold themselves.

Analyzing the moral views that undergird the culture wars helps explain why a majority of evangelicals believe that gay rights activists have too much influence in society. Recent research puts the figure at 57 percent of theologically conservative Protestants who believe that gay rights groups have too much influence, compared to 43 percent of all other Americans who believe this. Homosexuals were also the only group that a majority of theologically conservative Protestants, 51 percent, said they would not want as a neighbor. Only 38 percent of other Americans held this view of gay neighbors. Even so, the percentage of evangelicals or even fundamentalists who support "hate crime" legislation to protect gays and lesbians is not statistically different from the percentage of other Americans who support such laws. A small minority of evangelicals even have what could be characterized as quite open attitudes toward gays. Some of these evangelicals oppose Christian Right arguments that gays undermine society and instead support a live-and-let-live attitude toward homosexuality. As one such evangelical said, "I don't agree with homosexual marriage. I think it's really sick and twisted. But you know, if they want to, I guess it's fine. . . . I don't think it is right, but I wouldn't try to get a law against them." Another even more open evangelical said, "I don't believe it is right or wrong to be a homosexual. I don't think it is my place to judge a person."[56] Granted, this level of openness toward homosexuality is the minority view for evangelicals. The vast majority of evangelicals believe that homosexual practice is a sin, but how they apply such a theological belief in the social, cultural, and political realms is much less predictable. The range goes from those who believe their views on homosexuality are private and should not apply to the public square to those who are evangelical culture warriors and want the state to take a clear stand on the side of traditional sexual morality.

Conclusion

When it comes to gender, race, and gay issues, it is not just that evangelicals as a group hold to a range of views. Rather, even individual evangelicals hold views that are fluid and unpredictable on these and many other questions. One evangelical touts wifely submission while also describing marriage as an equal partnership. Another evangelical believes racial prejudice is a sin yet still holds that African Americans lag behind whites economically because black people lack initiative. As Smith's research shows, homosexuality is the issue where evangelicals differ the most from all other Americans, but even here an evangelical may believe that homosexuality is sinful and that a gay person would not be a good neighbor or president while still believing that gays should have equal, and in some cases special, legal protection. Certainly, there are evangelicals who practice wifely submission while being prejudiced against minorities and generally intolerant of gay people. A large and unified social bloc of such evangelicals, however, exists more in the imagination of some culture warriors than in the real world.

Notes

1. "Report of the Baptist Faith and Message Study Committee to the Southern Baptist Convention," June 9, 1998. See Barry Hankins, *Uneasy in Babylon: Southern Baptist Conservatives and American Culture* (Tuscaloosa: University of Alabama Press, 2002), 200–39.

2. Susan Juster, *Disorderly Women: Sexual Politics and Evangelicalism in Revolutionary New England* (Ithaca, New York: Cornell University Press), 5–6.

3. Juster, *Disorderly Women*, 7.

4. These are words from the trial record as quoted in Juster, *Disorderly Women*, 1.

5. Catherine Brekus, *Strangers and Pilgrims: Female Preaching in America, 1740–1845* (Chapel Hill: University of North Carolina Press, 1998), 3–17.

6. Betty DeBerg, *Ungodly Women: Gender and the First Wave of American Fundamentalism* (Minneapolis, Minnesota: Fortress Press, 1990), 122.

7. Quoted in Margaret Lamberts Bendroth, *Fundamentalism and Gender, 1875 to the Present* (New Haven, Connecticut: Yale University Press, 1993), 3.

8. Bendroth, *Fundamentalism and Gender*, 3.

9. Matthew 28:18–20 (in part). All scriptural passages come from *The Holy Bible: New International Version* (Grand Rapids, Michigan: Zondervan Publishing House, 1988).

10. William Vance Trollinger, Jr., *God's Empire: William Bell Riley and Midwestern Fundamentalism* (Madison: University of Wisconsin Press, 1990), 104–5.

11. Quoted in Trollinger, *God's Empire*, 105.

12. Quoted in Trollinger, *God's Empire*, 106.

13. Quoted in Trollinger, *God's Empire*, 107.

14. Janette Hassey, *No Time for Silence: Evangelical Women in Public Ministry around the Turn of the Century* (Grand Rapids, Michigan: Academie, 1986), 137.

15. Quoted in Bendroth, *Fundamentalism and Gender*, 110–11.

16. Bendroth, *Fundamentalism and Gender*, 111.

17. Quoted in Bendroth, *Fundamentalism and Gender*, 111.

18. Bendroth, *Fundamentalism and Gender*, 110.

19. Bendroth, *Fundamentalism and Gender*, 105.

20. Ephesians 5:22–24.

21. James M. Ault Jr., *Spirit and Flesh: Life in a Fundamentalist Baptist Church* (New York: Vintage Books, 2004), 90–91.

22. Quoted in Ault, *Spirit and Flesh*, 91–92.

23. Ault, *Spirit and Flesh*, 50–51.

24. Ault, *Spirit and Flesh*, 103.

25. Ault, *Spirit and Flesh*, 254.

26. Quoted in Ault, *Spirit and Flesh*, 316.

27. Ault, *Spirit and Flesh*, 316.

28. Ault, *Spirit and Flesh*, 317.

29. Quoted in Ault, *Spirit and Flesh*, 318.

30. Christian Smith, *Christian America?: What Evangelicals Really Want* (Berkeley: University of California Press, 2000), 186.

31. Sally K. Gallagher, "Symbolic Traditionalism and Pragmatic Egalitarianism: Contemporary Evangelicals, Families, and Gender." The report on this study is available on the website of the Hartford Institute for Religion Research.

32. Smith, *Christian America?*, 172; Brenda Brasher, *Godly Women: Fundamentalism and Female Power* (New Brunswick, New Jersey: Rutgers University Press, 1998), 4; R. Marie Griffith, *God's Daughters: Evangelical Women and the Power of Submission* (Berkeley: University of California Press, 1997), 22.

33. Mark Chaves, *Ordaining Women: Culture and Conflict in Religious Organizations* (Cambridge, Massachusetts: Harvard University Press, 1997), 6.

34. Ault, *Spirit and Flesh*, 254.

35. "The Danvers Statement," The Council on Biblical Manhood and Womanhood, accessible at www.cbmw.org.

36. "The Danvers Statement," The Council on Biblical Manhood and Womanhood, accessible at www.cbmw.org.

37. See www.cbeinternational.org.

38. "Christians for Biblical Equality: Statement on Men, Women and Biblical Equality," www.cbeinternational.org.

39. Mark Noll, *The Civil War as a Theological Crisis* (Chapel Hill: University of North Carolina Press, 2006), 50. Both scripture verses from *The Holy Bible: New International Version*, 1333–34.

40. Noll, *The Civil War as a Theological Crisis*, 73.

41. Noll, *The Civil War as a Theological Crisis*, 161.

42. David Chappell, *A Stone of Hope: Prophetic Religion and the Death of Jim Crow* (Chapel Hill: University of North Carolina Press, 2004), 6 and 8, quote on 8.

43. Chappell, *A Stone of Hope*, 119–20 and 143–45.

44. Both verses from *The Holy Bible: New International Version*, 1333–34.

45. See Charles Marsh, *God's Long Summer: Stories of Faith and Civil Rights* (Princeton, New Jersey: Princeton University Press, 1997).

46. Michael Emerson and Christian Smith, *Divided by Faith: Evangelical Religion and the Problem of Race in America* (New York: Oxford University Press, 2000), 3.

47. Emerson and Smith, *Divided by Faith*, 7.

48. Emerson and Smith, *Divided by Faith*, 18.

49. Quoted in Emerson and Smith, *Divided by Faith*, 68.

50. Emerson and Smith, *Divided by Faith*, 76–79.

51. Quoted in Emerson and Smith, *Divided by Faith*, 79.

52. Emerson and Smith, *Divided by Faith*, 96–97.

53. Quoted in Emerson and Smith, *Divided by Faith*, 107.

54. Emerson and Smith, 107–8, citing the work of sociologists Mary Jackman and Marie Crane.

55. James Davison Hunter, *Culture Wars: The Struggle to Define America* (New York: Basic Books, 1991).

56. Smith, *Christian America?*, 212, 214, and 53, quotes on 53.

CHAPTER SIX

~

Inspired Politics

Evangelical Religion in the Political Marketplace

The presidential election of 1980 saw three "born-again" evangelical candidates run for the presidency—incumbent Jimmy Carter, a lifelong Southern Baptist and longtime Sunday school teacher; Carter's Republican challenger and eventual winner Ronald Reagan; and John Anderson, an evangelical Republican congressmember who ran as an independent. During the campaign that year the Christian Right, at that time called the New Religious Right, burst onto the political scene led by Jerry Falwell and his organization called the Moral Majority. In the two decades between 1980 and 2000, the Christian Right succeeded in pushing religion onto center stage in American politics. This was a remarkable feat when one considers that before 1976, when Jimmy Carter ran for the first time openly as an evangelical, there was a common rule of decorum that said one should not mix religion and politics. Of course, there had always been a good deal of religion in American politics, but the dictum stipulated that for campaign purposes candidates should not bring their personal religion into play, and the media should not probe the subject. There was an exception made for President John F. Kennedy, the first and only Roman Catholic president in American history, but that exception seemed to prove the rule. Inquiries into Kennedy's religion were significant primarily because they violated the general rule of decorum.

Political Liberalism and the Public Role of Religion

The view that religion is a private matter that should not play a role in the public square has its own philosophical justification. Known as political liberalism, the chief theorist of this view was John Rawls of Harvard University. Rawls and other devotees of political liberalism see themselves as embodying the liberal tradition started by seventeenth-century philosopher John Locke. The modern form of political liberalism holds that in a pluralistic democracy it is uncivil and unfair to bring what Rawls called "comprehensive doctrines" into matters of law and politics. A comprehensive doctrine is any worldview that seeks to say comprehensively what is good, right, or just. For Rawls, this restriction on comprehensive doctrines in the public square applied primarily to matters of constitutional law, but other liberal theorists have applied it to all of politics, arguing that one has a civic duty to keep comprehensive doctrines out of political matters. They believe that in a pluralistic society people will never be able to agree on what constitutes the good, so that question must be bracketed from politics and left for individuals to decide. If law reflected a comprehensive doctrine, this would be an imposition of one group's notion of the good onto others who do not share that comprehensive doctrine. The only answer, therefore, is to give individuals maximum freedom to decide for themselves what the good is. Some liberal theorists, Robert Audi for example, believe that while it may be acceptable for religious people to formulate their political views based on their religion (i.e., their comprehensive doctrines), when they enter the public arena they should find nonreligious arguments for their positions. If they cannot find arguments that are separate from their comprehensive doctrines, then they should refrain from expressing their views in the public square. This is to ensure that there are public reasons for coercive laws, which in turn ensures that no law is based on sectarian religious views or any other comprehensive doctrine.

The most thoroughgoing upshot of liberal political theory is the idea that religion is a private matter, not suitable for public affairs. This view that religion is private helps explain why for so long in American politics there existed the general rule of decorum that religion and politics should not mix. It was considered bad manners, at the least, and uncivil, at the worst, to probe a candidate's personal religious views during a political campaign. It was like prying into the candidate's private sexual life. Some even argued that to probe a candidate's religious views amounted to a religious test for office, which is forbidden by the constitution when done by a governmental entity. As anyone who follows politics today knows, political candidates' personal affairs, religious or sexual, are no longer off limits.

The Old Religious Right

While many Americans accepted the argument of political liberalism, most without knowing its origin, many evangelicals and fundamentalists before 1980 stayed clear of mixing religion and politics for other reasons. As discussed earlier in this book, fundamentalists believed in theological and cultural separatism. Even many evangelicals who were not fundamentalist separatists believed that politics was a worldly pursuit that diverted attention away from evangelism and missions, which were held up jointly as the primary tasks of churches. When Martin Luther King Jr. was joined by many liberal Protestants in the Civil Rights movement of the 1960s, Jerry Falwell spoke for virtually all fundamentalists and many evangelicals when he preached a sermon entitled "Ministers and Marchers," in which he said he would never get involved in politics because his call was to preach the gospel. Falwell's statement hearkened back to the nineteenth century, especially in the South, and the phenomenon that scholars have called "the spiritualization of the church." This was the view that the church was to deal with spiritual matters only; politics was the realm of the nonspiritual. There were exceptions made when a political issue had moral overtones, such as gambling or alcohol. Southern Christians often supported legislation regulating or outlawing these practices because they were considered immoral, but in doing so they still sought to hold on to the fiction that the churches should not be involved in politics.

Even with the view that evangelicals should not be involved in politics, there were exceptions. From the 1930s to the 1970s a smattering of individual fundamentalists were deeply involved in politics and are often referred to as the Old Religious Right. Of course, this name did not surface until there was a New Religious Right against which to compare the old. The Old Religious Right consisted primarily of fundamentalists who rejected liberal political theory and the spiritualization of the church in order to engage in selected political causes, chiefly anticommunism during the Cold War era. Carl McIntire was a key figure, as was Billy James Hargis. They used radio to preach a combination of fundamentalist religion, American patriotism, and virulent anticommunism. The Old Religious Right leaders were given to conspiracy theories about Communist infiltration and clandestine plots to destabilize America. One of the more outlandish conspiracies was the belief held by several Old Religious Right preachers that fluoridation of water supplies, done ostensibly to protect children from tooth decay, was really part of a Communist plot to deny individual choice and foist governmental control onto the American people.

The Old Religious Right was part of what has been called "the lunatic fringe" and "radical right" of American politics, and often with good reason. In the 1960s, for example, McIntire ran afoul of Federal Communications Commission regulations on radio programs. Instead of complying with the FCC, he moved his broadcast onto a ship off the east coast in international waters, outside the jurisdiction of the federal government. From the ship he broadcast to shore in the style of Radio Free Europe. Radio Free Europe was a U.S.-sponsored radio program that blasted program signals into Communist countries. McIntire seemed to think that he was doing the same by sending his illegal signal into the United States. In 1948, a year before the Soviet Union successfully tested its first atomic bomb, McIntire advocated a preemptive strike against Russia. "[F]or us to have the atom bomb and in the name of a false morality, born of a perverted sense of self-respect and pacifist propaganda, to await the hour when Russia has her bombs to precipitate an atomic war, is the height of insanity and will, when the fateful hour comes, be a just punishment upon us. We believe that Almighty God holds us responsible."[1] McIntire was saying that the United States had a duty under God to attack the Soviet Union with atomic weapons.

Like McIntire, Billy James Hargis was also a virulent anti-Communist. Hargis was a Church of Christ minister in Oklahoma who by the 1960s had a radio program, fledgling Bible college, and an organization called the Christian Crusade, which was as much a crusade against communism as for the gospel. He liked to say that he preached "God and country, always God and country." Hargis and many in the Old Religious Right took aim at sex education in schools as a primary example of government-sponsored attempts to undermine traditional morality. Hargis's organization published a book by a Michigan man named Gordon Drake entitled *Is the School House the Proper Place to Teach Raw Sex?* Hargis claimed to have sold over 1 million copies. Hargis and Drake hit the road together and barnstormed the country, Drake leading with the antisex education message followed by Hargis's God and country sermons. Ironically, Hargis's empire crashed temporarily when he was involved in a sex scandal in the 1970s. A newly married couple from his Bible college confessed to each other that each had had sex with Hargis. Hargis had performed their wedding ceremony. Members of the school's traveling choir also came forward with similar allegations. Hargis denied them.

While most leaders of the Old Religious Right were not as blatantly hypocritical as Hargis, many were nearly as outrageous. Still, they had vast mailing lists and tens of thousands of subscribers to their periodicals. At its peak, Hargis's *Christian Crusade* had more than 98,000 subscribers. McIntire's *Christian Beacon* had more than 66,000, and contributions to his organization called the Twentieth Century Reformation were more than 3 million dollars per year. Hargis's radio program was broadcast seven nights a week from a powerful station in Mexico.[2] Even though various preachers had thousands of radio listeners, these conspiracy theorists were not taken seriously by reputable political activists, nor by a very large percentage of evangelicals. The political parties largely ignored their rantings.

The Rise of the (New Religious) Christian Right

The New Religious Right, or Christian Right as it is called today, would be different, primarily by entering the mainstream of American politics and becoming the major constituency of the Republican Party. How did this happen? The answer lies in the movement's history. In the 1960s and early 1970s, there were significant movements to resist sex education in schools, many of which were far more temperate and reasonable than Hargis's efforts mentioned above. In Anaheim, California; Kanawha County, West Virginia; and other places, conservative Christian women led movements to stop sex education in their local public schools. Because the sex education materials failed to take a clear stand against homosexuality and sex outside of marriage, many conservative Christians were convinced that sex education was an effort by the government to indoctrinate their children with anti-Christian morality. The conservative activists believed that the act of sex was being divorced from the morality of sex. In 1969, on the heels of a sex education controversy in Anaheim, California, there was a meeting in Chicago called the National Convention on the Crisis in Education that was largely an antisex education gathering. Some 350 representatives from parent groups in twenty-two states gathered. In addition to opposing sex education, the National Convention also announced its plans to get prayer back into the schools.[3] The U.S. Supreme Court had ruled in 1962 and 1963 that organized prayer in public schools was an unconstitutional establishment of religion. Combining these prayer decisions with the advent of sex education, Christian conservatives liked to say that the government had taken God out of the schools and put sex in. In his study of the rise of the Christian Right, sociologist William Martin concluded that the sex education controversies taught Christian conservatives an important lesson. They learned "that by marshaling their arguments, organizing their forces, and stomping on the hottest buttons, they could exert influence out of all proportion to their numbers or the true popularity of their positions."[4]

As Christian conservatives began to mobilize at the grassroots level around sex education, the broader political right was also developing. In

1964, conservative political activists in the Republican Party supported Barry Goldwater for their party's presidential nomination. Goldwater won the nomination but was then trounced by incumbent president Lyndon B. Johnson in the general election. It looked as if the conservative movement in the Republican Party was moribund, but party conservatives learned valuable lessons from the 1964 debacle and redoubled their efforts to win the party again in the future. In 1966, Hollywood actor Ronald Reagan was elected governor of California. Reagan had become a popular conservative spokesperson, and his election in California renewed hope for party conservatives. Reagan made a bid for the Republican presidential nomination in 1968 but was defeated by Richard Nixon, who went on to win the general election over Democrat Hubert Humphrey. This should have set the stage for Reagan to win the nomination in 1976, after Nixon's second term, except that Nixon was forced to resign in 1974 due to the infamous Watergate scandal. He was succeeded by his vice president Gerald Ford, who was then eligible to run for reelection in 1976. It is, of course, very difficult to unseat an incumbent president for nomination within one's own party, and Reagan was unsuccessful in running against Ford in the Republican primaries of 1976. He would have to wait until 1980 before finally winning the Republican nomination and leading the conservative wing of the party to victory in the presidential election that year.

While Reagan would be the overwhelming favorite of the Christian Right, Jimmy Carter's victory in the 1976 election was very important in further energizing evangelicals in politics. Nixon had courted Christian conservatives, but he was not an evangelical himself and was unable to stir their imaginations. The Watergate scandal, moreover, served to confirm the belief that politics was dirty business of which Christians should steer clear. Carter, by contrast, was a born-again evangelical who regularly taught Sunday school in his Baptist church in Plains, Georgia. With the general rule of decorum against the mixing of religion and politics still in force, it was unusual for a presidential candidate to claim born-again status. Actually, it was not so much that Carter touted his own religion as it was that the press discovered it and was intrigued. Commenting on the candidate's reticence to use religion for political advantage, Carter's press secretary remarked during the campaign that Carter read more scripture and quoted less than other recent candidates. Kenneth Briggs, a religion reporter with *The New York Times*, recalled later that when Carter casually mentioned that he was an evangelical, the news media was sent scurrying to figure out what Carter meant. As Briggs said later, "The mainstream press in this country didn't really know what an evangelical was. And what they did know harkened back to the days of the Scopes trial and fundamentalism and a kind of backwoods yahoo-ism that they found very distasteful. No one was sure that a presidential candidate should be talking about such things as private 'born-again' experiences and conversions." NBC News anchor John Chancellor sought to put his television viewers at ease by telling them awkwardly, "We have checked on the religious meaning of Carter's profound experience. It is described by other Baptists as a common experience, not something out of the ordinary."[5] The whole idea of an evangelical presidential candidate stirred so much interest and coverage that *Newsweek* magazine proclaimed 1976 "The Year of the Evangelical."

There is considerable evidence that Carter drew evangelicals into politics. For many, he was the first major political figure in their lifetime to talk openly about his own personal religious commitments. The problem for Carter was that he was not conservative politically as were most evangelicals, and thus the initial enthusiasm evangelicals showed for having one of their own as president dissipated over the four years that Carter was in the White House. Carter believed that he needed to be careful not to impose his own religious and even moral views on others. Like most other Americans, he was sensitive to the dictum of political liberalism that religious coercion is unjust. Carter was also a Baptist, and Baptists have a long history of supporting religious liberty and the separation of church and state. Carter's sensitivity to religious coercion extended even to his personal moral views. For example, although not at that time supportive of homosexuality as an acceptable lifestyle, Carter nevertheless believed that gay people had rights that should be protected, just like everyone else. Although his administration was instrumental in organizing a major national conference on the family, conference participants were so diverse that they could not agree on what a family was. Christian conservatives began to back away from Carter. Moreover, Carter was not as theologically or socially conservative as most evangelicals. He admired the writings of the liberal theologian Reinhold Niebuhr, who had also influenced Martin Luther King Jr., and he drank alcohol occasionally and in moderation, which troubled many evangelicals and fundamentalists.

A key issue that turned many evangelicals against Carter was his administration's attempt to regulate Christian schools. In 1975, the IRS stripped Bob Jones University of its tax-exempt status because the college prohibited interracial dating. The university sued, and eventually in 1983 the case was heard by the U.S. Supreme Court, which ruled against the university. In the meantime, in 1978, the IRS attempted to revoke the tax-exempt status of any private school that did not meet certain racial integration standards.

Christian schools were proliferating across the nation, and in some places such schools were "segregation academies," a name developed for schools created to allow whites to escape integration. Many of the Christian schools were not segregation academies, however, but were formed because of increasing concerns about sex education and other curricular developments in public schools. As conservative activist Paul Weyrich, a key person in the development of the Moral Majority organization in 1980, would say later, "What galvanized the Christian community was not abortion, school prayer, or the ERA [Equal Rights Amendment]. . . . I was trying to get those people interested in those issues and I utterly failed. What changed their mind was Jimmy Carter's intervention against the Christian schools, trying to deny them tax-exempt status on the basis of so-called de facto segregation."[6]

Weyrich went on to explain that Christians believed they could resist the abortion decisions, the ERA, and the school prayer decisions privately. That is, they could teach their young women not to have abortions, run their families and churches according to their own ideas of distinct gender differences, and get around the prayer decisions and sex education courses by putting their kids in private Christian schools. When the government came after those schools, however, many evangelicals perceived this as an attack on their ability to live their lives in accordance with their own private religious views. While these policies were the result of decisions in government agencies, Carter seemed to agree with them, and he bore the brunt of criticism.

Most troubling by 1980 was Carter's pro-choice stance on abortion. During the late 1970s abortion became a hot-button issue much like sex education and prayer in schools. Many of the evangelicals drawn into politics in 1976 during Carter's first campaign were by 1980 thoroughly disenchanted with him. After a meeting Carter held with leading evangelical and fundamentalist preachers Jerry Falwell, Oral Roberts, Rex Humbard, Jim Bakker, D. James Kennedy, Charles Stanley, and Tim LaHaye, LaHaye said it was clear that "we had a man in the White House who professed to be a Christian, but didn't understand how un-Christian his administration was." LaHaye said he prayed, "God we have got to get this man out of the White House and get someone in here who will be aggressive about bringing back traditional moral values."[7] LaHaye said he learned shortly thereafter that several of the others at that meeting were praying the same prayer. In the election of 1980 they would all support Ronald Reagan, whose political views better fit with the majority of evangelicals.

During the 1970s, as the issues discussed above turned evangelicals away from Carter, Francis Schaeffer (1912–1984) was the key individual in galvanizing evangelicals for political action against the forces of secularism.

Until the 1970s, Schaeffer's message was almost completely apolitical, as we see in chapter seven. He emphasized the importance of Christian intellectual engagement with culture, writing several books that urged evangelicals to think seriously about philosophy, theology, the visual arts, music, and literature. In the 1970s, Schaeffer's books turned to films, and his message turned political. The first film appeared in 1976 and was called *How Should We Then Live?*. In this film and the accompanying book by the same title, Schaeffer's message changed from a call for cultural engagement to a call for culture war. He argued that the U.S. government was under the influence of secular humanism and that this anti-Christian worldview had become virtually the established religion of a secular state that was increasingly hostile to Christians. Grassroots activists such as those involved in the antisex education campaigns began to pick up Schaeffer's rhetoric against secular humanism. In 1979, Schaeffer produced his second film, *Whatever Happened to the Human Race?*. Joined by physician C. Everett Koop, who would later serve as Surgeon General in the Reagan administration, this film played a major role in galvanizing evangelicals for political action on the abortion issue. Schaeffer and Koop connected abortion, infanticide, and euthanasia, calling these issues collectively "a culture of death" reminiscent of Nazism.[8]

Schaeffer published *A Christian Manifesto* in 1982. Reprising and developing in more detail the culture warrior call he had first issued in *How Should We Then Live?*, in *Manifesto* Schaeffer called the Reagan presidency and Republican ascendancy a "window of opportunity" for evangelicals to assert themselves politically. Schaeffer helped convince many evangelicals that they could turn the country away from secular humanism and back toward what he called the nation's "Christian base." Privately, Schaeffer mentored fundamentalist minister Jerry Falwell, but his larger significance was in convincing evangelicals who had viewed politics as dirty business that it was time to put that notion to rest and get involved. Schaeffer died of cancer in 1984 and therefore did not live to see the full flowering of politically activist evangelicalism. Falwell and others led that effort.

Through the antisex education campaigns, the issues of prayer in schools and abortion, the government attempt to regulate private Christian schools, and the role Carter's presidency and Schaeffer's books and films played in bringing evangelicals into politics, the stage was set by 1979 for the development of the New Religious Right. In May of that year conservative Republican activists Weyrich, Howard Phillips, Ed McAteer, and Robert Billings met with fundamentalist preacher Falwell at the Holiday Inn in Lynchburg, Virginia, where Falwell pastored Thomas Road Baptist Church, produced the *Old Time Gospel Hour* television program, and led his fledgling Liberty University. Weyrich and other political operatives understood that evangelicals were overwhelmingly conservative in their politics and needed only to be energized and organized. The "sleeping giant," as some called evangelicals, had been substantially awakened during the seventies. What remained was to organize them behind effective leadership, bringing them into the Republican Party as a solid voting bloc. Weyrich and the others at the 1979 meeting believed Falwell (d. 2007) was the key person for this effort.

Falwell grew up as a roughneck unbeliever in Lynchburg, Virginia. His mother, Helen, was a pious Christian, while his father, Carey, was a businessperson, bootlegger, and alcoholic who shot and killed his own brother in a duel in 1931. Carey died of cirrhosis of the liver in 1948 when Jerry was fifteen years old. Falwell and his twin brother were baptized at the age of twelve, but Falwell says it was merely an outward ritual for them. Of the baptism Falwell would say later, "We went in dry sinners and came out wet sinners."[9] After graduating valedictorian of his high school, Falwell attended Lynchburg College for two years and planned to go to Virginia Tech his final two years to study engineering. During his second year of college, however, he had a conversion experience at a Sunday evening service at Park Avenue Baptist Church in Lynchburg. He became quite serious about his newfound faith and even considered becoming a preacher. Falwell, therefore, decided to attend Bible college. His pastor at Park Avenue Baptist encouraged him to attend Baptist Bible College in Springfield, Missouri, where the pastor's father was a professor. Falwell enrolled in the fall of 1952.

Fundamentalists who had split off from J. Frank Norris's church and seminary in Fort Worth, Texas, organized Baptist Bible College. Norris was the rabble-rousing fundamentalist covered in chapter two. Those who split off from Norris did so largely because of his dictatorial methods of running his religious empire, which consisted of First Baptist Church, Fort Worth; his seminary; and from 1935–1950 Temple Baptist Church, Detroit, Michigan, which he pastored simultaneously with First Baptist. Norris was one of the most infamous fundamentalists of the first generation of American fundamentalism.[10] As Falwell has put it, he was trained by men who were trained by J. Frank Norris, but neither they nor Falwell were the theological rascals that Norris was. They did, however, preach and teach the same militantly fundamentalist theology as Norris.

Falwell graduated from Baptist Bible College in 1955 and returned to Lynchburg, where he founded Thomas Road Baptist Church in June 1956. The church started with about thirty-five members in a building that formerly housed a soft-drink bottling company. Shortly thereafter, Falwell started radio and television ministries reminiscent of Charles Fuller's *Old Fashioned Revival Hour* radio broadcast, which his mother had played in the Falwell home hoping it would have an effect on her boys. Falwell spent the first three decades of his ministry as a militantly separatist fundamentalist, and like most others in that movement, he steered clear of political involvement. He came to believe in the 1970s, however, that fundamentalists and other evangelicals had to enter the political arena.[11] A man of considerable charm and a large television audience, Falwell was the ideal leader of the New Religious Right.

When they met in Lynchburg that day in May 1979, Weyrich began by telling Falwell, "Out there is what one might call a moral majority—people who would agree on principles based on the Decalogue [Ten Commandments], for example—but they have been separated by geographical and denominational differences and that has caused them to vote differently. The key to any kind of political impact is to get these people united in some way, so they can see that they are battling the same thing and need to be unified." As Weyrich tells the story, Falwell stopped him and said, "Go back to what you said earlier." Weyrich backtracked, but Falwell interrupted. "No, no," Falwell said. "You started out saying that there is something out there . . . what did you call that?" Weyrich thought for a moment and answered, "Oh, I said there is a moral majority." Falwell replied, "That's it," turned to his own associate in the meeting and said, "That's the name of the organization." The Moral Majority was born.[12]

As Falwell associate Ed Dobson (not to be confused with James Dobson, who is discussed below) said in explaining how formerly separatist fundamentalists entered politics in 1980, "The miracle of the Moral Majority was that, in just a matter of months, that whole concept [fundamentalist separatism] was shattered, and [fundamentalists] began registering to vote and getting involved."[13] It was not quite a miracle when one considers how the events of the seventies prepared fundamentalists and evangelicals for political involvement, but it appeared to many observers that the Moral Majority and the broader New Religious Right burst onto the political scene out of nowhere during the election of 1980.

During the election, the Moral Majority was only the most influential and visible of New Religious Right organizations. Another was a more loosely organized coalition called the Religious Roundtable. At a meeting held by the Religious Roundtable in Dallas, Reagan was the only candidate who appeared. Knowing it would be hostile territory, Carter declined the invitation, as did independent candidate John Anderson. At that meeting Reagan used a line suggested to him by evangelical Texas preacher James Robison. In a nod to the old rule of decorum that religion and politics should not mix and that preachers should not endorse candidates, Reagan told the group, "I know you can't endorse me, but I want you to know that I endorse you."

With the help of the New Religious Right, Reagan defeated Carter by a landslide in the electoral college (489 to 49) and 51 percent to 41 percent in the popular vote (independent John Anderson received 6.6 percent of the popular vote). While the Lou Harris Poll and some other analysts argued that Reagan would have lost had it not been for evangelical support, later analyses concluded that Reagan may have won even without the help of the New Religious Right. Regardless of which argument is ultimately correct, more significant from our vantage point today is that the election of 1980 marked the beginning of a political shift that would see evangelicals become a solid Republican voting bloc, while the New Religious Right would amass tremendous influence within the party. The election signaled that evangelicals and even many who had been separatist fundamentalists were willing to become more active in politics than ever before. The fact that the Moral Majority welcomed all kinds of religious conservatives, including Roman Catholics and Jews, also signaled the beginning of alliances between evangelicals and Catholics that was unheard of previously. The election of 1980 showed that evangelicals could partner with and be tutored by secular conservatives who had been working since the Goldwater defeat in 1964 to bring conservatism to the forefront of the Republican Party.

As a result of their desire to be part of the party apparatus, the Moral Majority and other New Religious Right organizations took strong positions not only on abortion, prayer in schools, and other issues that had animated Christian conservatives but also on the free-market economic policies of the Reagan administration, opposition to the Strategic Arms Limitation Treaty that the Carter administration had been pursuing with the Soviet Union, and even opposition to the agreement that led eventually to the United States relinquishing control over the Panama Canal. Like other lobby organizations, some New Religious Right groups issued voter report cards that tabulated the voting records of congressional representatives and senators. One such report card issued by an organization called Christian Voice purported to measure the morality of various votes even on issues such as reinstatement of the 1955 U.S. defense treaty with Taiwan, abolition of ethnic or gender quotas in higher education, and support for a constitutional amendment requiring a balanced budget. These issues were grouped together with prayer in schools and federal funding of abortion. Clearly this report card measured conservative voting habits but not necessarily morality. Some congressional representatives who were active Christians and generally known to be morally incorruptible scored quite low, while one who had been indicted in a FBI sting operation scored very high. A number of liberal Democratic congressional representatives who were targeted by the New Religious Right went down to defeat as the Republicans not only won the White House but also the Senate as well.[14]

The Christian Right

In 1980 and for some years thereafter, Falwell's Moral Majority garnered the lion's share of media attention among New Religious Right groups. It is debatable whether the Moral Majority was actually the most important organization in the movement. By 1990, the Moral Majority was defunct, and Pat Robertson's Christian Coalition would become the most visible Religious Right group. Because his organization had the word "Christian" in the title, the name for the entire movement changed from New Religious Right to Christian Right, which remains to this day the most popular term. Robertson had not been included in the group of pastors who helped Falwell develop the Moral Majority. While we cannot be sure just why Robertson was not consulted, it may have been because of a rivalry between Falwell and Robertson. Both had huge religious empires in Virginia, and both were accustomed to getting their own way more often than not.[15]

In addition to the rivalry, Falwell and Robertson also have an important theological difference. Although ordained as a Southern Baptist minister in 1960, Robertson is charismatic. Charismatic evangelicals are those who experience the Pentecostal gifts of the spirit but are not in Pentecostal denominations. The gifts of the spirit that Pentecostals and charismatics experience that other evangelicals do not are speaking in tongues, faith healing, and word of prophecy. Although these were experienced by New Testament Christians and are discussed in the Bible, all dispensationalist fundamentalists and many evangelicals believe such gifts are no longer operative. A typical point of view among noncharismatic evangelicals is that the ecstatic gifts of tongues and prophecy were sent by God to launch the church but ceased to be necessary in subsequent centuries. With regard to the charismatic gifts of the spirit, Martin says flatly, "Without question . . . the major reason for Robertson's exclusion [from early New Religious Right leadership] was his theology."[16]

Robertson is also quite different from Falwell in background and upbringing. Robertson was the son of an influential Virginia senator and graduated from the prestigious Washington and Lee College and Yale University Law School. After a conversion experience in 1956, he took a theological degree from New York Theological Seminary. Unlike Falwell, Tim LaHaye, D. James Kennedy, James Robison, and the other key figures in the early years of the New Religious Right, Robertson is not really a preacher. Although ordained, he has never pastored a church and rarely if ever preaches. Rather, he is a religious broadcaster. He founded WYAH-TV in Norfolk, Virginia, in 1961, the first television station in the country devoted solely to religious broadcasting. Within a few years the station evolved into the Christian Broadcasting Network (CBN) with the 700 Club as its flagship program. He would be primarily a religious broadcaster for the rest of his career. By the late 1990s, CBN had developed a variety of religious educational entities including the fully accredited Regent University and a fully accredited graduate school with programs in communications, business, counseling, theology, education, law, and public policy.[17] The 700 Club television broadcast combines talk show and nightly news formats. Much of the airtime is taken with Robertson talking to guests, talk-show style, and he usually has a sidekick, much as the famous talk-show host Johnny Carson of the seventies and eighties had Ed McMahan. Robertson spends a good deal of his broadcast time interpreting current events in light of scripture and sometimes in light of his own word of prophecy that he receives directly from God. Like other Pentecostal and charismatic television personalities, he sometimes performs faith healing on the air for television viewers scattered across America.

Like Falwell, throughout the sixties and seventies Robertson eschewed politics. In 1966 he even refused to use his considerable influence in Virginia to help his father's Senate reelection bid. His father lost by 600 votes. Even as late as the early 1980s, as others launched the Moral Majority, Robertson was staying clear of politics, even declaring at one point in 1980 that "active partisan politics is the wrong path for true evangelicals."[18] Within a few years, however, he could no longer resist the new wave of evangelical political engagement. He began to believe that while the Moral Majority, Christian Voice, Religious Roundtable, and other New Religious Right organizations attempted to influence elections at the highest levels, grassroots efforts might be more effective. Just months after saying that he was uninterested in politics, he reversed himself and formed the Freedom Council with a stated goal of putting trained Christian activists in every political precinct in America to influence the political system from the bottom up.

By the mid-1980s, Robertson was deeply involved in politics and even began to test the waters for a presidential bid of his own. In the spring of 1987, Robertson developed a campaign apparatus and later announced his candidacy. In early state primaries and caucuses Robertson did well. He might have won Michigan had it not been for a successful effort on the part of Vice President George H. W. Bush's team to gerrymander the precinct races in Bush's favor. Robertson challenged the maneuver in court, but the suit was eventually dismissed. To this day, Robertson believes he won Michigan. In the ever-important Iowa caucus, Robertson finished second behind Senator Robert Dole but ahead of Bush and Congressman Jack Kemp. Robertson's showing in Michigan and Iowa gave him momentum going into the New Hampshire primary, but it became clear there that his novice campaigners were outorganized. Bush won New Hampshire, beating Dole and Kemp, while Robertson finished fifth. Robertson's last chance to revive his flagging campaign was the Super Tuesday primaries that included many southern states, which he thought would be his strongest base of support. Bush won every Super Tuesday primary, while Robertson finished third in his own state of Virginia. Robertson had said he had to win South Carolina in order to remain a viable candidate. He did not and ceased to be a serious contender. He remained in the race for some months thereafter, but only to keep Religious Right issues before the people; he had no chance to win.[19]

No political scientist or commentator believes that Robertson could actually have won the presidency. Even the seasoned politicos in the New Religious Right understood this. At one point when Robertson informed Weyrich that God had told him he would be president, the longtime political organizer responded, "Did [God] say when? Because it isn't going to be this year."[20]

Making Robertson's bid all the more difficult were the infamous televangelist scandals of 1987 and 1988. First, Jim Bakker of the PTL (Praise the Lord or People That Love) network's husband and wife team of Jim and Tammy Faye admitted to a sexual tryst with former church secretary Jessica Hahn. The *Charlotte Observer* reported the brief affair and also that one of Bakker's associates had paid Hahn more than a quarter million dollars to keep quiet. That was just the tip of the iceberg. The IRS, the Federal Communications Commission, and the Justice Department for years had investigated the PTL and the Bakker's Christian amusement park called Heritage USA for alleged financial mismanagement. The Bakkers lived an extravagant lifestyle on the millions they raked in from their broadcasts, often through questionable appeals and promises to viewers. When the empire came down as a result of fraudulent fund-raising, Bakker was sentenced to forty-five years in prison for having defrauded his viewers of $158 million, and the ministry was sued by the IRS for $56 million in back taxes. The public also learned that Tammy Faye had done a stint in the Betty Ford Clinic for drug dependency, while Jim admitted to being an abuser of valium. He would be in prison until 1994. The entire story broke in early 1987 as

Robertson was trying to repackage himself as a serious politician and not a television preacher. Robertson, Falwell, and many other television ministries suffered a precipitous drop in contributions, and a *New York Times* poll found that 65 percent of Americans had an unfavorable opinion of television evangelists.[21]

The second scandal broke in 1988 after the New Hampshire primary, while Robertson was gearing up for Super Tuesday. Pentecostal television preacher Jimmy Swaggart in Baton Rouge, Louisiana, was one of the most popular television preachers in terms of viewing audience. A cousin of rock-and-roll legend Jerry Lee Lewis, Swaggart was a honky-tonk piano man himself and often played on his television show. He was an even better preacher, usually pacing back and forth across his immense stage, leather Bible opened in hand, weeping as he spoke, just before launching into a fearsome denunciation of sin followed by a call to repentance. In 1988, Swaggart was photographed taking a prostitute into a motel on the outskirts of New Orleans. Swaggart's was purely a sex scandal, much less complicated but no less shocking to his followers than the PTL debacle, which Swaggart had helped expose. Embarrassed by yet another televangelist scandal, Robertson accused the Bush campaign of leaking the Swaggart story to the press to tar all television ministries once again.

Actually, another Assemblies of God minister, Marvin Gorman, was responsible for the photographs. He had hired a private detective to shadow Swaggart in retaliation for Swaggart exposing to their Assemblies of God denomination Gorman's sexual affair the year before. Gorman confronted Swaggart after taking the photos and demanded that Swaggart come clean publicly. When Swaggart refused, Gorman reported the matter to the Assemblies of God headquarters in Springfield, Missouri. Apparently, a Bakker associate who was angry at Swaggart for his scathing criticism of the Bakkers scandal had a hand in leaking the story to Ted Koppel of ABC's *Nightline* program. Swaggart eventually gave a weeping confession to his followers but then refused to accept his denomination's disciplinary action because it would have required him to stay off the air for up to a year. Three years later, in 1991, he was pulled over by police in Indio, California, for driving on the wrong side of the street. With him was another prostitute. This time Swaggart told his drastically diminished congregation and television audience that his personal life was none of their business.[22]

While the Bakker and Swaggart scandals hurt many evangelical television ministries, they were not the reason that Robertson was unsuccessful in his bid for the presidency. It is fairly clear now that Robertson could not garner even a majority of the evangelical vote. Most of Robertson's support came from the charismatic wing of evangelicalism. As an evangelical aid in the Bush camp put it, many evangelicals would not vote for Robertson for the same reasons nonevangelicals would not vote for him.[23] Many evangelicals, including Southern Baptists, the largest Protestant denomination in America, are suspicious of tongues speaking, faith healing, and, more significantly, directing hurricanes. While in prayer in 1985 on a *700 Club* broadcast, Robertson ordered Hurricane Gloria to turn away from the Virginia coast. The hurricane moved north, hitting Long Island. Later Robertson linked the event to his political ambitions, saying that "if I couldn't move a hurricane, I could hardly move a nation."[24] Among evangelicals, charismatics and Pentecostals are virtually the only ones who would put much stock in such a claim, and fundamentalists reject charismatic gifts outright. The most reputable study of the political behavior of evangelical preachers in the election of 1988 showed that 43 percent of charismatic and Pentecostal preachers named Robertson as their first choice, 28 percent of Baptists, 18 percent of fundamentalists, and 10 percent of Holiness and Adventists.[25] Falwell and most other New Religious Right leaders supported Bush.

The most significant outgrowth of Robertson's quixotic bid for the presidency was the development of the Christian Coalition, which would become the most visible and important Christian Right organization of the 1990s. After the election, Robertson received a call from a friend telling him that local Robertson campaign groups all over the country needed direction. The campaign had started a grassroots Christian Right movement that needed to be sustained. In January 1989, Robertson attended a dinner in Washington, D.C., held in his honor by a conservative organization called Students for America, which had designated Robertson their "Man of the Year." Seated next to him was Ralph Reed, a young Republican activist who was writing a Ph.D. dissertation at Emory University. Reed and Robertson had met once before at Dartmouth College during the New Hampshire primary. During the dinner, Robertson told Reed about his idea for a new political organization and asked Reed to be part of it. Soon thereafter Reed sent a memo to Robertson with ideas for the new group, then heard nothing from Robertson for months. When Reed attended the kickoff meeting for the new organization, which had no name at the time, Robertson introduced Reed as the first staff member. Reed was as surprised as everyone else at this announcement.[26]

Reed was not yet thirty when the Christian Coalition began. A talented historian, Reed was awarded best undergraduate senior essay in history at the University of Georgia in 1983, and the essay was then published in the *Georgia Historical Quarterly* as "'Fighting the Devil with Fire': Carl Vinson's Victory over Tom Watson in the 1918 Tenth District Democratic Primary."[27] That same year Reed experienced an evangelical conversion at the Pentecostal Evangel Assembly of God Church in Camp Springs, Maryland. He would later become Presbyterian. Following his conversion, he continued his college interest in politics. He had already been active as a volunteer for the Reagan campaign in 1980, as a Senate intern in the summer of 1981, and as executive director of the National College Republicans from 1983 to 1985. Reed aided conservative North Carolina Senator Jesse Helms in his 1984 re-election bid, and, ironically, supported congressional representative Jack Kemp's presidential effort in 1988, not Robertson's. Reed's interest in history also continued as he entered the Ph.D. program at Emory University, where he wrote his dissertation with prominent historian Dan Carter. The dissertation was titled "Fortresses of Faith: Design and Experience at Southern Evangelical Colleges, 1830–1900."

Reed accepted Robertson's appointment, and the new organization took the name Christian Coalition. Reed headed the effort to create a grassroots approach to Christian Right politics. He proved to be a genius at political mobilization, and, moreover, put a youthful, friendly, choirboy face on evangelical activism. Under Reed, the Christian Coalition began to assemble state and local chapters that helped Christians become activists. The national Christian Coalition chartered the state chapters, and the charters had to be renewed each year. Local chapters were affiliates of the state chapters that were affiliated with the national organization, but state and local units received no funding from the national organization. This chartering arrangement allowed for a certain degree of autonomy for state and local chapters but also gave the national Christian Coalition the ability to disavow local groups that became loose cannons. As long as state and local chapters stayed in line, the national Christian Coalition would provide training for local activists, helping them run for school boards and other offices, teaching them how to lobby congressmembers and influence the local media, and helping them set up voter registration drives. This approach proved highly successful. By 1995 the Coalition had 1.6 million members, 50 state affiliates, and 1,600 local chapters. Beginning in 1992, the Christian Coalition held an annual "Road to Victory" rally where representatives from Coalition affiliates around the country gathered to hear prominent conservative politicians and nationally recognized Christian political activists.[28]

In conjunction with its grassroots vision, the Christian Coalition was led by laypeople from evangelical churches rather than by pastors. This was a marked difference from Falwell's Moral Majority, where nearly all the leaders were preachers. This facilitated the major difference between the two organizations. The Christian Coalition wanted to influence the political system from the bottom up, rather than starting with the presidency and expecting the influence to filter down. Moreover, the Christian Coalition institution-alized evangelical political activism rather than having it geared to election cycles. In other words, local activists were going to be an ongoing presence in politics, not merely visible during national campaigns every two years for Congress and four years for the presidency. As Reed put it, "The Christian community got it backwards in the 1980s. We tried to charge Washington when we should have been focusing on the states. The real battles of concern to Christians are in the neighborhoods, school boards, city councils and state legislatures."[29] This institutionalization of evangelical politics resulted in the most significant achievement of the Christian Coalition—the Christian Right became a constituency of the Republican Party. As political scientist Duane Oldfield puts it, "Whereas previous movement groups had had inci-dental dealings with the party, the coalition, from its beginnings, made or-ganizing within the party a central focus of its overall activity."[30] At the 1992 Republican National Convention, it was reported that 300 of the 2,000 del-egates were from the Christian Coalition, and by 1996 the figure had climbed to 500.[31]

Along the way toward institutionalizing the Christian Right as a major constituency of the Republican Party, Reed and the organization had to withstand a good deal of criticism, some of it of their own making. Reed made a few ominous statements about using "stealth" candidates, painting his face, and using guerilla warfare tactics to win elections. The secular me-dia used these statements to argue that there was something sinister and un-derhanded about the Christian Coalition. Reed also said, "We think the Lord is going to give us this nation back one precinct at a time."[32] He came to re-alize, however, that the so-called profamily conservative voter was about one-third of the electorate. Most of the Christian Coalition's success is at-tributable to the mobilization of previously untapped conservative resources in the form of evangelical Christians, conservative Roman Catholics, and a few Orthodox Jews. Reed and the Christian Coalition concentrated on niche marketing to mobilize this sizeable minority rather than following the Moral Majority model of presuming to speak for the majority of Americans.

By the mid-nineties, the mantle of leadership in the Christian Right had passed from the Moral Majority, which had gone out of existence in 1989, to the Christian Coalition. Reed resigned from the Christian Coalition in 1997, however, and since then the organization has not enjoyed nearly the visibil-ity it did under his leadership. By the late 1990s, the Christian Coalition had been so successful in institutionalizing the larger Christian Right into the Republican Party that there was no longer the need for a single organization.

Today there are a variety of Christian Right organizations and individuals, all with varying degrees of influence within the Republican Party. One of these is James Dobson and Focus on the Family. Dobson earned a Ph.D. in psychology at the University of Southern California in 1967 and served for fourteen years as a clinical professor at the University of Southern California School of Medicine. In 1970 he wrote a book entitled *Dare to Discipline* that became immensely popular with parents, eventually selling more than 4.5 million copies. He followed with a string of books on marital relationships and child rearing that sold millions of copies, allowing him to found Focus on the Family in 1977, a nonprofit organization headquartered in Colorado Springs, Colorado. A major feature of Focus is Dobson's daily radio program that is broadcast on more than 3,000 stations in North America and to 160 countries worldwide in seven different languages.

Dobson's first foray into politics was his founding of the Family Research Council lobby group in Washington, D.C., in 1983, which has been active in Washington politics ever since. In 2004, Dobson spun out Focus on the Family Action, which unlike the original Focus on the Family, is not tax-exempt and can therefore be active in partisan electoral politics. He was also instrumental in the founding of the "I Vote Values" campaign, which was a Christian Right effort to help secure George W. Bush's reelection as president. Some estimate that 7 to 9 million new evangelical voters attended the polls in the election, presumably to vote for Bush.[33] More than any other Christian Right leader in the past, Dobson commands respect from a wide array of evangelicals who take their political cues from him. In addition to the abortion issue, he has taken the lead in opposing gay rights and particularly gay marriage.

The Evangelical Left and Others

While the most visible manifestation of evangelical politics is the Christian Right, there is a smaller but nevertheless significant evangelical left as well. While there are many organizations that could be considered, the longest running and most influential evangelical left group is the Sojourners Community.

Sojourners was founded by Jim Wallis, who is still its driving force. Wallis was from the Detroit area and grew up in an evangelical church. Like many evangelicals who came of age in the 1960s Civil Rights era, he became concerned and somewhat disillusioned by the racism he saw manifested in his own church and noticed how little evangelical emphasis there was on the issue of poverty. Moreover, like many young people, he was opposed to the Vietnam War. In 1971, he and others of like mind at Trinity Evangelical Divinity School near Chicago founded a magazine that was originally called the *The Post American*, a title that reflected the group's desire to extricate the teachings of the gospel from its captivity to middle-class American values, especially materialism and nationalism. *The Post American* emphasized the biblical notions of peace and justice. Wallis likes to tell how the early group once took a copy of the New Testament and cut out all the passages that dealt with poverty. The Bible literally fell apart once those portions were excised, Wallis's point being that the Christian gospel cannot hold together without a biblical emphasis on justice for the poor.

In 1975, the group moved to one of the poorest regions of Washington, D.C., called Columbia Heights, and changed the name of the magazine to *Sojourners*, a biblical metaphor that means that Christians live fully in the present world but as pilgrims committed to a different order. Living among the poor and disenfranchised was part of the design of this alternative expression of evangelical Christianity. For many years, the Sojourners members lived in a community, sharing their goods and incomes in common, resembling a monastic order. Identifying with the poor of their neighborhood, they started after-school tutoring for children along with a variety of other programs. Over the years, they succeeded in sending a string of poor kids from the ghetto to college and then into successful careers. At the same time the group ministered locally, members also took leadership positions in national and international peace and justice movements such as the Nuclear Freeze of the 1980s, the Free South Africa movement, Witness for Peace, and more recently the Call to Renewal. The latter effort has, among other things, stressed that overcoming poverty should be a nonpartisan issue.[34]

Over the years, Wallis has written a number of books, including his 2005 *God's Politics: Why the Right Gets It Wrong and the Left Doesn't Get It.*[35] The title reflects Wallis's belief that Christian involvement in politics should not be tied to either party, a criticism he often makes about the Christian Right's residence within the Republican Party. Wallis himself risked such party identification with the Democrats when he took on increased visibility nationally after the 2004 presidential election. Democratic Party leaders reached out to him, fearing that the party was viewed as a secular entity uninterested in religious issues and incapable of attracting religious voters. Party leaders consulted Wallis, who had developed a reputation for being orthodox, biblical, and even conservative theologically while for the most part being liberal politically. They recognized that the inability to speak in religious terms was a serious liability in today's political climate.

As the Sojourners Community took root in Washington, *Sojourners* magazine became the staple periodical of the evangelical left. Carrying a variety of articles on everything from worship and theology to culture and political activism, the general tone of the magazine could be characterized as politically liberal, the counterpoint to the Christian Right. Whereas voices in the Christian Right often emphasize America's Christian roots, *Sojourners* stresses that America, like all nations, will come under the judgment of God for how it treats the poor and underprivileged of society. While the Christian Right has recently made opposition to gay rights and gay marriage a leading part of its agenda, *Sojourners*, while not fully affirming the gay lifestyle, is often more concerned about homophobia and discrimination against gay people by evangelicals and others who go by the name Christian. There is one issue on which the Christian Right and the evangelical left are in agreement, and that is abortion. Even here, however, there is a difference. Wallis and *Sojourners* have adopted the "seamless garment" ethic that was articulated by the late Joseph Cardinal Bernardin, Pope John Paul II, and other Roman Catholics. This ethic joins concern for the poor, opposition to war and other forms of violence, opposition to capital punishment, and opposition to abortion. The seamless garment stance is also called "consistent life."

Conclusion

Clearly, as we have seen in this chapter, whatever evangelicals believe about politics, those views are more prevalent in the public square today than was the case before 1980. After Carter's successful run for the presidency in 1976, the general rule of decorum and political liberalism's dictum concerning religion and politics began to erode significantly. From 1980 to 2000, bringing one's religion into political campaigns was not nearly as politically risky as before, but it was still optional. In 2000, George W. Bush ran against Vice President Al Gore, and Joseph Lieberman was Gore's vice-presidential running mate. Bush was a born-again Methodist who spoke openly of his conversion in the 1980s. Gore, a lifelong Southern Baptist, joined Bush in talking openly about how his faith helped form his political views and policies, while Lieberman, an orthodox Jew, joined in with his own rendition of the integration of faith and politics. From that election forward, discussing how religion relates to one's political positions was no longer just optional. Rather, after 2000 the American people seemed to expect their candidates for office to be forthcoming about their personal faith and how it relates to politics. In the 2004 presidential campaign when Bush ran for reelection against Senator John Kerry, a Roman Catholic, Bush was by this time accustomed to talking about religion. Kerry, being a liberal New Englander, was from the old school where the general rule of decorum and political liberalism still reigned. Religion was a private matter for him. When it became clear that his campaign was faltering in part because of his reluctance to discuss faith, he attempted to bring religion into his speeches. Unaccustomed to discussing religion publicly, he seemed uncomfortable, despite the fact that he was a devout Catholic believer. In the meantime, the "I Vote Values" campaign energized another swath of evangelical voters, and Bush won reelection 51 percent to 48 percent in the popular vote and 286 to 252 in the electoral college.

For better or worse, religion now appears to be a prerequisite topic of campaign conversation for presidential candidates. This remarkable change from the general rule of decorum and political liberalism of a generation ago is attributable largely to the work of the Christian Right. Efforts of key figures such as Francis Schaeffer, Jerry Falwell, Pat Robertson, and James Dobson are responsible for the Christian Right taking a status in the Republican Party today similar to that of labor unions in the Democratic Party in the 1960s. The Christian Right is the largest constituency of the Republican Party, and evangelicals are the most reliable Republican voters. Once seen as a dangerous threat to the democratic process, most scholars and many commentators now concede that the Christian Right is a staple of American politics and will be for the foreseeable future.

Still, a 2006 study by the Pew Research Center found that only about 20 percent of white evangelicals consider themselves members of the Religious Right, while only 7 percent of white evangelicals consider themselves members of the Religious Left.[36] Sociologist Christian Smith's research in the late 1990s yielded similar findings. For every evangelical he interviewed who supported a Christian Right leader or organization, he found another who opposed the Christian Right.[37] Because they are so much in the public eye, these two groups, Christian Right and evangelical left, are worth trying to understand. We must keep in mind, however, that just as is the case with the issues of gender, race, and gay rights covered in the previous chapters, so it is in politics. Evangelicals are not just diverse as a group. Rather, even individual evangelicals hold views that are fluid and unpredictable. As Smith wrote in 2000, "It is not simply a matter of a dominant evangelical view qualified by internal diversity. Nor is there simply a spectrum of evangelical political views. More accurately, evangelicals express a range of assumptions, beliefs, thoughts, and feelings on a variety of distinct issues that intersect and combine in complicated and sometimes improbable ways."[38]

What do evangelicals want to do with their political power? Paint their faces, travel at night, support stealth candidates, and take over America one precinct at a time? Hardly. About 40 percent of evangelicals doubt whether

America ever was a Christian nation, and the majority of evangelicals who do believe this mean at least six different things when they say America was once Christian. These six are (1) a nation of religious freedom; (2) a nation that once had a majority of Christians; (3) a nation whose government was once based on Christian principles; (4) a nation that had theistic Founding Fathers; (5) a nation whose people once held to Christian principles and values; and (6) a nation where the public and official expression of Christian values was once the norm.[39] In other words, there is no one idea in mind when the majority of evangelicals say America was once a Christian nation. As Smith found in his study, the vast majority of evangelicals support and practice civility and tolerance of non-Christian views and almost universally reject efforts to force Christian values on non-Christians. The core method evangelicals espouse for influencing the culture is through personal example built on relationships with unbelievers.[40] Evangelicals want from politics what most Americans want—to know that their voices are heard and their interests considered. As law professor and church-state expert Douglas Laycock has said, in a nation where all groups are minorities—religious, ethnic, or otherwise—almost everyone at some time fears that they could be persecuted by the majority made up of everyone else. Evangelicals are no different. In Smith's study, almost all of the evangelicals interviewed acknowledged that they do not personally experience discrimination, yet they still identified discrimination against evangelicals as a major problem.[41]

Certainly, there are evangelicals in the Christian Right who want to take over the country and impose their values, but the same is true of some secular groups as well. To believe that evangelicals can best be summed up by the most outrageous statements made by Christian Right leaders covered in this chapter is to confuse what some sociologists call "report talk" with "rapport talk." Report talk consists of a group's actual intentions, while rapport talk is what groups use to maintain their own identity. This helps explain why one study of the Christian Coalition in the 1990s found two distinct languages used. One was a language of "restoration" that Christian Coalition leaders used in their rallies. They spoke of restoring a Christian America, a thought that is frightening for non-Christians. In the political campaigns in public, however, these same Christian Coalition leaders seemed to accept the fact that no one group is ever going to dominate the country. They not only spoke but also acted as if they were just one group among many in the contest for political influence. In public they used the language of "recognition," arguing that they wanted their concerns heard and addressed. The author of this study concluded that the language of restoration was like rapport talk used to rally the troops and create and maintain a group identity. Recognition was like report talk—i.e., what evangelicals really wanted, which was to know that their concerns were recognized as legitimate in a pluralist democracy.[42]

Notes

1. Quoted in William Martin, *With God on Our Side: The Rise of the Religious Right in America* (New York: Broadway Books, 1996), 36. This book is the most thorough study of the rise of the New Religious Right through 1996 when the book appeared. It was the companion volume to a PBS film documentary of the same title.

2. Statistics from Martin, *With God on Our Side*, 76.

3. For the stories of the sex education battles in Anaheim and Kanawha County, see Martin, *With God on Our Side*. Martin devotes a chapter to each controversy.

4. Martin, *With God on Our Side*, 114.

5. Both quotes in Martin, *With God on Our Side*, 149–50.

6. Quoted in Martin, *With God on Our Side*, 173.

7. Quoted in Martin, *With God on Our Side*, 189. See Barry Hankins, *Francis Schaeffer: Fundamentalist Warrior, Evangelical Prophet* (Grand Rapids, Michigan: Eerdmans, 2009).

8. Quoted in Dinesh D'Souza, *Falwell: Before the Millennium: A Critical Biography* (Chicago: Regnery Gateway, 1984), 42.

9. See Barry Hankins, *God's Rascal: J. Frank Norris and the Beginnings of Southern Fundamentalism* (Lexington: University Press of Kentucky, 1996).

10. Susan Friend Harding, *The Book of Jerry Falwell: Fundamentalist Language and Politics* (Princeton, New Jersey: Princeton University Press, 2000), 17–18.

11. Martin, *With God on Our Side*, 200; see also D'Souza, *Falwell: Before the Millennium*, 105–14.

12. Quoted in Martin, *With God on Our Side*, 202.

13. Erling Jorstad, *The Politics of Moralism: The New Christian Right in American Life* (Minneapolis, Minnesota: Augsburg Publishing House, 1981).

14. Martin, *With God on Our Side*, 258.

15. Martin, *With God on Our Side*, 258.

16. Justin Watson, *The Christian Coalition: Dreams of Restoration, Demands for Recognition* (New York: St. Martin's Press, 1997), 30.

17. Quoted in Martin, *With God on Our Side*, 259.

18. For a more detailed coverage of Robertson's campaign, see Martin, *With God on Our Side*, 258–98.

19. Quoted in Martin, *With God on Our Side*, 294.

20. Martin, *With God on Our Side*, 273–74.

21. At the time this chapter was written, Swaggart's confession could be accessed at www.americanrhetoric.com/speeches/jswaggartapologysermon.html. For the Bakker/PTL scandal see articles in *Time* magazine, March 30, 1987, 70; April 6, 1987, 60–64; May 4, 1987, 82; May 18, 1987, 65; June 8, 1987, 70–74; August 3, 1987,

48–49; and October 16, 1989, 65. For the Swaggart scandals see *Time*, March 7, 1988, 46–48; April 18, 1988, 33; July 22, 1991, 28; October 28, 1991, 35.

22. Martin, *With God on Our Side*, 290.

23. Quoted in Martin, *With God on Our Side*, 268.

24. Martin, *With God on Our Side*, 295, citing the work of political scientist John Green.

25. Watson, *The Christian Coalition*, 51–52.

26. Reed's article can be found in the *Georgia Historical Quarterly* 67:4 (Winter 1983): 451–79.

27. Watson, *The Christian Coalition*, 54.

28. Quoted in Watson, *The Christian Coalition*, 63.

29. Quoted in Watson, *The Christian Coalition*, 64. Watson cites Duane M. Old-field, *The Right and the Righteousness: The Christian Right Confronts the Republican Party* (Lanham, Maryland: Rowman & Littlefield, 1996), 190.

30. Watson, *The Christian Coalition*, 64.

31. Quoted in Watson, *The Christian Coalition*, 77.

32. Peter Heltzel, *Lion on the Loose: Jesus, Evangelicals, and American Politics, 1996–2006* (New Haven, Connecticut: Yale University Press, forthcoming).

33. The Sojourners Web site can be accessed at www.sojourners.com.

34. Jim Wallis, *God's Politics: Why the Right Gets It Wrong and the Left Doesn't Get It* (San Francisco, California: HarpersSanFrancisco, 2005).

35. "Many Americans Uneasy with Mix of Religion and Politics," The Pew Forum on Religion and Public Life, August 24, 2006. This and other Pew research on religion and American culture can be found on the Web site www.pewforum.org.

36. Smith, *Christian America?*, 122.

37. Smith, *Christian America?*, 94.

38. Smith, *Christian America?*, 26–35.

39. Smith, *Christian America?*, 42–45.

40. Smith, *Christian America?*, 70.

41. The "report talk" and "rapport talk" imagery comes from Smith, *Christian America?*, 56. He is relying on Deborah Tannen, *You Just Don't Understand: Women and Men in Conversation* (New York: Ballantine Books, 1990). The study of the Christian Coalition is in Justin Watson, *The Christian Coalition: Dreams of Restoration, Demands for Recognition*, cited earlier in this chapter.

CHAPTER SEVEN

~

Back to the Academy

Evangelical Scholars and the American Mind

As key leaders in the Christian Right have succeeded in getting evangelicals to be more politically active, another very different set of evangelical elites has encouraged evangelicals to think more and act less. This is a difficult challenge for people who have been marked by activism throughout their history. While twentieth-century evangelicals ranged from militant separatism to moderate cultural reengagement and even the political activism of the Christian Right, they were never at the forefront of academic endeavors. Many critics and commentators believed that fundamentalism was inherently anti-intellectual. Columbia University historian Richard Hofstadter included fundamentalists prominently in his 1963 Pulitzer Prize–winning book *Anti-Intellectualism in American Life*. Moving almost seamlessly, sometimes in the same sentence, from the Ku Klux Klan to the Scopes trial to the defense of Prohibition and the campaign against Al Smith, Hofstadter portrayed antimodernist fundamentalism as "frantic," "desperate," panic stricken, and rhetorically violent. Hofstadter almost certainly had not read *The Fundamentals*, whose moderate tone defied these descriptions. Billy Sunday was his favorite example, and all the fundamentalists Hofstadter mentioned in his chapter on "The Revolt against Modernity" were militant and rabid—J. Frank Norris, the Fort Worth pastor who shot and killed a man in his own church office; Carl McIntire, the famous red-baiting anticommunist who tried to portray Billy Graham as a left-leaning heretic; the anti-Semitic Gerald L. K. Smith; and the fascist-leaning Gerald Winrod. The only mention of the erudite fundamentalist scholar J. Gresham Machen was to say that McIntire had once been associated with him.

Hofstadter spoke of fundamentalism in the 1920s as being in the "waning phase of its history" and as experiencing a "shrinkage in its numbers," neither of which were true. Whereas an earlier scholar had written that after 1800 Americans were given the hard choice of being either religious or intelligent, Hofstadter merely corrected the date to argue that this actually did not occur until the rise of modernism in the late nineteenth century. Hofstadter had a very loose working definition of anti-intellectualism, if indeed he had one at all, and he acknowledged in his Prefatory Note that his work lacked documentation and was "largely a personal book, whose factual details are organized and dominated by my views." It is thus hard to read the book today as anything other than a genteel expression of prejudice in which Hofstadter characterizes nearly every type of thinking other than his own as anti-intellectual. This was evident even more in his discussion of Catholicism than of fundamentalism. He stated flatly that the Catholic Church had "failed to develop an intellectual tradition in America or to produce its own class of intellectuals capable either of exercising authority among Catholics or of mediating between the Catholic mind and the secular or Protestant mind." A significant part of the problem, according to Hofstadter, was not enough Catholic millionaires to endow universities and the fact that "there is not known to me one Bishop, Archbishop or Cardinal whose father or mother was a college graduate."[1]

The Scandal of the Evangelical Mind

The current view of evangelical intellectual life is more sophisticated than Hofstadter's interpretation was. His charge of fundamentalist anti-intellectualism is partly true but overlysimplistic. In 1994, evangelical historian Mark Noll wrote *The Scandal of the Evangelical Mind*, in which he argued that the twentieth century had indeed been a disaster for evangelical thinking. Noll's argument helps explain why there was a noticeable absence of evangelical participation in twentieth-century scholarly conversation. Noll was not talking about an absence of Christian colleges, for there are many of these. Evangelical liberal arts colleges, however, exist to train undergraduates from a Christian perspective in disciplines whose core features and trends are set by the larger secular academy. Such colleges do not attempt to set or even influence the intellectual agendas of academic life. Beyond this institutional reason for the scandal of evangelical thinking was the problem of the evangelical culture. The evangelical ethos, Noll argues, generally has been activist, populist, pragmatic, and utilitarian. Recall that activism is one of Bebbington's four evangelical characteristics that we have been using throughout this book.

When evangelicals engage in activism, they do so in populist, pragmatic, and utilitarian ways. This means that rather than reflecting deeply on social and intellectual problems, evangelicals in the twentieth century had a tendency to act immediately to remedy perceived ills. The populist tendency meant that the masses of believers serve as the court of adjudication as to which ideas evangelicals would adopt. As one would expect, the ideas that win popular approval are the ones that seem pragmatically useful, in essence a utilitarian approach to ideas.

This has not always been so for evangelicals. The scandal that resulted from twentieth-century evangelical developments stood in stark contrast to the history of evangelical scholarship in the eighteenth and nineteenth centuries. As discussed in chapter one, Jonathan Edwards, a key figure in the development of American evangelicalism, was also the leading intellectual in America during his lifetime and one of the few truly original thinkers America has ever produced. In the late eighteenth century and into the nineteenth evangelicals continued this tradition of serious intellectual endeavor, largely by appropriating Scottish Common Sense Realism. Evangelical Protestant thinkers at some of the most prestigious Ivy League universities developed a compelling synthesis of the Scottish Enlightenment and Protestant theology, the result being a theology that was in many ways central to intellectual conversation in America into the late nineteenth century.

During the era when nineteenth-century evangelical Protestants were at the forefront of public intellectual conversations, most of the leading colleges and even some of the elite state universities had preacher presidents, and the intellectual life of these universities was at least broadly Protestant if not overtly evangelical. Before the advent of the professionalized, elective undergraduate curriculum pioneered at Harvard and the German model of graduate education that came to America at Johns Hopkins, the classical liberal arts education was the norm. Many colleges required seniors to take a capstone course in moral philosophy that was often taught by the university president. This course brought together the arts and sciences under an integrated rubric of Christian moral thought.

Even when evangelicalism was in its intellectual heyday, however, evangelical thinkers were developing bad habits that would hurt their cause later. Specifically, they were unself-conscious and unreflective about their synthesis of evangelicalism and the Enlightenment, the result being that they assumed the best of science and theory would always harmonize easily with the best of theology. Such harmony had been the case when Baconian science and Common Sense Realism dominated American intellectual life, but it was not so when the scientific world began to shift away from the inductive

Baconian emphasis on categorization of plain facts to a more theoretical approach to science such as Darwinism. In effect, the wider academic world of the late nineteenth century came to view the entire universe differently than had been the case earlier. Through the eighteenth century, virtually all scholars viewed the universe as static and mechanistic—that is, its basic features were created by God and fixed. Beginning in the early nineteenth century, then exploding onto the academic scene after Darwin, was the view that the universe was dynamic and organic—that is, ever changing and evolving. In conjunction with this shift in basic worldview was a larger shift in higher education itself toward scholarship that was judged on the basis of its usefulness in reforming and building a culture rather than judged according to transcendent standards of what is true.

American Protestants responded in different ways to this intellectual revolution. As we saw in our discussion of the fundamentalist-modernist controversy in chapter two, modernist or liberal Protestants adjusted theology to fit modern modes of thought. Theological truths themselves came to be viewed as dynamic and organic, ever changing, ever evolving, and ever progressing. Fundamentalists responded with the militant defense of the traditional faith in the face of the modernist challenges. Most people, as is the case in most culture wars, were somewhere in between these two responses.

When the fundamentalist-modernist controversy seemed to signal that the modernist adjustment of theology to science resulted in the loss of key theological truths, evangelical intellectual confidence gave way to bewilderment. That confidence had been forged through the synthesis of Baconian science and the Scottish Enlightenment with Protestant theology; the bewilderment resulted from the fact that the evangelical synthesis that had been in the mainstream in the 1870s was by 1925 something of a laughingstock. Faced with what now seemed like a scientific threat, evangelicals and fundamentalists began to opt out of mainstream intellectual endeavors and adopt the warfare approach to science that resulted in the Scopes trial, which became a symbol of the evangelical tendency to move out of the mainstream of intellectual life in other areas as well. It was not that evangelicals were becoming anti-intellectual, they just found themselves to be intellectual in a way that differed from the norm in the universities. Fundamentalists still emphasized the importance of study, but they wanted study of the Bible disconnected from the concerns of mainstream science, the social sciences, and the humanities. Their easy assumption that Protestant thinking would always harmonize with the best secular thinking, and their unself-conscious and unreflective appropriation of Baconian science and the Scottish Enlightenment, left them unprepared to develop distinctly Christian ways of thinking about a variety of academic subjects. Noll calls all this "the intellectual disaster of fundamentalism," and it took most of the rest of the twentieth century for evangelicals to start to overcome the disaster.

Science was particularly disastrous for evangelical thinking. As discussed in chapter three, nearly all fundamentalists and many evangelicals moved from the antievolution of the Scopes era to Creation Science as an alternative to mainstream scientific conversations that take place in universities and at scholarly conferences. Evangelicals did this largely because they move intuitively and literally from the text of Genesis 1 and 2 to the area of science. Essentially, this was an example of Bebbington's Biblicism and activism coming together in a populist, pragmatic, and utilitarian way. Antievolutionism and Creation Science were populist, having wide appeal among the masses of evangelicals, largely because these movements seem intuitively to honor scripture. In other words, when Creation Science billed itself as science wrought straight out of the Bible, the movement appealed to evangelical Biblicism. Antievolutionism and Creation Science were also pragmatic movements in that they addressed practically the challenges modern science posed for evangelicals. These movements were utilitarian in that they were useful in the fundamentalist and evangelical desire to resist secular culture. The scholarly alternative of carefully developing scientific thinking from Christian perspectives that might take a couple of generations was, by contrast, unappealing to evangelicals who tend to address problems with a great sense of immediacy. As Noll wrote in *The Scandal of the Evangelical Mind:* "The tendency of American evangelicals, when confronted with a problem, is to act. For the sake of Christian thinking, that tendency must be suppressed."[2] In the area of science, evangelical activism was not suppressed.

The situation has been only marginally better for Intelligent Design. Again, as we saw in chapter three, ID started as a movement among some serious scientists and mathematicians with the potential for substantive dialogue within mainstream science. Fairly quickly, however, ID became significantly political with populist ID proponents encouraging school districts to adopt a "teach the controversy" policy when in fact there is virtually no controversy in the academic world over the question of whether or not evolution is a fact. Rather, controversy in the academy almost exclusively has to do with how evolution took place. Once again, as with Creation Science, it seems that evangelicals have proven too populist, pragmatic, and utilitarian, not to mention impatient, to wait for ID to work its way through academic, scholarly channels, a process that might take a century. Instead, ID has moved to political strategies and has appealed to the masses in order to further an evangelical agenda.

This tendency to opt out of mainstream science for activist, populist, pragmatic, and utilitarian reasons has not been the strategy of science professors in evangelical colleges. Most science professors in such schools are theistic evolutionists or progressive creationists attempting to harmonize their faith with science, much as their nineteenth-century evangelical forebears did. In this respect, not only do the masses of evangelicals oppose mainstream science but they also pay little attention to their own evangelical college professors who attempt to remain in contact with the broader scientific community. Creation Science and now ID serve as the preferred science for tens of millions of evangelicals, not only in America but also around the world. According to Noll, the adoption of Creation Science is particularly puzzling in that it relies on a biblical interpretation, specifically flood geology, that no responsible Christian teacher in the history of the church ever endorsed before the twentieth century. It nevertheless came to dominate worldwide evangelicalism.[3]

In *The Scandal of the Evangelical Mind* Noll critiqued not only Creation Science but dispensational premillennialism as well. *Scandal* appeared in 1994, just three years after the first Gulf War in which UN forces led by U.S. president George H. W. Bush drove Saddam Hussein and his Iraqi forces out of Kuwait. Within months of the start of the war, a spate of prophecy books appeared from evangelical presses. The authors of these books did not attempt to understand the Middle East crisis on the basis of current geopolitical considerations or even in terms of the contentious history of the region. Rather, the evangelical prophecy authors tried to decipher just how the Gulf War fit into the dispensational framework. In some important areas of study, the Middle East as a prime example, dispensationalists rarely study current events and recent historical developments on their own merits. Rather, such events are viewed through the grid of dispensationalism and accepted as important almost exclusively for what they can tell us about end-times. As with science, evangelicals tend to opt out of mainstream academic discourse, rarely developing a distinctly Christian way of analyzing serious world events.

In addition to evangelical Creation Science and prophecy belief, Noll also critiqued the "victorious life" or higher spirituality emphasized by Pentecostals and many other evangelicals that can lead to a disregard for the plight of this world in order to focus on one's inner spirituality and the "victory over sin" individuals can achieve through the power of the Holy Spirit. This sort of emphasis on inner spirituality, often called the holiness impulse, was part of the revivalist tradition of evangelicalism. One could argue that without it, certainly without the revivals, there would be no American evangelicalism, at least as we know it today. At the same time, however, scholars of evangelicalism recognize that the type of revivalism that gave rise to modern evangelicalism was not conducive to a life of the mind. Instead, it had the effect of turning evangelicals inward in an effort to develop personal holiness and outward toward an immediate and activist life that was divorced from serious intellectual work. In other words, the revivalist emphasis tends toward inner spiritual holiness followed by immediate activist reform, skipping the process of deep intellectual reflection as to the nature of the problems evangelicals want to address. Again, as is the case with Creation Science and prophecy belief, the victorious life mentality has devalued serious study of the world. Evangelicalism has only recently begun to recover from the intellectual disaster of the early twentieth century.

The Recovery

A leading influence in the recovery of evangelical intellectual life was Francis Schaeffer, the same person we met in the previous chapter as the guru of Christian Right activism. Before Schaeffer was politicized by the abortion issue, his message was largely intellectual and cultural. Schaeffer was a product of fundamentalism in the 1930s and was associated with some of the most militant and antimodernist fundamentalists of the first half of the twentieth century. His early life as a militantly antimodernist fundamentalist and his late career as a leader in Christian Right politics make him an unlikely evangelical intellectual, but that is precisely what he was for the middle third of his life, at least in a popular sense. From 1948 until nearly the end of his life in 1984 he lived in Switzerland, where he and his wife Edith founded a Christian community called L'Abri, which is French for "the shelter." Young people throughout the fifties, sixties, and seventies could stay at L'Abri temporarily for a very nominal fee and listen to Schaeffer talk about intellectual issues. By the 1960s, when hippies and assorted other young people were dropping out of college and society to roam across the world, L'Abri became a popular stopping off point, partly because it was a cheap place to stay. In the evenings, everyone would gather in a large living area with a fireplace, and Schaeffer would sit on an elevated chair that was cut from an old barrel. The conversations were unstructured. Schaeffer would talk for a while, then the young people asked questions. Typically, a question might take a few seconds, and Schaeffer's answer as much as thirty or forty minutes. Schaeffer was a genius at engaging the minds of those who came to L'Abri. He learned enough about modern modes of thought to speak intelligently about everything from art to philosophy. The conversations often extended well past midnight, and many young people who had been searching for the meaning of life through drug use, sexual liberation, and political radicalism converted to evangelical Christianity. They had arrived at L'Abri on the verge of despair but left believing they had found intellectual and spiritual answers to the deepest questions facing humankind.[4]

Having seemingly left his fundamentalism behind, by the sixties Schaeffer was spinning out lectures on the intellectual history of the West and how the Christian worldview that had been normative through the mid-nineteenth century had given way to "secular humanism." Until the 1970s, Schaeffer's message had virtually no political overtones. Rather, he tried to show through logical argument that modern worldviews such as existentialism, various forms of atheism, and secular humanism were incoherent. No one, he argued, could actually live as if life had no meaning. He traced the development of these modern worldviews from sources in the Middle Ages, through the Renaissance and Reformation, into the Enlightenment of the eighteenth century, to Hegel and Kierkegaard in the nineteenth century, then to existentialists such as John Paul Sartre and Albert Camus in the twentieth. Along the way he even discussed the visual arts and rock music as modern expressions of despair and meaninglessness.

In 1964, Schaeffer was invited by evangelical university students at Harvard, Boston University, and other universities in the Boston area to deliver a series of lectures. From that time forward he became a popular speaker on evangelical college campuses across America, and more and more Americans traveled to Switzerland to study at L'Abri. His lectures were taped, the tapes transcribed, and the transcriptions edited into books. His first three books became his trilogy and contained Schaeffer's basic argument about the relationship between Christianity and Western intellectual history. They were titled *The God Who Is There*, *Escape from Reason*, and *He Is There and He Is Not Silent*. The campus lectures and these three books made Schaeffer an evangelical star. Before he died there would be more than twenty books published from his lectures.

None of Schaeffer's arguments would have gone very far in graduate seminars in universities. He routinely erred in his details and almost completely missed the boat in his interpretation of key intellectual figures such as Thomas Aquinas and Soren Kierkegaard. However, he successfully inspired a generation of intelligent young evangelical college students to take seriously the life of the mind. These students had been raised in the wake of the scandal of the evangelical mind and also with the telltale influence of fundamentalist cultural separatism. They had been taught by their parents and churches to shun the secular world. Christian education for many of these young evangelicals in the 1950s and 1960s was about learning technical skills to make a living and just enough about secular ideas to know how to steer clear of them. Schaeffer told these students to take secular ideas seriously, study them boldly, and develop a Christian intellectual life that could stand in the ring and battle the best the world had to offer. Many of these students responded to Schaeffer's challenge, went off to the best graduate schools, and became scholars. As such, they were continuing a tradition already started by the founders of neoevangelicalism in the 1940s and 1950s, but Schaeffer did more than any other neoevangelical scholar to popularize the idea that evangelicals should engage culture and take the intellectual world seriously. This was ironic because living in Switzerland, he was isolated from the development of the neoevangelical movement of the 1950s. It was also ironic in that Schaeffer himself was not a scholar in the professional sense. He did not have a Ph.D., and he never held an academic position. Rather, he was a preacher and evangelist, albeit one who saw intellectual arguments as central to his form of evangelism.

One of the first campuses where Schaeffer appeared following his visit to Boston was Wheaton College. Schaeffer lectured there for a week in 1965 and energized the students in ways not seen for some time. In the audience at these lectures was Mark Noll, at the time a Wheaton undergraduate. It should be noted that Wheaton already had several fine professors doing what Schaeffer advocated, but Schaeffer had a knack for packaging and popularizing the intellectual message better than any other evangelical of his time, certainly better than most professors were capable of doing. Noll hesitates to list Schaeffer's influence as decisive, but he acknowledges nevertheless that Schaeffer was helpful in inspiring Noll's generation of evangelicals to think seriously about ideas. Many traveled to L'Abri to study with Schaeffer, including historian George Marsden, who has done as much for the mainstreaming of evangelical scholarship as anyone else living today.

Marsden is finishing out a brilliant career as a historian. In 1968, when Marsden was a young assistant professor at Calvin College, he wrote an article in an underground newspaper covering Schaeffer's very successful visit to the campus. Marsden wrote, "For a Calvin Faculty member the most startling aspect of this achievement is that Mr. Schaeffer, without displaying any particular academic credentials and with an apparent disregard for the usual academic standards and precautions, did exactly what we always have hoped to do—make Christianity appear intellectually relevant to the contemporary era."[5] As is the case for Noll, it would be a mistake to claim that Schaeffer's influence was decisive for Marsden. Nevertheless, Marsden set out to do in academic life exactly what Schaeffer did on a popular level—that is, "make

Christianity appear intellectually relevant to the contemporary era." Specifically, Marsden and a few others would take the lead in making Christianity relevant to historical scholarship, and Marsden would do so while remedying Schaeffer's lack of academic credentials and "apparent disregard for the usual academic standards and precautions." After receiving his Ph.D. from Yale University, Marsden essentially published his way from Calvin College to Duke Divinity School then to an endowed chair at Notre Dame where he retired in 2008, only to be replaced by Noll, who had spent the previous thirty years at his alma mater, Wheaton.

Marsden and Noll are the twentieth-century's most important scholars studying evangelicalism, and as such they have been equally important for overcoming the scandal of the evangelical mind. Marsden has done this by helping to push evangelical scholarship into the mainstream of academic life, first by publishing a series of books in the 1980s and early 1990s on fundamentalism and evangelicalism. These books were widely recognized as superb examples of scholarship, and they were all done from Marsden's broadly evangelical perspective. He is a product of the Reformed, or Calvinist, wing of American evangelicalism. In many respects, he stands in the same theological and intellectual tradition as Jonathan Edwards, about whom he wrote an award-winning biography published in 2003. In between his work on fundamentalism and his biography of Edwards, Marsden wrote a book entitled *The Soul of the American University: From Protestant Establishment to Established Nonbelief.* In this book Marsden traced how America's elite universities moved from a broadly Protestant establishment in the nineteenth century to a position in the late twentieth century where religious points of view were considered illegitimate for scholars in the mainstream academy. Part of his point was that neither position was equitable. In the nineteenth century, state-supported universities probably should not have been so Protestant given that the nation was becoming increasingly diverse and pluralistic. In other words, it was not necessarily right for Catholics and other non-Protestants to be required to support broadly Protestant universities with their tax dollars. By the same token, however, neither was it fair that by the mid-twentieth century religious points of view were excluded from the mainstream academy on the basis of what has been called Enlightenment objectivity, a position related to the political liberalism discussed in the previous chapter.

In his "Concluding Unscientific Postscript" to *The Soul of the American University,* Marsden suggested some ways that faith-informed scholars of whatever religion might helpfully integrate religious perspectives with academic scholarship. This postscript fueled an already existing debate about the role of religious points of view in academic circles, a debate that was covered by *The Chronicle of Higher Education*, which serves as the newspaper of academic life and is read by many academics across the country. (Since *The Chronicle* carries the advertisements for academic positions at colleges and universities, it is likely that virtually every academic reads it at one time or another.) On the cover of *The Chronicle* appeared a photo of the unassuming Marsden sitting on the Notre Dame campus in front of the famous "touchdown Jesus." In the article Marsden was quoted as saying, "Why should it be taken for granted that religious perspectives should be out of bounds? Feminists say that one's biography is relevant to one's scholarship. I'm saying that about religion as well."[6] Among those taking issue with Marsden was Bruce Kuklick at the University of Pennsylvania who responded by saying the idea that personal beliefs were compatible with academic scholarship was "loony," reflecting "a self-indulgent professoriate." "George Marsden is a conservative Christian and he feels marginalized in the secular academy. And I'm sorry about that," Kuklick continued, but he also argued that race and gender were empirical categories and therefore legitimate bases from which scholarship should proceed. Religion, being nonempirical, was out of bounds as a point of view from which to engage in scholarly activity.[7]

The rest of the *Chronicle* article related anecdotes of discrimination against religious professors in the secular academy and charges of Christian professors or instructors using their positions to attempt to advance their faith. One Christian professor of computer science said that when he was a teaching assistant in graduate school he was pressured to remove Christian literature from the door of his office and to stop publicizing Christian activities on a department-wide computer network. He was puzzled, however, when a colleague was allowed to keep gay-rights literature on his door. Another university dismissed a biology instructor who told his class he was a creationist and gave an assignment where students were to compare and contrast creationism and evolution.[8] Marsden and most of the other prominent Christian scholars said that using one's academic position to proselytize was inappropriate, but theologian Stanley Hauerwas of Duke Divinity School took a different view. The often controversial Hauerwas, who would later appear on the cover of *Time* magazine as America's most important theologian, said he had little interest in helping his students make up their own minds because, in his words, "I don't think they have minds worth making up. When they're finished, I want them to think just like me."[9] It is worth noting that Hauerwas does not teach college undergraduates, but rather teaches in a graduate divinity school where the students are older, more mature, and enrolled specifically to study religion.

Because Marsden's "Concluding Unscientific Postscript" touched off something of a firestorm, he decided to develop his views more fully in a little book titled *The Outrageous Idea of Christian Scholarship*. The point of the book is that the notion that scholarship can be shaped in part by a Christian point of view is actually not very outrageous, especially in light of the fact that all sorts of other points of view—feminism, Afrocentrism, African American, Marxist, gay and lesbian, etc.—are acknowledged as legitimate starting places for scholarly work in the humanities and social sciences. Marsden asked why it was that when religion was part of the discussion, it was as if it were "high-noon of the Enlightenment" where everyone was suddenly supposed to set aside their points of view and work objectively. The notion of scholarly objectivity had been thoroughly debunked, it seemed, for every point of view save religion.[10] As he had argued in *The Soul of the American University*, Marsden understood that Protestantism had to be disestablished as the dominant force shaping American universities, and he summarized that argument in *The Outrageous Idea of Christian Scholarship*. In moving from Protestant establishment to established nonbelief, however, universities had overcorrected, he argued. "This passion for disestablishment, nondiscrimination, and justice," Marsden wrote, "led to an ironic result. Explicitly Christian views had been the problem, so eliminating them had seemed the solution. An understandable reaction had become an over-reaction. . . . Today there is no realistic prospect for the reestablishment of the dominance of Christianity in America's leading universities. Yet the biases against speaking about Christian perspectives persist."[11] Marsden made it clear that he did not believe that the marginalization and even exclusion of faith perspectives from the academy was the result of a conspiracy of secularists. Rather, the exclusion resulted from a reaction and overreaction "to the problems of having a quasi-established religion in a pluralistic modern society," as had been the case in the late nineteenth and early twentieth centuries. He even criticized evangelicals in the Christian Right for overstating the extent to which secular humanism dominates society and for attributing that dominance to a conspiracy of secular humanists, as Francis Schaeffer had done late in his life.

While the flap over Marsden's "Concluding Unscientific Postscript" showed that evangelical scholarship was still a controversial idea in some quarters, by the 1990s in history circles the work of Marsden, Noll, and some others had shown convincingly that evangelicals, working as evangelicals, could be fine scholars. Noll is currently the most prolific of all scholars of religion in America and along with Marsden is one of the four or five most important historians of religion in America for the entire twentieth and twenty-first centuries. So successful have they been that there has even developed an internal debate among evangelicals themselves as to whether Noll, Marsden, and others like them should be more bold and overt in their application of faith to scholarship. Yale historian Harry Stout squared off with a small cadre of Christian historians working largely outside the mainstream academy. The debate centered on Stout's biography of Great Awakening preacher George Whitefield. Stout's approach to scholarship is much like Marsden's and Noll's, and his opponents wondered how a professing evangelical could write about Whitefield's revivals without acknowledging the work of the Holy Spirit as part of historical causation. Stout answered in a way that most, but not all, evangelical scholars would. He said simply that the work of the Holy Spirit, while real, was outside the bounds of study for professional historians. In other words, historians interpret earthly events and report on what seem to be their natural causes.

Marsden called this approach "methodological secularization," and he uses the analogy of a pilot landing an airplane. Most passengers, no matter how religious, hope the pilot flying the airplane will rely on the control tower radar, not the Holy Spirit, when landing the plane. Likewise, for many academic exercises a methodological secularization is appropriate. Marsden, however, cited a difference between methodological secularization and methodological atheism, which has more often than not been the rule in academic life. As Marsden put it, "Methodological secularization means only that for limited ad hoc purposes we will focus on natural phenomena accessible to all, while not denying their spiritual dimensions as created and ordered by God or forgetting that there is much more to the picture."[12] Specifically, Marsden and most other evangelical historians believe they should do no "special pleading." Special pleading is the claim that one is privy to knowledge unbelievers do not have. Rather, Marsden argues merely that Christians of various types will likely have perspectives that are different from the perspectives of those who practice no faith. Marsden, Stout, and most evangelical historians acknowledge that to engage in special pleading is to set oneself outside the rules of the game. It is one thing to say that a scholar's point of view shapes the way he or she looks at the evidence or even shapes what evidence a scholar deems important; it is quite another to say that one can go beyond the evidence and claim that God revealed an interpretation directly to the scholar.

Many professional academics ask what difference such faith perspectives could possibly make for historical interpretation, and admittedly the end result of evangelical scholarship is often not much different from the work of nonevangelical scholars. Still, Marsden answers, on several fronts faith perspectives will make a difference, and, moreover, even where the end result is just good scholarship pretty much indistinguishable from scholarship that does not emanate from a faith perspective, there is much to be gained and little threat when evangelicals reflect on how their faith informs their work. One area where an evangelical perspective does seem to make a difference is in the area of scholarly agendas. Evangelical scholars are likely to be interested in questions that others might not be.[13] Evangelicals have done most of the scholarship on evangelicals and fundamentalists carried out over the past thirty years, just as most women's history is done by women and much African American history done by African Americans. Even many nonevangelical scholars who study evangelicalism were raised evangelical but rejected their faith as adults. Such is the case for Paul Boyer, whose book *When Time Shall Be No More* was cited in chapter four on end-times prophecy belief, his University of Wisconsin colleague Ronald Numbers, whose book *The Creationists* was cited in chapter three on evangelicals and science, and William Martin, whose work on the Christian Right was covered in the previous chapter. It appears that faith-committed scholars as well as those raised in faith traditions have a heightened sensibility to the place of religion in history and are likely to study religious topics. In this way, religious points of view often help set scholarly agendas.

Beyond scholarly agendas, evangelical scholars, or scholars of any faith for that matter, are likely to see some things that others may not. Harry Stout's work on Puritans serves as a good example that Marsden cited. Stout acknowledges that one does not have to be a Christian to take the religious ideas of the Puritans seriously. Two giants in the history of Puritanism, Edmund Morgan and Perry Miller, were both atheists. Until Stout, however, no scholar had studied handwritten Puritan sermon manuscripts systematically, despite the fact that hundreds of these unprinted sermons are available in various archives. Stout established his career and landed at Yale as a result of his copious study of these sermons, which reveal different concerns than most printed versions. Moreover, Stout asked different questions of his sources. Whereas Miller had been interested primarily in how the Puritan mind helped forge the American nation, Stout was interested in how Puritan spiritual practices and sensibilities helped shape American Christianity.

Stout saw the Great Awakening revivals not merely as historical events that helped form the American nation but as spiritual events that could not be explained exhaustively by the use of historical methodologies.[14] The difference between Miller and Stout was that Miller focused on those aspects of Puritanism that had long-range implications for the development of a modern America where religion is far less central than it was in the days of the Puritans. By contrast, Stout focused on aspects of Puritanism that showed the extent to which humans are fundamentally religious and spiritual beings. In addition to personal religious sensibilities, the differences between Miller and Stout also have to do with the time periods in which they lived as scholars. Miller wrote his works in the period between the Scopes trial of 1925 and the development of the Christian Right in the 1980s—in other words, in the period when it looked as if modern scientific forces had relegated fundamentalism and evangelicalism to a side show of American history. By the time Stout wrote, it was clear that fundamentalism and evangelicalism were still very significant forces in American life, suggesting that the spiritual approach to life taken by Puritans was perhaps basic to human history and not a passing phase on the road to scientific maturity. Stout's spiritual life made it likely that he would see the Puritans differently than Miller.

In addition to scholarly agendas and challenging what is taken for granted, a third way that faith-informed scholarship makes a difference for evangelical scholars is in challenging reductionistic interpretations. Reductionism is the tendency in academic life to believe that all things can be explained in one way, usually by naturalistic, scientific, or empirical analysis. Here Marsden cites an analogy by the late scientist Donald McKay. McKay imagined an electronic sign. If an expert in electrical engineering were to analyze the sign, he or she would observe and report on its electrical components, which would be fine, unless the electrical engineer insisted that the sign's electrical properties exhausted the ways in which one could view the sign. Such a view would be especially deficient if the sign read, "Live Girls." In that case, the sign could be analyzed in a number of different ways. Sociologists would view its social implications, gender-studies scholars would likely see exploitation, ethicists its moral component, and aestheticians the sign's tackiness. All these interpretations would be important, yet there is a tendency in academic life for each discipline to act as if its interpretation exhausts the possibilities. Evangelical scholars, such as Marsden, argue that the religious influences help one see some aspects of historical and sociological problems that may not be readily apparent to other points of view.

In several academic disciplines, Christian scholars have created scholarly organizations that are affiliated with the discipline's main organization. For example, in the late 1960s, Christian historians, almost all of them evangelical, founded the Conference on Faith and History (CFH). At the time, the history profession was still largely under the influence of modern, scientific notions of Enlightenment objectivity that pervaded the social sciences and even to a degree the humanities (there is a long-running discussion concerning to what extent history is a social science or humanity). This emphasis on scientific objectivity held that scholars should essentially park their points of view outside their studies and classrooms and work objectively in-terpreting the facts. At the very time the CFH was being founded, this idea of objectivity was under severe attack from postmodernists who would shortly succeed in laying bare the myth of Enlightenment objectivity. The CFH and other societies of Christian scholars developed at a time when other subdisciplinary organizations also began. Feminist and Afrocentrist scholars were beginning to argue that their particular point of view made a difference in the way they interpreted history. For many Christian scholars the CFH was merely an organization created for professional and Christian fellowship, but a few Christian scholars were beginning to think more self-consciously and reflectively about how their faith influenced their work as historians. It took several years before the CFH was recognized by the Amer-ican Historical Association and accepted as an affiliated organization, and it is probably no accident that the president of the AHA at the time the CFH became a member was an African American scholar. He knew something about marginalization and was sympathetic to the place of Christian scholars within the academy. He also no doubt knew that point of view made a dif-ference. Today the CFH welcomes Christians of any persuasion—evangeli-cal, Roman Catholic, mainline Protestant, Orthodox, etc.—but is still heav-ily evangelical.

The Society of Christian Philosophers (SCP) was founded in 1978, about a decade after CFH, and has probably been the most successful or-ganization of Christian scholars. The organization seeks to promote reflec-tion on how Christian commitment influences philosophical thinking broadly, beyond just the philosophy of religion. Like the CFH, the SCP is affiliated with the largest professional philosophy organization, the Amer-ican Philosophical Association (APA). With over 1,000 members, the SCP is one of the largest subdisciplinary organizations of any kind affiliated with the APA. Membership of the SCP is open to Christians of any persuasion; there is no doctrinal creed. The SCP has been much more diverse than the CFH and much less dominated by evangelicals, but the ongoing secretary treasurer is an evangelical on the faculty of Calvin College. The organiza-tion's past presidents include evangelicals, Catholics, and other types of Christians, and some of those individuals also have served as presidents of various subdisciplinary divisions of the APA, which is among the highest honors possible in the philosophy profession. Both the Conference on Faith and History and the Society of Christian Philosophers publish schol-arly journals—*Fides et Historia* and *Faith and Philosophy* respectively. The latter is quite selective and regarded by many as the best English-language journal for the philosophy of religion. Along with the SCP there is also the

Evangelical Philosophical Society (EPS) that publishes a journal called *Philosophia Christi*. The EPS has a particular evangelical doctrinal statement to which members must agree.

Conclusion

The CFH, the SCP, and the EPS reflect the ways in which evangelical scholars and those of other Christian traditions have moved into the mainstream of academic life. As the debate in the *Chronicle of Higher Education* between Marsden and Kuklick shows, the idea that faith should inform how one does scholarly work can still be controversial. On the other hand, Marsden's 2003 biography *Jonathan Edwards: A Life*, won two of the most prestigious book awards in the history profession.[15] Here was a biography of an evangelical, by an evangelical, which was recognized as the best historical work published that year. This seems to suggest that evangelical scholarship is indeed mainstream.

Notes

1. Richard Hofstadter, *Anti-Intellectualism in American Life* (New York: Knopf, 1963), vii, 117–19, 123, 125, and 138–39.

2. Mark Noll, *The Scandal of the Evangelical Mind* (Grand Rapids, Michigan: Eerdmans, 1994), 243.

3. Noll, *The Scandal of the Evangelical Mind*, 14.

4. Barry Hankins, *Francis Schaeffer: Fundamentalist Warrior, Evangelical Prophet* (Grand Rapids, Michigan: Eerdmans, 2009).

5. George Marsden, "Twentieth Century Fox," *The Spectacle* 1:5 (November 1, 1968): 1

6. Carolyn J. Mooney, "Devout Professors on the Offensive," *Chronicle of Higher Education* (May 4, 1994): A18.

7. Mooney, "Devout Professors on the Offensive," A18.

8. Mooney, "Devout Professors on the Offensive," A21.

9. Mooney, "Devout Professors on the Offensive," A22.

10. George Marsden, *The Outrageous Idea of Christian Scholarship* (New York: Oxford University Press, 1997).

11. Marsden, *The Outrageous Idea of Christian Scholarship*, 23.

12. Marsden, *The Outrageous Idea of Christian Scholarship*, 91.

13. Marsden, *The Outrageous Idea of Christian Scholarship*, 63–65.

14. Marsden discusses the implications of Stout's work in *The Outrageous Idea of Christian Scholarship*, 70–71.

15. George Marsden, *Jonathan Edwards: A Life* (New Haven, Connecticut: Yale University Press, 2003). The book won both the Bancroft and the Curti prizes.

CHAPTER EIGHT

~

Conclusion

The evangelical scholars covered in the previous chapter defy the typical stereotypes of evangelicals. Evangelical scholars are not fundamentalists, they do not reject mainstream science, most oppose Christian Right politics, and they are not uniformly conservative in anything other than theology. Such is true for many other evangelicals as well, and a large part of this book has been devoted to understanding that while there is some basis for stereotypes, in reality evangelicals are a diverse lot and as a group not much different from other Americans.

While some view the diversity of evangelicals like a kaleidoscope, mosaic, or feudal kingdom, a more quintessentially American metaphor is athletics. Athletes come in all different shapes and sizes. Football players are heavy, strong, and fast; basketball players tall and quick; while baseball players, golfers, and tennis players possess great hand-eye coordination. If one stood LeBron James, Peyton Manning, Alex Rodriguez, Tiger Woods, and Serena Williams next to each other, they would appear to have little in common. As an NBA basketball player, James is a 6'8" African American from the Midwest who possesses tremendous strength, speed, and jumping ability. Manning is a white southerner with none of James's speed. Rodriguez is a powerful Latino American who has great hands and eyesight and is smooth in his movements. Woods's father was African American, his mother from Thailand. We do not know if Tiger can run fast or even if he can run at all, since he plays golf and therefore walks through his matches at a somewhat leisurely pace. Tennis star Williams, like James, is an African

American, but, of course, she is female and therefore quite different from the others.

As diverse as these five individuals are, every American sports fan views them as similar, and the five share a common bond, the result of their being dominant figures in their respective sports. They are instantly recognizable as great athletes, and they carry this identity with them at all times. Many other performers in these sports are not recognizable on the street. Only when in uniform practicing their craft do they appear athletic, yet their identity as athletes continues throughout their lives and usually becomes an internalized part of their self-image. As the recent friendship between Woods and tennis great Roger Federer attests, athletes can easily identify their commonalities, even if they play different sports, come from different nations, and speak different native languages. They can bridge cultural barriers more easily than people of similar ethnicity can strike up friendships with neighbors in their own towns.

Evangelicals can be as different from one another as our five great athletes. They are a diverse subculture, yet they share in common Bebbington's four distinctives—Biblicism, crucicentrism, conversionism, and activism. Moreover, just as athletes in the same sport are divided among a multitude of teams, evangelicals live out their faith in different denominations—Baptists, Methodists, Presbyterians, independents, and a host of smaller groups. These religious teams sometimes compete and sometimes cooperate. No one would think to contrast athletes and Americans, except perhaps in terms of the socioeconomic standing of professional athletes. Set professional sports aside, and the analogy works even better. It is not just that athletes ranging from the weekend duffer through the top collegiate all-Americans are like other Americans. They are American, as American as, well, baseball.

Evangelicals share Bebbington's four traits in common, making them a distinct subculture, but in most ways they resemble other Americans. Like most athletes, only when engaging in explicitly religious activities do evangelicals appear different, and even then they are diverse. If we look again at Bebbington's four distinctives we find that evangelicals are divided over two—Biblicism and activism—while sharing wide agreement over conversionism and crucicentrism.

Nearly all evangelicals agree that Biblicism means the authority of scripture above all other authorities. Still, evangelicals disagree often over whether the Bible is inerrant. In the 1980s, for example, the largest Protestant denomination in America, the Southern Baptist Convention, experienced a major controversy between moderates and conservatives, the latter usually referred to as fundamentalists. This controversy ripped the denomination apart and ended with the conservatives ousting the moderates from power. Ironically, by almost any historical or theological standard, including Bebbington's, both groups of Southern Baptists are biblicist evangelicals. This notwithstanding, the rallying cry of the conservatives against the moderates was "the inerrancy of scripture." In other words, the issue was over what Biblicism should mean. Moderates thought it enough to tout the authority of scripture; the conservatives believed that in addition to authority, evangelical Biblicism meant that scripture was without error even in matters of science and history.

This was hardly the first time that evangelicals had fought among themselves over Biblicism. In the 1970s, northern evangelicals were divided over this issue with inerrantists claiming that noninerrantists were not really evangelicals. Francis Schaeffer, who we met in chapters six and seven, argued routinely that to deny inerrancy was to cease being an evangelical. He and others knew well that the modernist liberals of the early twentieth century had denied inerrancy, and they believed that evangelicals who did likewise would become theological liberals in short order. Billy Graham was the only evangelical in the 1970s who was better known than Schaeffer, and he too affirmed inerrancy. Graham, however, was not so quick to write noninerrantists out of the evangelical arena.

As we saw in chapter six, evangelicals are also divided over activism. The Christian Right has far more adherents than the evangelical left, but the majority of evangelicals do not identify strongly with either of these political movements. The majority of evangelicals affirm either implicitly or explicitly activism that is nonpolitical. For these, evangelical activism means evangelism and volunteer work on behalf of "the least of these," to use a phrase that Jesus coined. While there are churches that are heavily active in politics, the more typical Sunday morning service in evangelical and fundamentalist churches consists of praise and worship, Bible study, and preaching that is usually devoid of explicit political references. Some denominations urge their congregations to set aside one Sunday a year for emphasis on human life issues, but this is a minority, and we do not know how widely such emphasis Sundays are observed in the individual churches. There are a variety of evangelical approaches even on a hot-button issue like abortion. While the most visible evangelicals march in the streets, engaging in civil disobedience in an effort to shut down Planned Parenthood clinics, the vast majority of evangelicals have never attended an antiabortion rally. For most evangelicals, activism on the abortion issue takes the form of prayer and voting for pro-life Republicans, not civil disobedience. That said, it is true that evangelicals are the strongest bloc of Republican voters. Roughly 78 percent of voting evangelicals cast their ballots for George W. Bush in 2004, but when many of them left the polls, their political activism was complete as they turned to other sorts of voluntary efforts that reflect evangelical activism.

Evangelicals are active inside and outside of their churches in a variety of ways. Recent research indicates that they donate more time than nonevangelicals. The full volume of evangelical volunteer work was undervalued for years because social scientists failed to count church participation along with participation in secular voluntary organizations. Again, as in other areas, volunteer work does not make evangelicals distinct from other Americans; rather, it merely makes them leaders in an area that is quite American. Americans have always been renowned for their volunteerism.

In the activism plank of evangelicalism, there is also diversity and disagreement over science. Christian Right activists insist that evolution should be resisted in the public schools and that either Intelligent Design or Creation Science should be given equal time. Many go so far as to say that the public schools are given over to secular humanism and are hostile to the faith. They advocate that evangelicals take their children out of what they term "government schools" and opt for either private schools or home schooling. Again, the Southern Baptist convention is instructive as to how calls for activism often divide evangelicals. In 2006 and 2007, a cadre of Southern Baptists attempted to get the denomination to pass a resolution calling on parents to take their children out of public schools. Neither resolution made it to the floor of the Southern Baptist Convention meetings, dying in committee instead. This is because the issue of how actively Christians should oppose the public schools is highly divisive. The vast majority of Southern Baptist children in America, like those of all other evangelical groups, still attend public schools, and their parents have no plans to remove them.

This division among evangelicals comes down to how vigorously or actively they should oppose the culture. As we have seen in this book, the evangelical stance toward culture was divisive throughout the twentieth century. Fundamentalists called for separation from and militant battle against the larger culture, while neoevangelicals and others called for engagement but not warfare. Such division over how to be active within the culture, how to apply one's Christian faith, continues among evangelicals. Only a minority of evangelicals could be described today as cultural separatists, and even they are usually active in some way in evangelism and missions. For the larger segment of evangelicalism, the distinction is between fundamentalistic evangelicals who militantly oppose the culture and more moderate types who try to be distinct from many secular norms but nevertheless live rather happily in the larger culture.

There is much less diversity among evangelicals with regard to conversionism than Biblicism or activism. Virtually all evangelicals believe in Christian conversion. It is impossible to be born a Christian, they believe; rather, individuals are born sinful and must at some point experience God's forgiveness and conversion, which is often called being born again, saved from sin, or converted. Most evangelicals believe in some form of revivalist conversion, but not all. For some evangelical groups, especially in the Reformed Calvinist tradition, which would include conservative Presbyterians, conversion is part of a process of catechization and nurture within the community of faith, but they still testify to having been saved, born again, or converted. Interestingly, the wives of both Francis Schaeffer and Billy Graham could not recall exactly when they were converted, but they knew they were and testified to that fact at every opportunity. The irony of this is that Graham has been the most influential revivalist in the history of the Christian faith, always calling for an immediate decision to follow Christ in the act of conversion.

Crucicentrism presents the least diversity in the Bebbington quadrilateral. Nearly all evangelicals believe that Christ's sacrificial death on the cross atones for sin. For them, Christ's death is not merely a moral statement or a witness to His obedience to God. Rather, it has supernatural power capable of redeeming sinful souls. Fittingly, while evangelicals exhibit the least diversity on this aspect of Bebbington's distinctives, it is here where they are most distinct from many other Americans. Traditional Roman Catholics share the crucicentrist point, but secular Americans, many liberal Christians, Jews, and other adherents of non-Christian faiths take exception to this very unmodern view of the uniqueness of Christ, and non-Christians often chafe at the idea that they need to be converted. To many modern and postmodern Americans, such a claim to uniqueness smacks of superiority, which is then compounded when evangelicals attempt to evangelize those of other faiths. In short, the insistence that people of other faiths also stand in need of Christ as the only way to God rubs up against modern views of tolerance and the postmodern belief that there is no transcendent overarching narrative.

Evangelicals sometimes turn this postmodern rejection of narratives on its head, however, using it to their advantage against modern rational views that reject supernaturalism. As we saw in the previous chapter, there was a time when the modern Enlightenment view reigned supreme in the academy. Calling as it did for scientific objectivity, this modern view often excluded faith-based positions from scholarly work because faith-based views were considered subjective, unscientific, and, therefore, not part of the body of knowledge. In the wake of the postmodern critique of Enlightenment objectivity, in an age where all intellectual endeavors are believed to have precommitments, presuppositions, and background beliefs, evangelicals may stand in a slightly better position than they did during much of the twentieth century. They can now say, "You have a narrative, we have a narrative, and there is no basis for excluding any narratives from the table of discourse." This, of course, will not satisfy all evangelicals because many of them are uncomfortable with pluralism. Some evangelicals pine for the days when evangelical Protestants ran the country, but as Christian Smith's research has shown, this is not a majority. Most want their concerns to be taking seriously even as they live with pluralism happily or begrudgingly.

Understanding evangelicals, therefore, is similar to understanding Americans. One must take into consideration what makes them distinct and different, while still acknowledging how much diversity there is within this loosely defined subculture. This is similar to the way that non-American commentators from Tocqueville to the present have viewed Americans. From a European or Asian perspective, there is much that is distinctive or even peculiar about Americans. At the same time, scholars and pundits recognize that Americans comprise a diverse, divided, and contentious nation. So it is with evangelicals in America: They are distinct and they are divided, they are diverse and share common beliefs, and they are contentious, among themselves and with nonevangelicals. Evangelicals have helped shape American culture and also have been shaped by it. They are outsiders in the same way so many other Americans are outsiders, but they are also insiders quite at home in the culture where they live. They emphasize individual choice, even in matters as fundamental as salvation and biblical interpretation, and they affirm the freedom to be what one wants to be, or, to use evangelical vernacular, to be what God wants one to be. They are often fiercely independent, while at other times conformist. Many evangelical practices are but thinly veiled covers of secular phenomenon, the Christian music and book industries serving as prime examples.

Evangelicals often critique each other for not being different enough from the larger culture. This is the most consistent criticism that fundamentalists make of other evangelicals—they are too much like other Americans. But evangelicals criticize each other for this same thing. Leftwing evangelical activists say Christian Right types have sold out to American capitalism, materialism, and nationalism, while the Right answers that the Left fails to take a strong enough stance against abortion and the gay lifestyle. Pentecostals and charismatics believe other evangelicals fail to appropriate the full power of God by failing to exercise all the gifts of the Holy Spirit, while noncharismatic evangelicals answer that focusing too much on miraculous experience distracts believers from the task of sober Bible study and serious theological reflection. The charge that evangelicals are pretty much like other Americans in most ways is one of the most serious accusations one can make, whether from within or without evangelicalism. The fact that this charge is made so often, and has recently been joined by a few secular scholars, brings us back to sociologist Alan Wolfe, mentioned in the preface. He sees evangelicals as quintessentially American. Evangelicals are more like other Americans than they are distinct, and Americans are more like evangelicals than they know. As Wolfe says, "We're all evangelicals now."

~

Bibliography

The Marsden Paradigm and Its Critics

Collins, Kenneth. *The Evangelical Moment: The Promise of an American Religion.* Grand Rapids, MI: Baker Academic, 2005.

Dayton, Donald and Robert K. Johnson, eds. *The Variety of American Evangelicalism.* Knoxville: University of Tennessee Press, 1991.

Hart, D. G. *Deconstructing Evangelicalism: Conservative Protestantism in the Age of Billy Graham.* Grand Rapids, MI: Baker Academic, 2004.

Marsden, George. *Fundamentalism and American Culture: The Shaping of Twentieth-Century Evangelicalism.* New York: Oxford University Press, 1980.

Marsden, George. *Reforming Fundamentalism: Fuller Seminary and the New Evangelicalism.* Grand Rapids, MI: Eerdmans, 1987.

Sandeen, Ernest. *The Roots of Fundamentalism: British and American Millenarianism, 1800–1930.* Chicago: University of Chicago Press, 1970.

Szasz, Ferenc Morton. *The Divided Mind of Protestant America, 1880–1930.* Tuscaloosa: University of Alabama Press, 1982.

Trollinger, Jr., William Vance and Douglas Jacobsen. *Re-forming the Center: American Protestantism, 1900 to the Present.* Grand Rapids, MI: Eerdmans, 1998.

Evangelical Biographies and Regional Studies

Abrams, Douglas Carl. *Selling the Old-Time Religion: American Fundamentalists and Mass Culture, 1920–1940.* Athens: University of Georgia Press, 2001.

Bahr, Robert. *Least of All Saints: The Story of Aimee Semple McPherson.* Englewood Cliffs, NJ: Prentice Hall, 1979.

Bendroth, Margaret Lamberts. *Fundamentalists in the City: Conflict and Division in Boston's Churches, 1885–1950*. New York: Oxford University Press, 2005.

Blumhofer, Edith. *Aimee Semple McPherson: Everybody's Sister*. Grand Rapids, MI: Eerdmans, 1993.

Brereton, Virginia. *Training God's Army: The American Bible School, 1880–1940*. Bloomington: Indiana University Press, 1990.

Carpenter, Joel. *Revive Us Again: The Reawakening of Fundamentalism*. New York: Oxford University Press, 1997.

Dalhouse, Mark Taylor. *An Island in the Lake of Fire: Bob Jones University, Fundamentalism, and the Separatist Movement*. Athens: University of Georgia Press, 1996.

Dochuk, Darren. "From Bible Belt to Sunbelt: Plain Folk Religion, Grassroots Politics, and the Southernization of Southern California, 1939–1969." Ph.D. dissertation, University of Notre Dame, 2005.

Dorsett, Lyle. *Billy Sunday and the Redemption of Urban America*. Grand Rapids, MI: Eerdmans, 1991.

Glass, William. *Strangers in Zion: Fundamentalists in the South, 1900–1950*. Macon, GA: Mercer University Press, 2001.

Hangen, Tona. *Redeeming the Dial: Radio, Religion, and Popular Culture in America*. Chapel Hill: University of North Carolina Press, 2002.

Hankins, Barry. *Francis Schaeffer: Fundamentalist Warrior, Evangelical Prophet*. Grand Rapids, MI: Eerdmans, 2009.

Hankins, Barry. *God's Rascal: J. Frank Norris and the Beginnings of Southern Fundamentalism*. Lexington: University Press of Kentucky, 1996.

Harding, Susan Friend. *The Book of Jerry Falwell: Fundamentalist Language and Politics*. Princeton, NJ: Princeton University Press, 2000.

Harrell, David Edwin, Jr. *Oral Roberts: An American Life*. Bloomington: Indiana University Press, 1985.

Harrell, David Edwin, Jr. *Pat Robertson: A Personal, Religious, and Political Portrait*. San Francisco, CA: Harper and Row, 1987.

Harrell, David Edwin, Jr., ed. *Varieties of Southern Evangelicalism*. Macon, GA: Mercer University Press, 1981.

Hart, D. G. *Defending the Faith: J. Gresham Machen and the Crisis of Conservative Protestantism in Modern America*. Baltimore, MD: Johns Hopkins University Press, 1994.

Hicks, L. Edward. *"Sometimes in the Wrong, but Never in Doubt": George S. Benson and the Education of the New Religious Right*. Knoxville: University of Tennessee Press, 1994.

Lately, Thomas. *Storming Heaven: The Lives and Turmoils of Minnie Kennedy and Aimee Semple McPherson*. New York: Morrow, 1970.

McLoughlin, William G. *Billy Sunday Was His Real Name*. Chicago, IL: University of Chicago Press, 1955.

Mathews, Mary Beth Swetnam. *Rethinking Zion: How the Print Media Placed Fundamentalism in the South*. Knoxville: University of Tennessee Press, 2006.

Stanley, Susie. *Feminist Pillar of Fire: The Life of Alma White*. Cleveland, OH: Pilgrim Press, 1993.

Sutton, Matthew. *Aimee Semple McPherson and the Resurrection of Christian America*. Cambridge, MA: Harvard University Press, 2007.

Trollinger, Jr., William Vance. *God's Empire: William Bell Riley and Midwestern Fundamentalism*. Madison: University of Wisconsin Press, 1990.

Turner, John G. "Selling Jesus to Modern America: Campus Crusade for Christ, Evangelical Culture, and Conservative Politics." Ph.D. dissertation, University of Notre Dame, 2006.

Wacker, Grant. *Augustus H. Strong and the Dilemma of Historical Consciousness*. Macon, GA: Mercer University Press, 1985.

Warner, R. Stephen. *New Wine in Old Wineskins: Evangelicals and Liberals in a Small-Town Church*. Berkeley: University of California Press, 1988.

The Christian Right

Balmer, Randall. *Mine Eyes Have Seen the Glory: A Journey into the Evangelical Subculture in America*, 4th ed. New York: Oxford University Press, 2006.

Balmer, Randall. *Thy Kingdom Come: An Evangelical's Lament*. New York: Basic Books, 2006.

Bruce, Steve. *The Rise and Fall of the New Christian Right*. Oxford: Clarendon Press, 1988.

Dempster, Murray and Augustus Cerillo, Jr. *Salt and Light: Evangelical Political Thought in Modern America*. Grand Rapids, MI: Baker, 1989.

Diamond, Sara. *Not by Politics Alone: The Enduring Influence of the Christian Right*. New York: Guilford Press, 1998.

Lienesch, Michael. *Redeeming America: Piety and Politics in the New Christian Right*. Chapel Hill: University of North Carolina Press, 1993.

Martin, William. *A Prophet with Honor: The Billy Graham Story*. New York: W. Morrow and Company, 1991.

Martin, William. *With God on Our Side: The Rise of the Religious Right in America*. New York: Broadway Books, 1996.

Skillen, James. *The Scattered Voice: Christians at Odds in the Public Square*. Edmonton, Alberta: Canadian Institute for Law, Theology, and Public Policy, 1996.

Watson, Justin. *The Christian Coalition: Dreams of Restoration, Demands for Recognition*. New York: St. Martin's Press, 1997.

Wilcox, Clyde and Carin Larson. *Onward Christian Soldiers?: The Religious Right in American Politics*, 3rd ed. Boulder, CO: Westview Press, 2006.

Evangelicals and Science

Conkin, Paul K. *When All the God's Trembled: Darwinism, Scopes, and American Intellectuals*. Lanham, MD: Rowman & Littlefield, 1998.

Ginger, Ray. *Six Days or Forever?: Tennessee v. John Thomas Scopes*. Boston: Beacon Press, 1958.

Israel, Charles A. *Before Scopes: Evangelicals, Education, and Evolution in Tennessee, 1870–1925*. Athens: University of Georgia Press, 2004.

Larson, Edward. *Summer for the Gods: The Scopes Trial and America's Continuing Debate over Science and Religion*. New York: Basic Books, 1997.

Livingstone, David N. *Darwin's Forgotten Defenders: The Encounter between Evangelical Theology and Evolutionary Thought*. Grand Rapids, MI: Eerdmans, 1987.

Livingstone, David N., D. G. Hart, and Mark A. Noll, eds. *Evangelicals and Science in Historical Perspective*. New York: Oxford University Press, 1999.

Lindberg, David and Ronald Numbers, eds. *God and Nature: Historical Essays on the Encounter between Christianity and Science*. Berkeley: University of California Press, 1986.

Numbers, Ronald L. *The Creationists: The Evolution of Scientific Creationism*. Berkeley: University of California Press, 1993.

Premillennial Prophecy Belief

Ariel, Yaakov. *On Behalf of Israel: American Fundamentalist Attitudes toward Jews, Judaism, and Zionism*. Brooklyn, NY: Carlson Publications, 1991.

Boyer, Paul. *When Time Shall Be No More: Prophecy Belief in Modern American Culture*. Cambridge, MA: Belknap Press of Harvard University Press, 1992.

Forbes, Bruce David and Jeanne Halgren Kilde, eds. *Rapture, Revelation, and the End Times: Exploring the* Left Behind *Series*. New York: Palgrave, 2004.

Frykholm, Amy Johnson. *Rapture Culture: Left Behind in Evangelical America*. New York: Oxford University Press, 2004.

Morgan, David T. *The New Brothers Grimm and Their Left Behind Fairy Tales*. Macon, GA: Mercer University Press, 2006.

Shuck, Glenn W. *Marks of the Beast: The* Left Behind *Novels and the Struggle for Evangelical Identity*. New York: New York University Press, 2005.

Smith, Christian. *American Evangelicalism: Embattled and Thriving*. Chicago, IL: University of Chicago Press, 1998.

Weber, Timothy P. *Living in the Shadow of the Second Coming: American Premillennialism, 1875–1925*. New York: Oxford University Press, 1979.

Weber, Timothy P. *Living in the Shadow of the Second Coming: American Premillennialism, 1875–1982*. Grand Rapids, MI: Zondervan's Academie Books, 1983.

Weber, Timothy P. *On the Road to Armageddon: How Evangelicals Became Israel's Best Friend*. Grand Rapids, MI: Baker Academic, 2004.

Evangelicals, Gender, and Race

Ammerman, Nancy. *Bible Believers: Fundamentalists in the Modern World*. New Brunswick, NJ: Rutgers University Press, 1987.

Ault, James, Jr. *Spirit and Flesh: Life in a Fundamentalist Baptist Church*. New York: Vintage Books, 2004.

Bebbington, David. *The Dominance of Evangelicalism: The Age of Spurgeon and Moody*. Downers Grove, IL: InterVarsity Press, 2005.

Bendroth, Margaret Lamberts. *Fundamentalism and Gender, 1875 to the Present*. New Haven, CT: Yale University Press, 1993.

Brasher, Brenda. *Godly Women: Fundamentalism and Female Power*. New Brunswick, NJ: Rutgers University Press, 1998.

Brereton, Virginia. *From Sin to Salvation: Stories of Women's Conversions, 1800 to the Present*. Bloomington: Indiana University Press, 1991.

Chaves, Mark. *Ordaining Women: Culture and Conflict in Religious Organizations*. Cambridge, MA: Harvard University Press, 1997.

DeBerg, Betty. *Ungodly Women: Gender and the First Wave of American Fundamentalism*. Minneapolis, MN: Fortress Press, 1990.

Denton, Michael. *Evolution: A Theory in Crisis*. Bethesda, MD: Adler & Adler.

Emerson, Michael and Christian Smith. *Divided by Faith: Evangelical Religion and the Problem of Race in America*. New York: Oxford University Press, 2000.

Gallagher, Susan K. *Evangelical Identity and Gendered Family Life*. New Brunswick, NJ: Rutgers University Press, 2003.

Griffith, R. Marie. *God's Daughters: Evangelical Women and the Power of Submission*. Berkeley: University of California Press, 1997.

Griffith, R. Marie. *Born Again Bodies: Flesh and Spirit in American Christianity*. Berkeley: University of California Press, 2004.

Hanking, Barry. *Uneasy in Babylon: Southern Baptist Conservatives and American Culture*. Tuscaloosa: University of Alabama Press, 2002.

Hassey, Janette. *No Time for Silence: Evangelical Women in Public Ministry around the Turn of the Century*. Grand Rapids, MI: Academie, 1986.

Hunter, James Davison. *American Evangelicalism: Conservative Religion and the Quandary of Modernity*. New Brunswick, NJ: Rutgers University Press, 1983.

Noll, Mark. *The Rise of Evangelicalism: The Age of Edwards, Whitefield, and the Wesleys*. Downers Grove, IL: InterVarsity Press, 2003.

Peshkin, Alan. *God's Choice: The Total World of a Fundamentalist Christian School*. Chicago: University of Chicago Press, 1986.

Pohl, Christine and Nicola Hoggard Creegan. *Living on the Boundaries: Evangelical Women, Feminism, and the Theological Academy*. Downers Grove, IL: InterVarsity Press, 2005.

Shibley, Mark. *Resurgent Evangelicalism in the United States: Mapping Cultural Change since 1970*. Columbia: University of South Carolina Press, 1996.

Smith, Christian. *Christian America?: What Evangelicals Really Want*. Berkeley: University of California Press, 2000.

Sweeney, Douglas A. *The American Evangelical Story: A History of the Movement*. Grand Rapids, MI: Baker Academic, 2005.

Wolfe, Alan. *The Transformation of American Religion: How We Actually Live Our Faith*. New York: Free Press, 2003.

Index

slavery, 14–15, 54, 123–24, 126, 132
Smith, Al, 163
Smith, Christian, 99, 117, 127, 159, 186
Smith, Gerald L.K., 163
Social control school, 14
Society of Christian Philosophers, 178–79
Sojourners community, 156–58
Sojourners magazine, 126, 158
South, the, 54, 58, 89, 123–24, 126, 128, 139
Southern Baptist (Convention), 24, 34,105, 113–14, 117–19, 122, 125, 137, 149, 158, 182, 184
Soviet Union, 93–95, 140, 148
speaking in tongues, 44, 149, 153
"spiritualization of the church," 139
Stanley, Charles, 144
Stone, Barton, 13
Stout, Harry, 175–77
Strategic Arms Limitation Treaty, 148
Summer for the Gods, 67
Sunday, Billy, 14, 163
Super Tuesday, 151–52
supernaturalism, 89, 185
Swaggart, Jimmy, 152
Switzerland, 4, 53, 169–71

Taiwan Defense Treaty (1955), 148
Temple Baptist Church (Detroit, Michigan), 35, 146
Ten Commandments, ix, 71, 147
Tennent, William, 10, 11
Thaxton, Charles, 76
The Enlightenment, 52
The Year of the Evangelical (1976), 143
Theological modernism, 14, 19–45, 58, 73, 90, 110–11, 164; and Charles Darwin, 23; defined, 19; evangelical response to, 27; and fundamentalist controversy, 30–31; and Germany, 59; and higher criticism, 24–26; and

romanticism, 20; as theological liberalism, 19
Thomas Road Baptist Church, 145–46
Time magazine, 67, 173
Tocqueville, Alexis, 186
touchdown Jesus, 173
Trinity Evangelical Divinity School, 156
Twentieth Century Reformation, 141

Uneasy Conscience of Modern Fundamentalism, 38–39
U.S. Supreme Court, 64, 68, 92, 141, 143

Vietnam War, 100, 127, 156
Vinson, Carl, 153
Virginia Tech, 74
Virginia, 20, 145–46, 149–51, 153

Wallis, Jim, 126, 156–58
Warfare model (of Science), 49–53, 57, 59, 73, 79, 166
Warfield, B. B., 57–58, 62
Washington and Lee, 149
Washington D.C., 153, 155–57
Watchman Examiner, 31
Watergate, 42, 142
West Virginia, 141
Westminster Confession of Faith, 29
Westminster Seminary, 33–36
Weyrich, Paul, 144–47, 151
Whatever Happened to the Human Race?, 145
Wheaton College, 41, 73, 112, 171
Whitcomb, John Jr., 73–75
White House, 143–44, 149
White, Andrew Dickson, 51–52, 57, 59
White, Ellen, 70–71, 73
Whitefield, George, 4–11, 14, 27, 40–41, 175
Williams, Serena, 181
Winrod, Gerald, 163

Witness for Peace, 157
Wolfe, Alan, x, 1, 187
women; and Christian Right, 96, 105,
    141, 144; in Baptist churches, 106;
    complementarity v. egalitarianism,
    119–30; evangelical view of,
    105–108; and feminism, 114; and
    fundamentalism, 109–18; as
    preachers, 11, 14–15, 107, 110;
    voting of, 61
Woods, Tiger, 181–82
word of prophecy, 149–50

World Vision, 37
World War I, 30–31, 42, 59, 61, 89; and
    dispensationalism, 90
World War II, 39, 111–13
Wright, George Frederick, 55, 58
Wright, J. Elwin, 35–36
WYAH-TV (Norfolk, Virginia), 150

Yale, 4, 37, 149, 172, 176
Youth for Christ, 37, 41

Zionist movement, 92

~

About the Author

Barry Hankins is professor of history and graduate program director in the
history department at Baylor University. He holds a B.A. in religion and an
M.A. in church-state studies from Baylor and a Ph.D. in history from Kansas
State University.

Among Hankins's books are his forthcoming biography, *Francis Schaeffer:
Fundamentalist Warrior, Evangelical Prophet*; *Uneasy in Babylon: Southern Baptist Conservatives and American Culture*; *God's Rascal: J. Frank Norris and the
Beginnings of Southern Fundamentalism*; and *The Second Great Awakening and
the Transcendentalists*.

Hankins lives with his wife Becky in Waco, Texas. In addition to his professional interests he is an avid fly fisherman, tennis player, and also performs
in a classic rock band called After Midnight.